AF841384

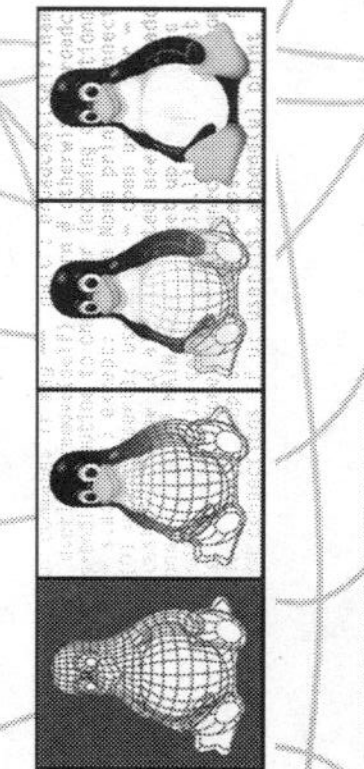

Integrating Your Network with Caldera OpenLinux 2.3

Send Us Your Comments:

To comment on this book or any other PRIMA TECH title, visit our reader response page on the Web at **www.prima-tech.com/comments**.

How to Order:

For information on quantity discounts, contact the publisher: Prima Publishing, P.O. Box 1260BK, Rocklin, CA 95677-1260; (916) 632-4400. On your letterhead, include information concerning the intended use of the books and the number of books you wish to purchase. For individual orders, visit PRIMA TECH's Web site at **www.prima-tech.com**.

Integrating Your Network With Caldera OpenLinux 2.3

Joe Cheek

Tony Ho

Matthew Coulson

Curtis Wilbar Jr.

PRIMA TECH

A Division of Prima Publishing

© 2000 by Prima Publishing. All rights reserved. No part of this book may be reproduced or transmitted in any form or by any means, electronic or mechanical, including photocopying, recording, or by any information storage or retrieval system without written permission from Prima Publishing, except for the inclusion of brief quotations in a review.

A Division of Prima Publishing

Prima Publishing and colophon are registered trademarks of Prima Communications, Inc. PRIMA TECH is a trademark of Prima Communications, Inc., Roseville, California 95661.

Caldera, the C-logo, OpenLinux, and DR-DOS are either registered trademarks or trademarks of Caldera, Inc.

Microsoft and Windows are registered trademarks of Microsoft Corporation.

Linux is a registered trademark of Linus Torvalds.

Tux, the penguin is the original creation of Larry Ewing using The Gimp. Modifications to Tux were made by Jim Thompson.

Important: If you have problems installing or running Caldera OpenLinux 2.3, go to Caldera's Web site at www.calderasystems.com. Prima Publishing cannot provide software support.

Prima Publishing and the authors have attempted throughout this book to distinguish proprietary trademarks from descriptive terms by following the capitalization style used by the manufacturer.

Information contained in this book has been obtained by Prima Publishing from sources believed to be reliable. However, because of the possibility of human or mechanical error by our sources, Prima Publishing, or others, the Publisher does not guarantee the accuracy, adequacy, or completeness of any information and is not responsible for any errors or omissions or the results obtained from the use of such information. Readers should be particularly aware of the fact that the Internet is an ever-changing entity. Some facts may have changed since this book went to press.

ISBN: 0-7615-2301-4

Library of Congress Catalog Card Number: 99-64757

Printed in the United States of America

00 01 02 03 04 BB 10 9 8 7 6 5 4 3 2 1

Publisher
Stacy L. Hiquet

Marketing Manager
Judi Taylor

Associate Marketing Manager
Jody Kennen

Managing Editor
Sandy Doell

Senior Acquisitions Editor
Kim Spilker

Senior Editor
Brian J. Thomasson

Editorial Assistant
Cathleen D. Snyder

Copy Editors
Chuck Brandstater
Theresa Wehrle

Technical Editor
Brandon Palmer

Developmental Editors
Jim Chalex
Kitty Jarrett

Interior Layout
Shawn Morningstar

Cover Design
Prima Design Team

Indexer
Joy Dean Lee

Proofreader
Theresa Wehrle

I would like to dedicate this book to my wife Liza and my daughter Rachel, the two most important women in my life.

Joe

Thank the Lord for blessing me with His grace, my family for their love and support and to the many innovative people making advances in Open Source software.

Tony

To my wife and son for their silent support, despite my neglect. Thanks to Linus, and the thousands of humble developers who helped make Linux what it is today.

Matthew

I would like to thank my wife Nicola. Without her love and support I might not have taken this project on.

Curtis

Contents at a Glance

Contents

Introduction

In this book we have endeavoured to write about the types of networks that are in use in today's business environment, and to which Caldera OpenLinux is well-suited. This book discusses the use of OpenLinux as a file and print server in a small to medium-sized organization, and as an Internet and E-mail server in a medium to large organization.

Assumptions

In order to limit the scope of this book, we have made some assumptions about you as a reader, and about the types of networks with which you will be working. First, we have assumed that you are familiar with computer networks and what they are used to accomplish, and that you have had some experience with them before.

Perhaps you have worked with other network servers, such as UNIX, NetWare, or Windows NT-based networks, or even another distribution of Linux. You are familiar with the basic hardware necessary to implement a network, and have in place the necessary hardware, including machines, cables, network cards, and so on.

We have also assumed some things about the network that you are using. This book discusses Ethernet networking, even though OpenLinux supports many other types, such as Token Ring, Frame Relay, and AX.25. This book covers only services typically used on a LAN(*Local Area Network*); it assumes that your OpenLinux machine will be used as a LAN server, and that the only WAN(*Wide Area Network*) connections that OpenLinux will be responsible for are simple Ethernet connections such as DSL, cable modem, or perhaps PPP over a modem.

Many steps to installing an OpenLinux server (such as partitioning hard drives or creating users) will not be discussed in this book; many aspects of maintaining an OpenLinux server (such as account maintenance or file system maintenance) will not be discussed either. We will assume that you know your way around a Linux or UNIX system to some degree, and have root-level access to the machines on which you will be working with this book. This book assumes that you are already moderately familiar with networking concepts and generic server maintenance. Finally, this book assumes that you will be logged in as the root user on your OpenLinux server; nearly all of the commands we ask you to use or tell you about require root access in order to function properly.

About This Book

This book is the fifth volume in the Prima Tech Linux series. It gives readers a look into one aspect of the Linux operating system. Other books in the series explore applications developed for Linux, as well as distributions of the operating system itself.

Many helpful elements are included, which offer insight and key information related to the topic being discussed.

TIP

Tips tell you about new and faster ways to accomplish a task.

NOTE

Notes delve into background information regarding a given topic.

CAUTION

Cautions warn about possible pitfalls and glitches involved with a procedure.

PART I

Introduction to Networking with Caldera OpenLinux

Chapter 1: Introduction to Caldera OpenLinux 2.3

Distinguishing Features of Caldera OpenLinux

New Features of Caldera OpenLinux 2.3

Additional Required Software

Networking Support in Caldera OpenLinux 2.3

Caldera Systems, Inc. calls its distribution of Linux *OpenLinux*, in part to convey the open-source nature of the Linux kernel and many of the available add-ons. OpenLinux, which is consistently ranked in the top three commercial Linux operating systems in the United States, is Caldera's second Linux product. Caldera Systems' first Linux product, the Caldera Network Desktop, was a customized version of Red Hat's Linux distribution and is no longer available. OpenLinux came into being as Caldera merged its Linux product with the Linux Support Team's LST Linux distribution.

Distinguishing Features of Caldera OpenLinux

Linux distributions vary greatly in their method of installation and in their system administration functions. Each Linux distribution comes with its own set of tools to accomplish these tasks. OpenLinux uses a tool called *lizard* (Linux Wizard) to do the installation, and one called *COAS* (Caldera Open Administration System) for administration. Both are new features of OpenLinux version 2. *COAS* provides a front end for editing configuration files whereas *lizard* is a great new installation routine. This book discusses editing the configuration files by hand, as opposed to using *COAS* (which is not yet mature enough to do everything discussed in this book).

NOTE

> Although *lizard* and *COAS* are new, OpenLinux also includes the old installation and administration utility, *lisa* (Linux Installation and System Administration). Although *lisa* can still be used to install and administer your OpenLinux system, typically the only time it is necessary to use *lisa* is when *lizard* and *COAS* don't work as expected.

OpenLinux's tagline is "Linux for Business"; Caldera aims its product squarely at the business user. Most people currently using Linux are home users, but this is starting to change as Linux gets more and more notice from the business world. Caldera wants to position itself as the Linux distribution of choice for business users, and it is well poised to do so. Business users need a stable, reliable, and capable operating system, and are prepared to pay for support when necessary. Caldera's close ties to Novell makes its distribution the clear choice for NetWare network integration; Caldera included both NetWare 3.x and 4.x client and administration utilities, and offers the NetWare for Linux product, which allows a Linux server to emulate a NetWare server.

New Features of Caldera OpenLinux 2.3

Caldera OpenLinux 2.3 has added some key new features. Following are some of the most impressive additions:

The Linux Wizard: lizard

Using *lizard* is a completely new way to install Linux. In the past, Linux installations were text-based, requiring users to know lots of technical details about their hardware. The *lizard*, however, is entirely graphical and mouse-driven, and probes the hardware for most of the settings necessary. The ingenious *lizard* installer also takes advantage of the multitasking nature of Linux, by installing software packages in the background while you configure user and video settings. By the time the system is fully configured, perhaps 30 percent or more of the operating system will be loaded.

Linux 2.2 Kernel

The 2.2 Linux kernel is the latest production-ready Linux kernel. Improvements upon its predecessor, kernel 2.0, include enhanced driver support, better scalability, and symmetric processing for up to 16 processors.

The Gnu C Library: glibc 2.1

The Gnu C Library, *glibc*, is the core of many of the programs included with Linux. OpenLinux supports the latest *glibc*, version 2.1, as well as the older version, known as *libc5*. When programs are built for Linux, they are built for one version or the other, but not both. Caldera's support of both versions allows it to run programs built for both newer and older Linux systems, with no major compatibility problems.

COAS

COAS is Caldera's administration package. This interface allows for quick and easy editing of popular configuration parameters, supporting both a textual and graphical interface. Unfortunately, this interface tool is not nearly complete, and the user still needs to configure many parameters by editing text files.

Additional Required Software

OpenLinux includes many of the features necessary for integration into typical networks, but it does lack some of the features to implement all the services described in this book. The packages in the following sections are necessary for a full OpenLinux network.

The Secure Shell: ssh

The Secure Shell, *ssh*, is a secure replacement for remote login services, such as *telnet* and *rlogin*. Its main benefit is that information passed over the network through *ssh* is encrypted so it cannot be easily intercepted and decoded. Information passed via *telnet* or *rlogin* is not encrypted; anyone can intercept sensitive information sent this way, and can gain account names, passwords, and other information that would allow for compromise of your systems. Many system administrators use *ssh* to prevent unauthorized access to sensitive information. Obtaining and installing *ssh* is discussed in Chapter 13, "Configuring telnet, ssh, and DHCP Services."

NOTE

> Because *ssh* uses encryption that is stronger than allowed by United States export control laws, it cannot be bundled with OpenLinux or this book.

Remote Authentication Dial-In User Service: radiusd

Radius (Remote Authentication Dial-In User Service) is a protocol typically used for an Internet service provider that has one machine dedicated for user dial-up and one machine configured as an Internet server. In this book, we assume the Internet server is your Linux machine, and the dial-up machine is a Lucent (formerly Livingston) Portmaster.

The Linux program that talks to the Portmaster and tracks which users are authenticated and which are not is *radiusd*. This program must be obtained from Lucent, built on your Linux machine, and configured for your use. Chapter 10, "Configuring Radius with Lucent's radiusd," explains how to do this.

The Proxy Server: squid

OpenLinux's HTTP and FTP proxy server is called *squid*. It allows for faster access of frequently visited Web sites and more security on an Internet connection. You must download and install *squid* from the Internet. Its installation is described in Chapter 12, "Configuring the squid Proxy Server."

Networking Support in Caldera OpenLinux 2.3

This book discusses the types of networks that are in use in today's business environment, and to which Caldera OpenLinux is well-suited. The use of OpenLinux as a file and print server in a small- to medium-sized organization, and as an Internet server in a medium- to large-sized organization, will also be examined.

File and Printer Sharing Services Provided by OpenLinux

Chapters 3 and 4 describe how to use OpenLinux as a file and print server in a number of standard network environments.

Integration with Windows NT and UNIX networks are described in separate chapters. In the real world, most networks are not single-vendor, and you might find it necessary to configure your OpenLinux server to connect with more than one type of network. Fortunately, OpenLinux allows you to do this; using one type of networking does not preclude your using one or more other types, and OpenLinux can handle all types simultaneously.

Before OpenLinux can be used as a network server, some basic configuration is required. Chapter 2 describes how to do the tasks necessary for all network services, such as finding and loading drivers and managing IP addresses and IP routing.

Samba and the SMB File System

The word *Samba* comes from SMB, the Server Message Block, which is the foundation for Windows NT networking. *Samba* is a free program developed by a team led by Andrew Tridgell, and can be used to emulate a Windows machine on a network. It can act as a peer in a Windows 9x network, or as a server or domain controller in a Windows NT network.

Chapter 3, "Using Samba and SMBFS for Windows NT File and Printer Sharing," describes how to set up and use OpenLinux's *Samba* server. It explains the server programs, *smbd* and *nmbd*, along with the associated clients *smbclient* and *smbmount*. It also covers some of the SMB support in the OpenLinux kernel.

Microsoft's Windows 2000, the next version of Windows, extends the SMB functionality with Active Directory, which places objects in a tree-like directory instead of a flat database, such as that with the NT 4 domain model. Currently, *Samba* does not support Active Directory, although that probably will change as development progresses. *Samba* provides file and printer sharing for Windows machines, and is a good place to start when integrating an OpenLinux server with Windows desktop machines on a LAN.

NFS and LPRng

NFS (*Network File System*) and LPR (*Line Printer protocol*) have long been the mainstay of UNIX networks. OpenLinux supports NFS version 2, and an enhanced version of LPR known as LPRng (*LPR next generation*). OpenLinux's NFS implementation was written from scratch by the Linux kernel developers, and LPRng was written by Patrick Powell of AStart Technologies. These combine to form the file and printer sharing components of OpenLinux.

CAUTION

> Sun Microsystems, the originator of NFS, created NFS version 3. It is important to know that the NFS implementations in OpenLinux (and other Linux distributions) have had problems connecting to Sun Microsystems' Solaris servers in the past.

Although the NFS version 2 in OpenLinux is a subset of Sun Microsystems' reference NFS implementation, LPRng is not a subset of standard LPR printing. LPRng extends standard LPR into a more robust, secure, and intuitive package, while maintaining nearly 100 percent backward compatibility.

OpenLinux can act as both NFS and LPRng client and server, and both are discussed in Chapter 4, "Using NFS and LPRng for UNIX File and Printer Sharing." In Chapter 4, we discuss how to connect your OpenLinux server to UNIX networks, as well as how to connect to other machines that implement these protocols. In particular, LPR printing is included in many network-aware printers, such as the Hewlett-Packard N-series laser printers, the Hewlett-Packard JetDirect printing interfaces, and the Intel NetPort Express.

NOTE

> LPR printing is sometimes called LPR/LPD printing, because the standard name of the daemon that handles the printer spooling is the *lpd* (Line Printer Daemon).

Internet Services Provided by OpenLinux

The services described in the rest of the book typically are used in an Internet setting, although they can just as easily be used on a company intranet or for other projects. These chapters are written with a medium to large company in mind, or for a specialized company such as an Internet service provider or Internet presence provider. There are a great many different services that OpenLinux can provide for Internet-related networking, and the topics covered here are by no means exhaustive. We chose these topics carefully to represent the services most used on OpenLinux networks.

bind, a Domain Name System Server

The Berkeley Internet Name Daemon (*bind*) handles DNS (*Domain Name System*) services for OpenLinux. Maintenance of *bind* is done by the Internet Software

Consortium, a non-profit company funded primarily through grants. Most of the Internet's name servers are powered by *bind*, which is a very popular package. The acronym "*bind*" is typically used to represent *named*, the main program of the package; the complete package also includes an application programming interface for DNS resolution and associated tools.

Both DNS server and client functions are performed by *named*; it can be told to provide name service resolution for your own domains as well as any other domains that it can access via the Internet or your local network. DNS is organized as a large distributed database. Each DNS server can host information for one or more domains. If a DNS server is asked about a domain it doesn't know about, it queries other DNS servers to find out about the domain. Whenever a DNS server finds something new, it caches the domain in memory so it doesn't need to perform the same query again.

Even if you are not hosting any domains on your servers, *bind* running on your OpenLinux machine can be beneficial just by providing easy and quick access to other domain names via its caching. I typically set up DNS on every server I install on a small network, or one on every network segment on a larger network. On a large network, this reduces network access times and bandwidth consumption; on a small network, it makes it easier to administer a single DNS server rather than maintain multiple host files.

The Domain Name System is more concerned with *zones* than with domains. Because DNS is a distributed database, and not all DNS servers are expected to be available 100 percent of the time, there are specific and detailed ways of controlling DNS replication. These concepts are explained in the DNS section of Chapter 5, "Configuring DNS and *bind*." We also explain in Chapter 5 how to install and configure *named*, and how to troubleshoot faulty DNS name resolution.

Apache, a Web Server

Apache, the world's most popular Web server, comes bundled with OpenLinux. *Apache* is an open-source Web server now written by the Apache Group, a non-profit association, and has versions available for most operating systems, including UNIX variants and Windows NT. The name "Apache" was used to mean "A Patchy" Web server, or a Web server written from various bits and pieces. It originally was based on the National Center for Supercomputing Applications' Web server, but has far outgrown those roots.

Because of its large installed base, *Apache* has plenty of support for integration with other programs, such as scripting languages and database and application servers. *Apache* also allows custom modules to be either compiled directly into the server itself, or executed as stand-alone applications. Many modules for *Apache* are available free on the Internet. Two of the most popular are *mod::perl*, which allows for *perl* execution faster than it would normally run via CGI, and *php* (*Hypertext Preprocessor*), a server-side scripting language similar in functionality to Microsoft's Active Server Pages. For instance, my Web site, **www.cheek.com**, is almost entirely written in *php*, which integrates the standard HTML and my Informix database server into a functional Web site.

Apache is very functional; besides being extensible via modules, the base package can support as many virtual hosts as your system can handle. These virtual Web sites all run from the same single *httpd* daemon *Apache* uses, so you can have many Web sites on the same IP address, many Web sites on many different IP addresses, or both. *Apache's* functionality is almost entirely controlled through its configuration files, which are hand-edited with OpenLinux. Chapter 6, "Configuring the Apache Web Server," explains the layout of these configuration files, and leads you through setting up your own Web sites and other sites as well. In that chapter, we also explain how to extend your server with modules.

An SMTP E-mail Server: sendmail

OpenLinux's default mail server is *sendmail*. More properly, *sendmail* is called an MTA (*Mail Transfer Agent*); this is in contrast to a MUA (*Mail User Agent*), which is the program that reads and displays and responds to mail. Typical MUAs are *pine* or *Netscape* mail on OpenLinux, or *Outlook* or *Eudora* on a Windows machine. In *sendmail*, mail is actually just received via SMTP *(Simple Mail Transfer Protocol)*. Other system daemons, such as *ipopd* and *imapd,* disperse the mail to the client through the POP3 (*Post Office Protocol*, version 3) and IMAP4 (*Internet Message Application Protocol*, version 4) protocols, respectively.

OpenLinux supports message transfer with other Mail Transfer Agents besides *sendmail*. Two of the most common of these are *smail* and *qmail*. Both are smaller, quicker, and easier to configure than *sendmail*, although *sendmail* is arguably the most versatile MTA. It is included as a default because it is the definite standard used on the Internet.

The single master configuration file used by *sendmail* is extremely complex and can be difficult to understand. Fortunately, not much needs to be changed to get mail services working on a standard OpenLinux machine. Even so, OpenLinux includes a meta-configuration program, called *m4*, which significantly simplifies the creation of *sendmail* configuration files.

You can receive e-mail for many domains and specify mail aliases and mail routing on a domain-by-domain or user-by-user level when you use *sendmail*. It delivers the mail itself to the message storage place on the server's hard drive, or allows for an *MDA (Message Delivery Agent)* to handle that task. Process Mail, also known as *procmail,* is also included with OpenLinux, and it is configured to handle the actual mail delivery; *procmail* can sort the mail into folders based on headers or content, set up automatic replies, provide for automatic or conditional forwarding, and much more. Chapter 7, "Configuring SMTP E-mail with sendmail and procmail," discusses how to configure *sendmail* and *procmail* for e-mail delivery on your network.

wu-ftpd, an FTP Server

Handling the FTP file transfer service for OpenLinux, is *wu-ftpd* (Washington University's File Transfer Protocol Daemon). By default, both private and public (anonymous) FTP are enabled. Configuring the *ftp* daemon is pretty easy, especially compared to configuring other bundled servers, such as the *Apache* Web server or the *sendmail* e-mail server. Chapter 8, "Configuring *FTP* Servers with wu-ftpd," explains normal *FTP* server configuration, and then goes into more advanced topics, such as restricting user rights and creating virtual services.

A UseNet NNTP Server: inn

UseNet has been called "the world's largest bulletin board." Hundreds of thousands of messages traverse UseNet each day, amounting to hundreds of megabytes of disk space. OpenLinux comes with the *inn* news package, which is maintained by the Internet Software Consortium, the same group that maintains the *bind* DNS server. As is standard with ISC products, the name *inn* is actually the name of the package, not the programs; the *inn* programs are *innd* and *nnrpd*. The UseNet network is distributed among hundreds of thousands of machines across the Internet, and the different UseNet servers are organized in a tree-like fashion similar to the way DNS servers are organized.

Unlike DNS, UseNet has no central starting place—no root server—so UseNet servers are distinguished by the other servers to which they connect. Upstream connections are called *feeders*, and these connections are used to receive UseNet articles. Downstream connections are called *readers*, and these connections are used to send UseNet articles to others, either an end user or another machine getting a news feed from your server.

The *inn* package is powerful and flexible, but requires configuring in great detail. Configuration is discussed in Chapter 9, "Configuring UseNet News with innd." We explain in Chapter 9 how to get your *inn* server working correctly so it can send and receive UseNet messages from upstream providers to your end users and other news servers.

Radius Authentication

Radius authentication is a method of providing user authentication across a network. It typically is used when there are enough remote users connecting to a server to warrant a separate machine handling just the remote connections and authentication.

Internet service providers and companies with a large number of remote employees set up their dedicated dial-in server, such as a Lucent Portmaster, along with other services on a machine such as an OpenLinux server.

Radius is the protocol that lets the Portmaster talk with the OpenLinux server, determining who is allowed to access network services and what they are permitted to do. It is described in Chapter 10, "Configuring Radius with Lucent's radiusd." That chapter explains how to obtain, install, and configure the server on the OpenLinux side, as well as the Portmaster. (Most of the information presented is applicable to other Radius clients, such as Lucent's Ascend MAX switches.)

OpenLinux can handle all aspects of remote access by itself, such as controlling the modems, providing authentication, and providing other services, such as Internet connectivity, but in large installations it is not always wise to have it do so. Having a single server provide remote access in addition to serving Web pages, *ftp* file transfers, LAN file and printer sharing, e-mail and Internet access, and more can tax even a large, dependable server. Offloading the remote access to a dedicated machine is a good way of reducing the burden on OpenLinux, allowing it more processing power for its other functions. Additionally, Radius provides logging and accounting information about remote access, giving companies all the details necessary for billing and statistical purposes. Portmasters are not the only Radius-enabled remote access solutions, but they are certainly the most common.

A Firewall Configuration Tool: ipchains

Companies interested in protecting their servers and data from exploitation on the Internet are deploying firewalls to restrict access to sensitive data. Firewalls, however, are not the only method of system security; other security methods, such as use of proxy servers and network address translation (*IP masquerading*), can provide more security than firewalls and might be better suited to your network environment.

The utility that controls firewall and network address translation configuration on OpenLinux is called *ipchains*. With *ipchains*, you can build a chain of rules for determining whether Internet Protocol packets are processed on your OpenLinux server. The name *ipchains* was used because of its use for configuring chains of IP packet rules. Each rule tells OpenLinux what to do with an IP packet it receives, whether to accept it, deny it, masquerade it, and so on. Security is enhanced when packets are stopped by the firewall, or other tools, so that attacks against your network can be minimized.

Whether a firewall, proxy server, or IP masquerading configuration is most applicable in your network depends greatly on your network setup and what security goals you wish to achieve. Chapter 11, "Building a Firewall with ipchains," discusses how to configure a firewall using the *ipchains* utility provided with OpenLinux.

Installing and configuring a proxy server is very different, and it warrants its own chapter; Chapter 12 is called "Configuring the squid Proxy Server." Whereas both firewalls and network address translation take an unhindered flow of traffic between two networks and restrict it, a proxy server takes two separate networks and provides a bridge to connect them when certain conditions are met. This can provide security because the two networks do not ever need to be logically connected. Unfortunately, *squid* only provides access to Web and FTP sites.

DHCP Servers, telnet, and ssh

These last few services round out typical Internet services. Both *telnet* and *ssh* provide command-line and GUI remote access to your OpenLinux server. However, *telnet* is bundled with OpenLinux and is not secure, meaning that it is susceptible to interception. As already mentioned, though, *ssh* is secure, meaning that if its transmissions are intercepted, they cannot be interpreted easily (but it is not bundled with OpenLinux and must be obtained separately).

DHCP, the *Dynamic Host Configuration Protocol*, provides a way for many machines to get IP addresses from a pool of available addresses, instead of having one specific address assigned to each machine. This can reduce administration time spent on client machines, because the entire pool of IP addresses can be managed from one machine, the DHCP server. Additionally, DHCP can provide dynamic numbers for other IP-related services, such as DNS servers and gateways.

Chapter 13, "Configuring telnet, ssh, and DHCP Services," explains how to configure all three of these services for typical use on your OpenLinux machine.

Chapter 2: Configuring OpenLinux's Basic Network

Finding and Installing Proper Network Drivers

Managing IP Routing

Managing Network Services

To use the information in this book, you need to have OpenLinux and proper network drivers installed on your server. This chapter explains how to get your OpenLinux server into a usable state, so the information in the chapters later in this book will be beneficial to you. You need to install OpenLinux 2.3 on your server, configure basic IP networking, and familiarize yourself with the basic network administration tools bundled with OpenLinux. (Other chapters show you how to change network settings or configure the system by using tools introduced in this chapter.)

Files Referenced in this Chapter

The following files are used by OpenLinux's base networking:

File	Purpose
`/etc/inetd.conf`	*inetd*'s configuration file tells which services it should run
`/etc/inittab`	The init table identifies different runlevels and tells what to execute on each
`/etc/sysconfig/network-scripts/ifcfg-routes`	This file defines static network routes

CAUTION

> As a root user, you have complete and total access to the OpenLinux system on which you are logged in. Do not be careless with this account, as you could easily compromise the security of the system, or destroy valuable data and programs while using it.

Finding and Installing Proper Network Drivers

The first necessary items to configure are the network drivers. OpenLinux needs to have the proper drivers for your network card loaded and available for use. You can load these drivers automatically by *lizard* (the *Linux Wizard*), Caldera's latest and greatest installer. You can also load them by hand, during or after installation by *lizard* or another installer.

Letting Caldera's lizard Installer Probe Your Network Card

lizard is the installer you most likely will use when you install OpenLinux. If you install OpenLinux from Windows, or boot directly from the CD contained in this book, you see the *lizard* graphical interface. This is the easiest way to configure networking; at a certain point in the installation routine, you are asked for details regarding your Ethernet, including IP address, subnet mask, DNS servers, gateway, and hostname. You can opt for an DHCP IP address or to join an NIS domain. You are not asked for the type of network card you have, as it is determined automatically by *lizard*.

You can opt not to configure networking at this point, although we advise against it. If you have more than one network card, you have the opportunity to configure only one (and *lizard* doesn't tell you which one you are configuring, unfortunately). If you have a token ring card, or some other type of network card instead of standard or fast Ethernet, you cannot configure it from *lizard*, but have to configure it manually after the installation is done.

lizard gives you several options for the type of install desired, such as a full installation, minimal installation, network server installation, and so on. Choose either the full installation (all packages) or network server installation. Choosing the full installation requires about 1.3 gigabytes of hard drive space, and installs the X Window System. The network server installation requires about 250 megabytes of hard drive space, and does not install the X Window System, instead forcing you to do all administration from the command line; nor does it install any development utilities (so that compiling such as that needed by *ssh* is disabled). Do not choose the Web server installation, as it does not load enough packages to be a fully functioning network server.

Loading Network Card Drivers with the lisa Installer

You can also load OpenLinux with Caldera's older installer, *lisa* (*Linux Installation and System Administration*), which is text-based. (It does not probe for as much information—more needs to be entered manually.) *lisa* is good to use when the *lizard* probe functions do not return valid information, or on rare occasions when the probe hangs your system.

To load OpenLinux with *lisa*, you first must create floppy disks. You can create these on a machine running either DOS or Windows, or on an existing Linux installation. The CD-ROM includes images of two floppy disks—a boot/install disk and a modules disk, which contains extra drivers. These images are located in the col/launch/lisa/floppy directory of the CD-ROM, as the files `install.144` and `modules.144` respectively. (Make sure you have a blank disk in your floppy drive before you start.) To create 1.44 megabyte disks from these images in DOS or Windows, use the `install.bat` and `modules.bat` batch files, also in this directory; in Linux, use the **dd** command twice.

```
dd if=install.144 of=/dev/fd0

dd if=modules.144 of=/dev/fd0
```

To install with *lisa*, insert the install floppy in your floppy drive, make sure the OpenLinux CD is still in the CD-ROM drive, and reboot. The installation starts automatically.

lisa does not automatically probe for network cards; it needs to be told to do so. It does find your hard drives and CD-ROM devices, and then asks if all is done. Choose "No" to tell it to probe for your network card also; it then searches for some of the more common network cards. If it finds one, it loads drivers for that card; if it does not, tell it to probe again, using the modules disk (which contains more drivers). If your card is not found with this modules disk, you must load it by hand after the installation of OpenLinux is done.

You are prompted for IP address information toward the end of the installation, but you are not given the choice of a dynamic IP address (using DHCP) at this point. You can choose to give it false information, if you want to use DHCP, or leave it unconfigured. You need to configure this after installation, using the tools described in the next section.

Loading Network Card Drivers by Hand after Installation

If you could not get your network card drivers loaded during the installation, you can use *COAS* (*Caldera Open Administration System*) to load them and configure them now. Because *COAS* has both a text-based and a graphical front end, it works with either a terminal window or the X Window System. To start it from the KDE menu, click on the Application Starter; then choose COAS, Network, Ethernet Interfaces (*COAS* does not configure token ring interfaces). This menu is shown in Figure 2-1.

You can also run *COAS* by hand, by entering the command `coastool` at the command prompt. This brings up the main menu, shown in Figure 2-2 (text mode) and Figure 2-3 (X Window mode).

Note that the menu contains the same information, just displayed differently. Choose Network Administration, Common Network Functions. You see the Ethernet Interface Configuration window, shown in Figure 2-4.

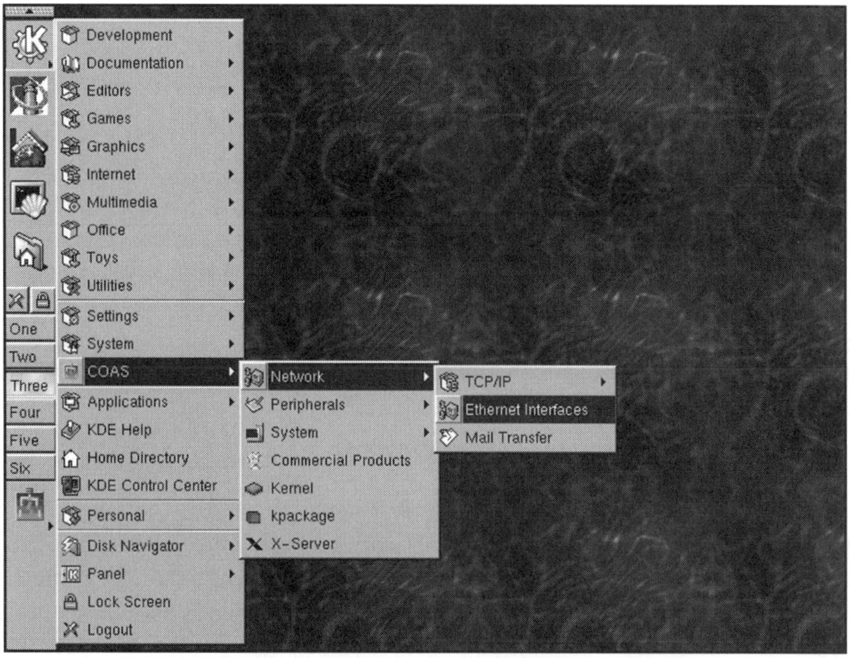

Figure 2-1 *Configuring your Ethernet via the COAS graphical interface*

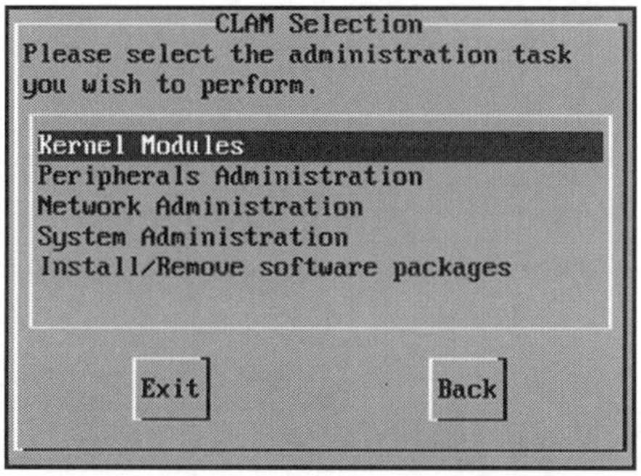

Figure 2-2 *The COAS main menu, in text mode*

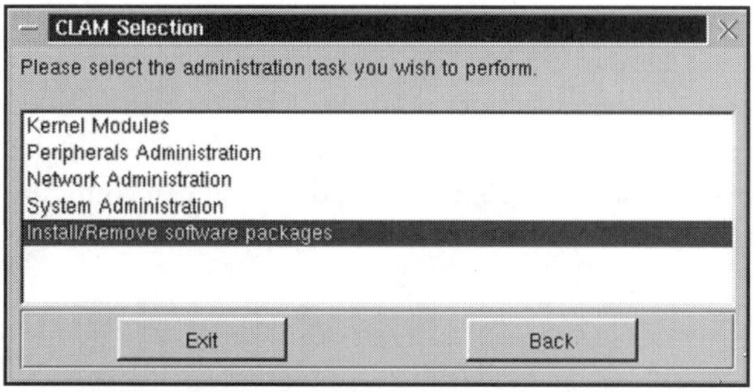

Figure 2-3 *The COAS main menu, in X mode*

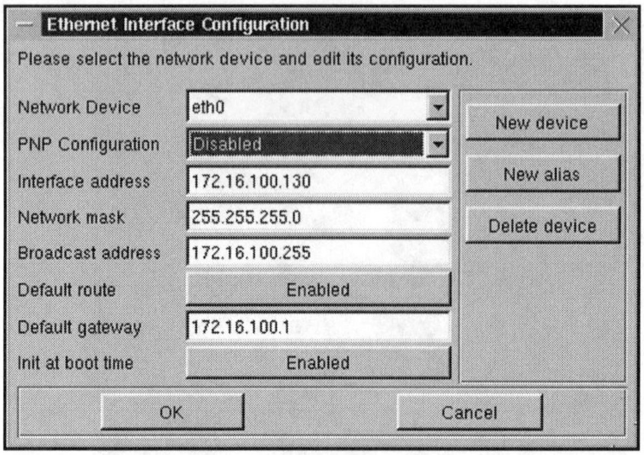

Figure 2-4 *The COAS Ethernet Interface Configuration screen*

Here you can configure the card's IP address, network mask, and broadcast address, as well as the gateway address. You can tell it to use DHCP instead of a static IP address. You can also tell it whether the network interface should be active at boot time.

If OpenLinux does not load the proper driver, you cannot configure your network card until you load a proper driver. From this window, choose New Device. This allows you to load a new driver, and brings up a list of devices, as shown in Figure 2-5.

After you select your card from the list, you are presented with options for setting up that card, which could be anything from an IRQ and base address to debugging and duplex options. After you enter this information, you can configure the card's IP address and more from *COAS*. (The options shown in Figure 2-6 are for an Intel EtherExpress 100 card.) If your card is not on this list, it is not supported by OpenLinux 2.3.

Assigning Multiple IP Addresses to an Interface

You might want to assign a second or third IP address to one network card. Known in OpenLinux parlance as IP Aliasing, you can easily accomplish this with the *COAS* tool. From the Ethernet Interface Configuration window, choose New Alias. You are prompted with a window looking almost exactly like the window you were just shown; the two differences are that this window does not have any information filled in, and the network device has a :0 appended to it, which stands for the first alias (:1 is the second alias, :2 is the third, and so on). From this window, you can configure the second IP address (or the third, or the fourth, and so on), just as you would the first. (See Figure 2-7.)

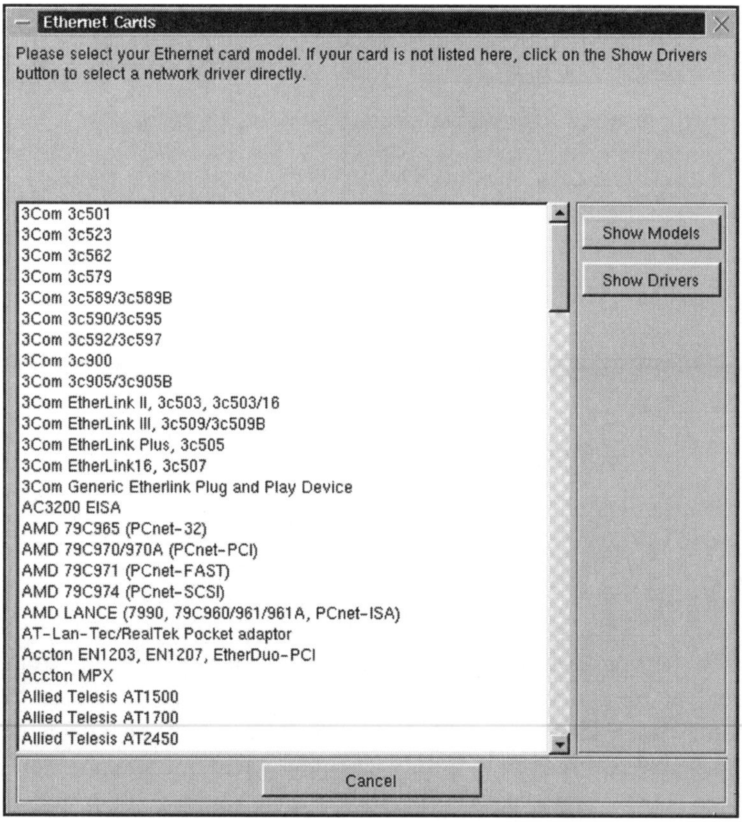

Figure 2-5 *The COAS Ethernet Cards device selection window*

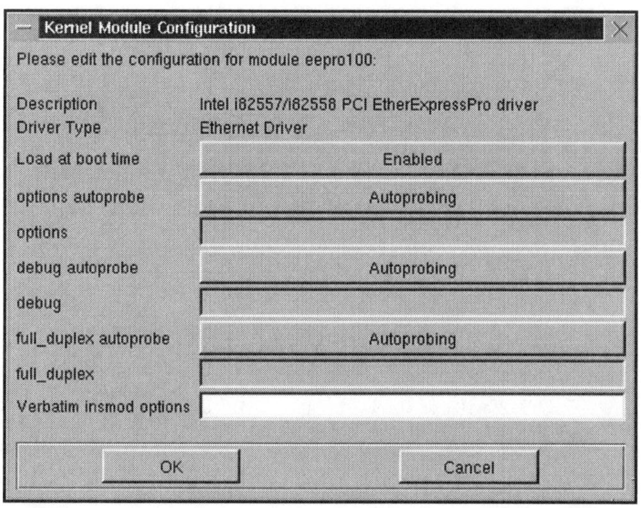

Figure 2-6 *Card-specific options for an Intel EtherExpress 100 network card*

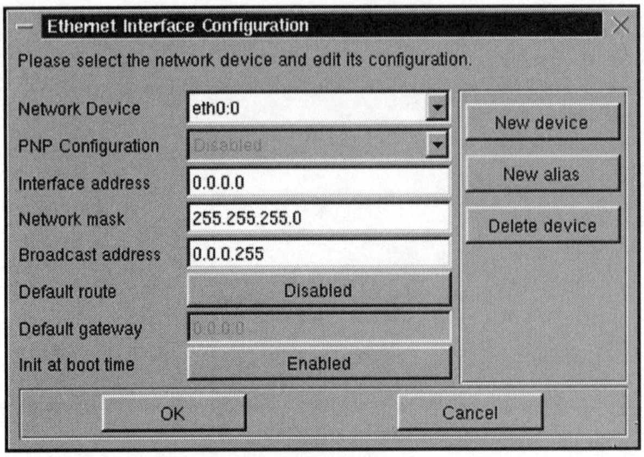

Figure 2-7 *The Ethernet Interface Configuration window for an aliased IP address*

Managing IP Routing

Routing is affected by settings within *COAS*, but cannot be managed directly from *COAS*—it must be done from a command prompt. The `route` command is used to view and alter routing tables. If you have only one network card, you probably have just three routes: one for your IP subnet, one for your gateway, and one for your loop-back interface. When you issue the `route` command (without options), information about them is displayed in the following form:

```
Kernel IP routing table
Destination    Gateway        Genmask        Flags   Metric  Ref   Use Iface
172.16.100.0   *              255.255.255.0  U       0       0     0 eth0
127.0.0.0      *              255.0.0.0      U       0       0     0 lo
default        172.16.100.1   0.0.0.0        UG      1       0     0 eth0
```

The preceding example is for a network card on the 172.16.100.0 subnet, with a mask of 255.255.255.0 and a gateway of 172.16.100.1. If you had a more complex network with multiple network cards, you might see something like the following:

```
Kernel IP routing table
Destination    Gateway        Genmask          Flags   Metric  Ref   Use Iface
208.12.12.128  0.0.0.0        255.255.255.224  U       0       0     0 eth0
192.168.1.0    0.0.0.0        255.255.255.0    U       0       0     0 eth1
127.0.0.0      0.0.0.0        255.0.0.0        U       0       0     0 lo
0.0.0.0        208.12.12.129  0.0.0.0          UG      0       0     0 eth0
```

In this example, two network cards (`eth0` and `eth1`) are shown with their own subnets: a 208.12.12.128/255.255.255.224 network and a 192.168.1.0/255.255.255.0 network, respectively, with a default gateway of 208.12.12.129 on the `eth0` interface. OpenLinux can be told to forward packets between the two networks, acting then as a gateway for one or both networks.

Enabling and Disabling IP Forwarding

IP Forwarding causes OpenLinux to act as a router: it takes packets sent from one network and destined for a different network and forwards them to the appropriate network. You can toggle IP Forwarding on (or off) from within *COAS*. (These settings are permanent, so they are saved after a server reboot.) From the *COAS* main menu, choose Network Administration, TCP/IP Network Options. This brings up the menu shown in Figure 2-8.

> NOTE
>
> For some reason, the *COAS* menu within the KDE desktop does not allow you to choose the TCP/IP Network Options window directly, as it does with other windows. You have to go to a command prompt, and then run `coastool` by hand to get that option.

Changing Routing from a Shell Prompt

Most routing automatically is in place if you set up your OpenLinux network correctly; if you have two network cards on different subnets, and want to route between them, all routing table entries are configured for you if you made the proper entries in *COAS*. Sometimes, however, it is beneficial to alter the routing table by hand, to either add or delete routes. This can be accomplished with the `route` command.

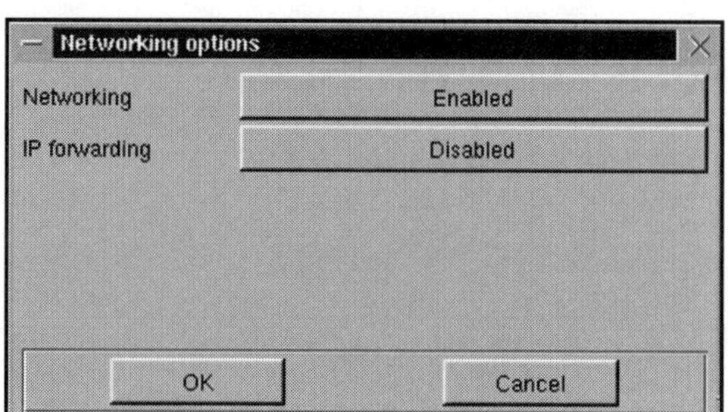

Figure 2-8 *The Networking Options window within COAS*

As explained earlier in this chapter, the `route` command shows the current routing table when called with no options. To add a new route, `route` must be called with the `add` parameter.

```
route add -net 208.12.12.128 netmask 255.255.255.224 dev eth0
```

This command adds a route to the 208.12.12.128/255.255.255.224 network on device `eth0`; basically, it states that all traffic bound for 208.12.12.128 through 208.12.12.159 should be sent out of the `eth0` interface. The `-net` parameter means that this route is for an entire network subnet. If I want to add a route for just one host, I use the `-host` parameter instead (in that case, no netmask is specified because a single host is not a network segment).

```
route add -host 192.168.1.1 dev eth0
```

Gateways can be added also. To add a default gateway, use a command similar to the following:

```
route add default gw 208.12.12.129
```

Routes can be deleted in a parallel manner. Substitute `del` for the `add` parameter with the `route` command. To delete the gateway just added, use the following:

```
route del default gw 208.12.12.129
```

Making Routing Changes Permanent

All of these `route` commands go into effect immediately, but they do not stay in effect after a system reboot. If you want to alter the routes on a permanent basis, you must add these commands to the `/etc/sysconfig/network-scripts/ifcfg-routes` file. This file is a shell script that is called after each system boot to alter the network routes. If you want to add a route to host 192.168.1.1 on device `eth0` permanently, use the following file (Listing 2-1).

Listing 2-1 A sample /etc/sysconfig/network-scripts/ifcfg-routes shell script

```
#!/bin/sh
#/etc/sysconfig/network-scripts/ifcfg-routes
# permanent server routing changes go here
route add -host 192.168.1.1 dev eth0
```

This file should be owned by the root user and group. It should be made executable for the root user with a command such as the following. (Note, though, that the file does not exist after a clean installation of OpenLinux; you need to create it.)

```
chmod +x /etc/sysconfig/network-scripts/ifcfg-routes
```

Managing Network Services

You can use *COAS* to bring the network up and down, and to enable and disable many system services (such as e-mail, DNS, and NFS). Some system services, notably those run from the *inetd* daemon, cannot be managed from *COAS*; you must configure these via shell commands and through changing of configuration files. This section shows you how to deal with these network management issues.

Bringing the Network Up and Down

COAS allows you to toggle networking on or off from the same screen that allows you to enable and disable IP Forwarding. (These settings are permanent, so they are saved after a server reboot.) From the *COAS* main menu, choose Network Administration, TCP/IP Network Options. This brings up the Networking Options menu shown previously in Figure 2-8.

Most of the time, instead of disabling networking permanently, you just want to take the network down to troubleshoot an issue; this is easily accomplished through the use of *runlevels*. Runlevels tell OpenLinux what state the server is in, whether it is booting, rebooting, coming up in single-user or multi-user mode, whether networking is enabled, and so on. There are seven defined runlevels in OpenLinux, shown in Table 2-1.

Table 2-1 Runlevels and their meanings in OpenLinux

Runlevel	Meaning
0	Halt (the system is going down for a halt).
1	Single-user mode (network cards are initialized, but the network is not up).
2	Multi-user mode (the network is up, but most network services are not).
3	Full multi-user mode (full networking, the default if X Windowing is not configured).
4	Unused.
5	Full multi-user mode with X Windowing (the same as 3, but an X Windowing logon is displayed).
6	Reboot (the system is going down for a reboot).

If you have the X Window System working and enabled, your standard runlevel is 5; otherwise it's 3. Telling the system to change its runlevel is the easiest way to bring network services up and down temporarily. I often take an OpenLinux system to runlevel 1 to troubleshoot and fix a core network problem, or to load a system-level patch; the easiest way to do this is by issuing the `init 1` command.

CAUTION

> Do not enter runlevel 1 if you are not at the console of the machine—if you are logged in remotely over a network connection, this shuts off your network connection and leaves the system in an unusable state.

This disables all networking and most system services, including X Window. All users will be logged off, and you will be left with a single shell prompt on a console terminal. (After doing your maintenance, you can re-enter runlevel 3 or 5.)

TIP

> If you are using a system purely as a server, you might want to boot to runlevel 3 instead of 5. Booting to runlevel 3 does not initialize the X Window System, which takes up a lot of memory on the server. To change this permanently, edit the `/etc/inittab` file, and change the line beginning with `id:5` to `id:3`.

Starting and Stopping rc Network Services

rc scripts control many network services. These services can be enabled or disabled through *COAS*'s System Administration menu. From the *COAS* KDE menu, choose System, Daemons. If you are running *coastool*, you must choose System Administration, Enable/disable system services. Either way brings you to the dialog box shown in Figure 2-9.

This window has many services listed, each with a checkbox to the left of the service name. Checked boxes are enabled at startup; unchecked ones are not. You can specify exactly which services you want to be enabled after a normal (runlevel 3 or 5) boot by checking and unchecking these services.

Unfortunately, altering these checkboxes in this dialog box does not immediately start or stop the particular service; it just tells OpenLinux whether to start the service after a reboot. To start or stop services immediately, you must do so by hand using that particular service's *rc* script. Each of these scripts is found in the `/etc/rc.d/init.d` directory, and can be called with parameters of `start` or `stop` to immediately start or stop the corresponding service. For instance, to stop the NFS service immediately, use the following command:

```
/etc/rc.d/init.d/nfs stop
```

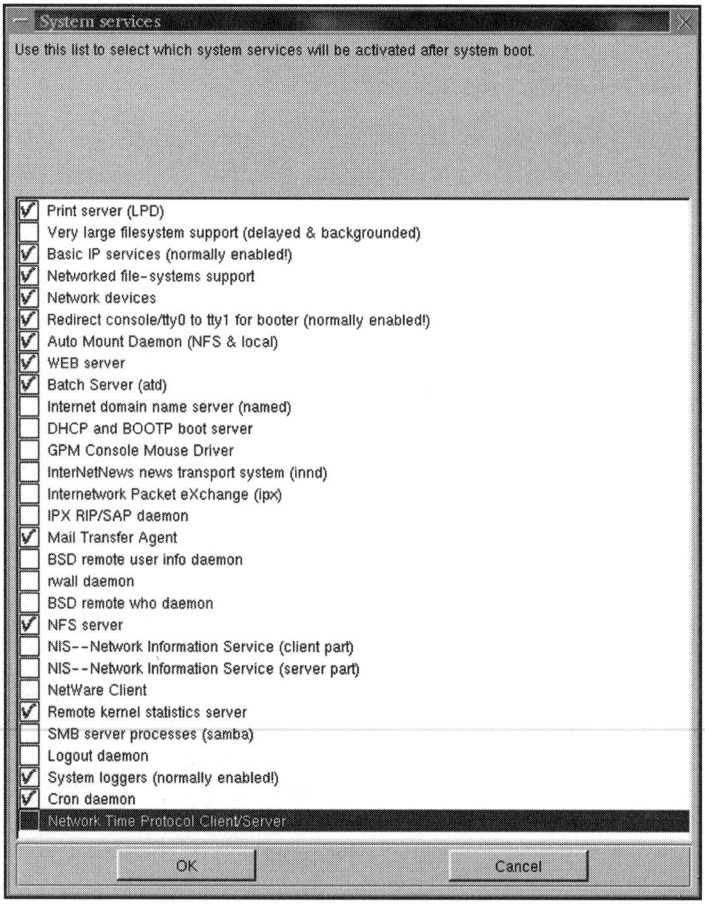

Figure 2-9 *The COAS System Services dialog box*

To start the DNS service, use the following command:

```
/etc/rc.d/init.d/named start
```

Starting and Stopping inetd Network Services

Some services are not managed by *rc* scripts at all, but rather by *inetd*. *inetd* is a superserver; it's job is to manage other system services, such as *rlogin* and *telnet*. *inetd* listens to a specified port, and when it gets a connection, it passes that along to the necessary program. All of these programs are enabled and disabled via the file `/etc/inetd.conf`. Each line in this file tells *inetd* what program to run when a connection is made. The lines in this file look like the following:

```
ftp      stream  tcp     nowait  root    /usr/sbin/tcpd in.ftpd -l -a
```

By default, almost all of the services in this file are active. To disable a particular service, comment it out with a hash mark. Conversely, to re-enable a system service, delete the hash mark from before the proper line.

Editing this file changes which services are started at system boot. To change which services are enabled currently, send the *inetd* program a signal after editing the `/etc/inetd.conf` file.

```
killall -HUP inetd
```

NOTE

> The parameter `-HUP`, a hangup signal; it is used in this case to tell *inetd* that its configuration file has changed, so that it will reread the file.

For More Information

Cheek Consulting's Linux Knowledge Base has an assortment of links to network and networking references on Linux at these two URLs.

URL	Resource Name
http://linuxkb.cheek.com/page.php?network	Linux Knowledge Base Network Card Information
http://linuxkb.cheek.com/page.php?networking	Linux Knowledge Base General Networking Information

PART II

Using Caldera OpenLinux for File and Printer Sharing

PART II

Using Caldera OpenLinux for File and Printer Sharing

Chapter 3: Using Samba and SMBFS for Windows NT File and Printer Sharing

Overview of Samba Networking

Installing Samba

Configuring Samba for File Sharing

Accessing SMB Shares with smbclient

Sending Winpopup Messages to a Windows Client

Additional Samba Utilities

Files Referenced in this Chapter

File	Purpose
`smb.conf`	The configuration file for the *Samba* suite.
`smbclient`	FTP-like client to access SMB/CIFS resources on servers.
`smbd`	Server to provide SMB/CIFS services to clients.
`smbmount`	Mount SMB file system.
`smbpasswd`	The *Samba* encrypted password file.
`smbrun`	Interface program between *smbd* and external programs.
`smbstatus`	Report on current *Samba* connections.
`smbtar`	Shell script for backing up SMB/CIFS shares directly to UNIX tape drives.
`smbtestparm`	Check an `smb.conf` configuration file for internal correctness.
`smbtestprns`	Check printer name for validity with *smbd.*
`smbumount`	Umount for normal users.
`samba`	Shell script to start or stop the *Samba* daemons.
`nmblookup`	Looks up NetBIOS names.
`findsmb`	Prints info on all *smb* responding machines on a subnet.
`nmbd`	*Samba* daemon to provide NetBIOS over IP naming services to clients.
`smbadduser`	Add *Samba* users to the `smbpasswd` file.
`smbd`	*Samba* daemon to provide SMB/CIFS services to clients.

Overview of Samba Networking

Samba is a collection of programs that allows file and printer sharing among computers running SMB. Microsoft operating systems, such as Windows 95/98/NT, use SMB. SMB is a network protocol developed by Microsoft. *Samba* is an open source suite of programs available on Linux and the various flavors of UNIX but also on other popular platforms, such as OS/2 and VMS to name a few. Of course, Windows 95/98/NT/2000 SMB support is native. There are other alternatives to *Samba*, such as NFS (Network File System), Appletalk, DECNet, NCP (Netware Core Protocol) in Netware, and Banyan VINES. All of these have strengths and weaknesses but only *Samba* is the most popular open-source suite of software for sharing files and printers with Microsoft Windows systems.

> SMB (Server Message Block) originated from NetBEUI (NetBIOS Extended User Interface), which was part of the NetBIOS protocol designed for small, isolated LANs. Consequently, the terms NetBEUI network, NetBIOS network, and Windows network mean the same thing. You might have heard of CIFS (Common Internet File System). This is Microsoft's extension of the Server Message Block (SMB) protocol. In this sense, *Samba* is an open source implementation of CIFS.

NOTE

> Andrew Tridgell was the person who started the work on *Samba*. To read an interesting account of how *Samba* was created, check out **http://us3.samba.org/samba/docs/SambaIntro.html**.

NOTE

Why Use Samba?

People use *Samba* to allow Microsoft desktop machines to access shared files or printers on their Linux or other non-Windows servers. Another reason is that people want their Microsoft servers to be accessible from their Linux or other non-Windows computers. Finally, people use *Samba* simply to replace their proprietary protocols (such as NFS and DECNet) with an open source one.

What Can Samba Do?

Besides providing file and print services, *Samba* can simply replace most services offered by Windows NT server. In a nutshell, *Samba* provides the following functions:

- File and print services.
- Authentication and authorization in a Windows network.
- Name resolution via the WINS nameserver.
- Service announcement or browsing (support Microsoft Windows Network Neighborhood browsing).

> Check out **http://anu.samba.org/samba/survey/** to get a glimpse of what others are doing with Samba!

NOTE

Samba Components

Samba consists of two key daemons: *smbd* and *nmbd.* These two daemons provide the functions listed previously.

smbd

This daemon provides file and print services to SMB clients, such as Windows 95/98/NT. Security via authentication and authorization is also provided. You can protect shared file and print services by requiring passwords. The simplest level of security is called the share level. A password is assigned to a shared directory or printer that is known by all users so anyone can use that share. The next level of security is user level security, which is the preferred level of security and the default setting. Each user has his or her own username and password. Consequently, access to shares can be granted or denied on an individual basis. The last two levels are server and domain security, which is of interest to advanced users. The server level security uses another SMB server (for example, NT server) to authenticate users. Domain level security is similar to the server level security but uses the Window's primary domain controller to authenticate uses.

The Windows NT Domain system (not the same as the Domain Name System, DNS) provides another level of security. The basic idea is that a user should only need to log in once to access the authorized shares on the network. This is accomplished by using an NT Domain Controller. An NT Domain basically is a group of computers on a network that share the same NT Domain Controller. Version 2 of *Samba* provides this Windows NT Domain Controller function. The configuration file for *smbd* is `/etc/samba.d/smb.conf`

nmbd

This daemon handles WINS name resolution and service announcement (browsing). These two services involve the management and distribution of lists of WINS names.

Name resolution takes two forms: broadcast and point-to-point. A machine can use one or both of these methods, depending on its configuration. A client looking for a server named Mickey broadcasts a message to the network and waits for the server named Mickey to answer with an IP address. All broadcast traffic is restricted to the subnet or local LAN. Point-to-point name resolution involves the use of an NBNS (NetBIOS Name Service) server, which holds a simple database of NetBIOS names and their IP addresses. Point-to-point name resolution works by having the SMB clients send their NetBIOS names and IP addresses to the NBNS server. When an SMB client wants to talk to another client, it sends the other client's name to the NBNS server. If the name is in the simple database, the NBNS server sends the IP address back to the requestor.

The other half of *nmbd* is service announcement, also known as browsing. This is not the same as browsing the Internet, but rather browsing a list of services (a service is a file and print share) offered by the computers on a network. On a LAN, one computer becomes the Local Master Browser (LMB). The purpose is to keep a list of available services so when you click on the Windows Network Neighborhood icon on your NT machine, you can see what available file and print shares are on the network.

Beside the LMBs, there are also Domain Master Browsers (DMBs), which coordinate browse lists among NT Domains. With assistance from the NBNS, an LMB can locate its DMB to exchange and combine browse lists with other LMBs. Consequently, the browse list is propagated throughout the NT Domain. This propagation time can be a few seconds to more than half an hour for a change on a remote subnet to appear in your Network Neighborhood. So if you don't see a service appear on your Network Neighborhood, you might have to wait a few more minutes or longer!

NOTE

> The delay depends on when the LMBs synchronized with DMB.

The configuration file for nmbd is `/etc/samba.d/smb.conf`.

Samba Utilities

Samba comes with a variety of utilities. The most commonly used are outlined in the following table.

Utility	Description
smbclient	This is an SMB client program with a simple FTP-like interface. This utility accesses shares on SMB servers, such as a Windows NT file and print server.
smbtestparm	This utility allows you to test your `smb.conf` configuration file for correctness.
smbtestprns	This utility allows you to test the printers defined in your `printcap` file.
smbstatus	This utility allows you to list current connections to the smbd server.
smbpasswd	This utility allows you to change SMB encrypted passwords on Samba and Windows NT servers.
mksmbcodepage	This utility allows you to create SMB code page definition files for your *smbd* server.
nmblookup	This is a NetBIOS name service client. *nmblookup* can find NetBIOS names on a network, look up their IP addresses, and query a remote machine for the list of names the machine believes it owns.
SWAT	The Samba Web Administration Tool (*SWAT*) allows you to configure *Samba* remotely, using a Web browser.

NOTE

> If you can't see the *SWAT* Web page when you enter **http://localhost:901** in your Web browser, edit the `/etc/hosts.deny` file so that a line like the following one appears.
>
> `swat:ALL EXCEPT 127.0.0.1`

SMB Filesystems for Linux

Windows NT can provide a file share as if it were a hard disk on your own machine. This drive looks like your own hard drive but it's really disk space on another computer, somewhere else on the network.

Your OpenLinux system can provide this service by using the SMB filesystem smbfs filesystem. For example, you can use *smbmount* to mount `C:\DATA` from your NT machine to the `/mnt/smb_share` directory on your Openlinux machine; then, you can read, write, edit, delete, and copy the files in that directory just as you would local files.

Setup and Management

Samba is configured by editing the parameters in the `/etc/samba.d/smb.conf` file. This is a simple text file designed to look a lot like the Windows .ini files used in Windows 95. If you are overwhelmed by the many parameters in `smb.conf`, you can use *SWAT* to present the information from a Web browser so it's easier to digest. For more details, please check the man pages on `smb.conf`.

SMB Servers

Before continuing our discussion on the SMB servers, it would be instructive to note the differences between workgroups and domains.

Workgroups

A workgroup is a collection of computers (workstations or servers) that maintain their own security information. The point is that security is distributed, not centralized.

Domains

A domain is a collection of computers whose security is maintained centrally. Each domain has one or more domain controllers. There is usually a primary domain controller (PDC) and several backup domain controllers (BDCs). The domain controllers maintain account information.

Security Levels

Samba supports four security levels. These are:

- Share
- User
- Server
- Domain

The Share Level

In the share level security, the client authenticates itself separately for each share with one or more passwords. The password determines what type of access is granted. It sends the password along with each share mount. The client expects a password to be associated with each share, independent of the user. This type of security is similar to what Windows 95/98 offers via the Access Control tab of the Network Control Panel.

If you don't want to create a UNIX account for each Windows account that can be used on your network, this is the security level you want *Samba* to be in. This is the simplest mode to set up and it is the least secure.

The User Level

This is the default security level and the most common security level used. In user level security, the client sends a session setup command directly after the protocol negotiation. This command contains a username and password. The server can either accept or reject that username and password combination. Note that at this stage the server has no idea what share the client eventually tries to connect to, so it can't base the accept/reject on anything other than the following:

- The username/password
- The machine on which the client is based

If the server accepts the username and password, then the client expects to be able to mount any share without specifying a password. Furthermore, it expects that all access rights are what the username and password specified in the session setup.

It is also possible for a client to send multiple session setup requests. When the server responds, it gives the client a uid to use as an authentication tag for that username and password.

If you want each Windows account to have its own account on the *Samba* server, then user level security is what you need.

The Server and Domain Level

If you want to add the *Samba* server to an existing NT Domain, consider using either the Security or Domain security level.

In server level security, the *Samba* server reports to the client that it is in user level security. The client then does a session setup as described earlier. The *Samba* server takes the username and password that the client sends and attempts to authenticate it by sending the same username and password that it got from the client to the password server (a PDC or another SMB server). If it accepts the password, then *Samba* accepts the client's connection. This allows the *Samba* server to use another SMB server as the password server.

You should also note that at the beginning of all this session startup, the server tells the client what security level and if it supports encryption. If it does, then the client sends all passwords in encrypted form. You have to configure *Samba* with encryption enabled to support this feature. A separate `smbpasswd` file is required which contains SMB-style encrypted passwords. It is cryptographically impossible to translate from UNIX-style encryption to SMB-style encryption.

Installing Samba

Surprise! The *Samba* suite is installed when you do NetServer installation, but you need to customize it to use it as a server.

If it's not installed for some reason, pop in your OpenLinux 2.3 CD or download the latest rpm package from **ftp://ftp.calderasystems.com/pub/OpenLinux/2.3/**.

As of this writing, the latest version is 2.0.5. You must be in root account to install the *Samba* packages. The examples in the following sections are in the directory containing the *Samba* installation files.

Installing the Binaries

From the shell prompt, issue the following command to install the *Samba* core binaries:

```
rpm -U samba-2.0.5-1.i386.rpm
```

Installing Samba Documentation

From the shell prompt, issue the following command:

```
rpm -U samba-doc-2.0.5-1.i386.rpm
```

This installs a comprehensive set of *Samba* documentation to `/usr/doc/samba-2.0.5/docs` and `/usr/doc/samba-2.0.5/examples`.

Installing SWAT

Issue the following command at the shell prompt:

```
rpm -U swat-2.0.5-1.i386.rpm
```

This installs the Web front end of the *Samba* administrative tool. From your Web browser, you can see and manage the *Samba* configuration file, `/etc/samba.d/smb.conf`.

Installing smbfs Tools

Issue the command:

```
rpm -U smbfs-2.0.5-1.i386.rpm
```

This installs the *smbmount* and *smbumount* tools to work with the SMB filesystem.

Starting and Stopping Samba

You must be in root to start or stop the *Samba* daemons.

Commands	Descriptions
`samba start`	Starts the *Samba* daemons (*smbd* and *nmbd*)
`samba stop`	Stops the *Samba* daemons
`lsmod	grep smbfs`	Sees if the *smbfs* module is running
`modprobe smbfs`	Loads the *smbfs* module
`rmmod smbfs`	Unloads the *smbfs* module

Configuring Samba for File Sharing

The standard OpenLinux installation creates a working *Samba* installation, but you can customize it to your needs. You need to create a `smb.conf` file and *Samba* password file. The easiest way to create the `smb.conf` file is to copy the sample one provided in the `/etc/samba.d` directory by issuing this command:

```
cp smb.conf.sample smb.conf
```

This `smb.conf` file provides the configuration parameters for *Samba*. The next step is to create the *Samba* password file by issuing this command:

```
cat /etc/passwd | mksmbpasswd > /etc/samba.d/smbpasswd
```

For the last step, set the Workgroup parameter in `smb.conf` to the name of your Windows workgroup. That's all that's required for a minimal *Samba* configuration.

All *Samba* configuration parameters are held in the `/etc/samba.d/smb.conf` file. At first, this file looks overwhelming, but it's actually organized into three main sections, as described in the following table.

Section	Description
Global	Parameters have global effects or are used as default values for other sections
Homes	Defines the shares for directories on the *Samba* server
Printers	Defines the shares for printers that are available on the *Samba* server

Although you can use your favorite text editor to edit the `smb.conf` file, for most configuration tasks I would recommend using *SWAT*.

These examples assume you can connect to *Samba* using a plain-text password. If you are using Windows 98 or NT 4 with Service Pack 3 or higher, you need to turn on encryption before you can open a connection or edit your registry key on the Windows client. See `/usr/docs/samba-2.0.5/docs/textdocs/WinNT.txt` for more details.

NOTE

> There is no need to restart your *Samba* daemons after modifications to `smb.conf` files. The *Samba* daemons read the `smb.conf` on a regular basis.

User Level Security

By default, *Samba* is configured for user level security. As mentioned, you need to create a UNIX account for each Windows account that needs to access your *Samba* file server. This is the most useful security level for *Samba* to be configured to share directories and printers. Looking at the `smbd.conf` file, you need to ensure the security parameter is set to `user`, as shown below.

```
[global]
workgroup = Workgroup
netbios name = SAMBA-OL23
server string = Samba Server running on OL23 in User Level
guest account = smbguest
security = user
```

This setting tells your *Samba* server that it belongs to the workgroup named Workgroup, has a NetBIOS name SAMBA-OL23, and displays the text "Samba Server running on OL23 in Share Level" from your Network Neighborhood icon. A UNIX account, smbguest, was created to be used as the *Samba* guest account, and *Samba* is running in user level security. You can create the smbguest account by using LISA's User Administration. The workgroup and machine names are limited to a maximum length of 15 characters.

Share Level Security

When *Samba* is configured to use share level security, there is no need to create a UNIX account for each Windows user who needs to access your *Samba* server. The only difference is the security parameter. Now, as opposed to the previous setting in user level security, the value is `share`. The configuration file looks like this:

```
[global]
workgroup = Workgroup
netbios name = SAMBA-OL23
server string = Samba Server running on OL23 in User Level
guest account = smbguest
security = share
```

Domain Security

From a general perspective, the server and domain security levels are very similar. Consequently, we examine domain level security because this model better emulates a Windows NT server. A basic configuration of a *Samba* server can be configured with at least four parameters.

```
[global]
netbios name = SAMBA-OL23
workgroup = NT-DOMAIN
password server = NT-DC
security = domain
```

Previous discussions about the guest account and password encryption still apply. The workgroup value should be the name of the NT domain of which you want to be a member. The password server values are a list of computers that can be used to perform authentication. This must be a list of a server in user level security (such as an NT Domain Controller or another *Samba* server using user level security). The values given here are the NetBIOS names of the machines to use.

Samba tries each machine of the password server line in the order in which they appear. *Samba* stops looking for the next machine if it gets an answer from one.

In other words, if a Domain Controller answers that the user does not exist, *Samba* doesn't try to connect to the next server to see if it can get a positive answer from it.

Creating Public Shares

To create a public share, add the parameter `public=yes` for each share listed in `smb.conf` file.

```
[public]
comment = Public Stuff
path = /home/public
browseable = yes
public = yes
writable = yes
```

The above lines tell *Samba* that there is a share called `public` and is mapped to `/home/public`. This share is described by the comment `Public Stuff` and is user writable. Anyone can access this share.

Creating Private Shares

The following is an example of creating a private share called `tonydir` for user `tho`. This writable share is described by the comment `Tony's Folder` and is mapped to `/home/tho`. Only the user called `tho` can access this share.

```
[tonydir]
comment = Tony's Folder
path = /home/tho
valid users = tho
public = no
writable = yes
```

Using Samba For Printer Sharing

Your standard OpenLinux installation should have created a printer queue for you. If this is the case, your Windows client sees a printer icon. The printer on the *Samba* server looks like any printer attached to your Windows machine. *Samba* does not do the actual printing; it simply accepts your print job and passes it to whatever print command you use on the OpenLinux server. So, if your OpenLinux server has no print queue then you won't be able to print using *Samba*!

Configuring Samba for Printer Sharing

The following code is the printers section from `smb.conf`. This automatically creates all the printer shares defined in `/etc/printcap`. The default settings should be sufficient to provide printing. If you need to make any changes to the print options for *Samba*, use the Printer Parameters page from *SWAT* to assist you.

```
[printers]
comment = All Printers
path = /var/spool/samba
browseable = no
# Set public = yes to allow user 'guest account' to print
guest ok = no
writable = no
printable = yes
create mask = 0700
```

Accessing SMB Shares with smbclient

To access any SMB shares on a *Samba* or Windows server, use the *smbclient* program. *smbclient* is very similar to *ftp* in terms of command syntax. Like *ftp*, *smbclient* is a text-based tool. Basically, *smbclient* allows you to use your OpenLinux system as a NetBIOS client in a Windows network.

Querying SMB Shares on an OpenLinux System

The following example shows a user querying what SMB shares are available on the OpenLinux system. The results are displayed in three sections. The first section lists the sharenames or SMB shares on that server. It shows that a folder called `public` and two printers called `ps` and `lp` are being shared on the OpenLinux system. The second section is the browse list of servers belonging to the workgroup or domain on which the server is located. The two SMB machines, `OL23` and `WinNT4`, are members of the workgroup called Workgroup. The last section displays the workgroup or domain known by this OpenLinux server. Here, `OL23` is the master browser for this workgroup. The `-N` switch uses the null password to connect to avoid being prompted for a password. This is equivalent to a guest connection to list shares.

```
[me@ol23 samba-2.0.5]$ smbclient -L localhost -N
Added interface ip=25.112.149.93 bcast=25.112.151.255 nmask=255.255.252.0
Password:
Domain=[WORKGROUP] OS=[Unix] Server=[Samba 2.0.5]
```

```
        Sharename      Type          Comment
        ———-           —             ——-
        public         Disk          Public Stuff
        IPC$           IPC           IPC Service (Samba Server on Caldera OpenLinux)
        ps             Printer
        lp             Printer

        Server         Comment
        ———-           ——-
        OL23           Samba Server on Caldera OpenLinux
        WinNT4         WinNT test box

        Workgroup      Master
        ———-           ——-
        WORKGROUP      OL23
[me@ol23 samba-2.0.5]$
```

Querying SMB Shares on an NT System

You can use *smbclient* to query what SMB shares are available on an NT system, as shown in the follwing example:

```
[me@ol23 samba-2.0.5]$ smbclient -L winNT
Added interface ip=25.112.149.193 bcast=25.112.151.255 nmask=255.255.252.0
session request to 25.112.149.251 failed
Password:
Domain=[WORKGROUP] OS=[Windows NT 4.0] Server=[NT LAN Manager 4.0]

Sharename             Type          Comment
———-                  —             ——-
ADMIN$                Disk          Remote Admin
IPC$                  IPC           Remote IPC
C$                    Disk          Default share
CDR                   Disk          Share CD
tony                  Disk          Tony's Folder
HPLaserJ              Printer       HP LaserJet 5L
TEMP                  Disk          Temporary Files
print$                Disk          Printer Drivers

                      Server        Comment
                      ——-           ——-
```

```
                    Workgroup     Master
                    -------       -------
[me@123 samba-2.0.5]$
```

Sending Winpopup Messages to a Windows Client

To send short text messages to a Windows client named `winNT` and have the message appear in the Winpopup window (see Figure 3-1), issue this command:

```
smbclient -M winNT
Added interface ip=25.112.149.93 bcast=25.112.151.255 nmask=255.255.252.0
Got a positive name query response from 25.112.149.254 ( 25.112.149.254 )
Connected. Type your message, ending it with a Control-D
Greetings Windows.  Take me to your Server!
sent 45 bytes
```

Additional Samba Utilities

Following are a number of useful *Samba* utilities included in the *Samba* package.

/usr/sbin/addtosmbpass

The awk script requires root privileges to execute and is used to add new entries to the `smbpasswd` files. Its syntax is:

```
addtosmbpass name1 [name2 ....] < smbpasswd.in >  smbpasswd.out
```

Arguments are account names, such as name1, name2, …, to add.

`smbpasswd.in` is the current *Samba* password file.

`smbpasswd.out` is the revised *Samba* password file.

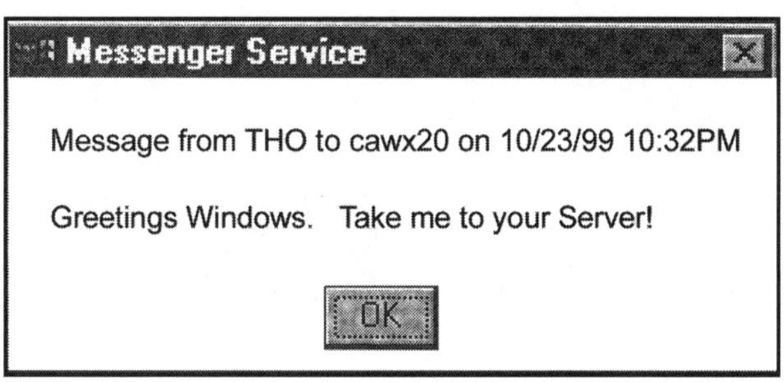

Figure 3-1 *A Winpopup message*

/usr/bin/smbstatus

This executable displays the status of current *Samba* connections.

```
[me@o123]$ smbstatus

Samba version 2.0.5
Service     uid      gid      pid     machine
---------------------------


No locked files


Share mode memory usage (bytes):
   1048464(99%) free + 56(0%) used + 56(0%) overhead = 1048576(100%) total
```

/usr/sbin/smbadduser

This perl script updates `/etc/samba.d/smbpasswd` and `/etc/samba.d/smbusers` files and executes smbpasswd for new users.

/usr/sbin/findsmb

This nice little perl script requires root privilege to execute and is useful to display information on all SMB machines on your subnet. Its syntax is:

```
findsmb [subnet broadcast address]
```

With no arguments, this lists the machines on the current subnet.

```
[root@o123.mydomain.org]# findsmb
IP ADDR          NETBIOS NAME   WORKGROUP/OS/VERSION
---------------------------------------------------

172.112.149.94  win98.mydomain.org
172.112.149.93  o123.mydomain.org
```

Troubleshooting

Samba creates a log file to help you troubleshoot problems. By default, the log files for *nmbd* and *smbd* are found in `/var/log/samba.d`. The degree of details in the log files is controlled by the log level parameter in `smb.conf`. Setting log level=3 logs in great details.

Don't forget to search the excellent archival and search site at **http://www.dejanews.com**. This site contains years of other people's questions and answers. For those of you who like to read USENET newsgroup, check out `comp.protocols.smb`.

To help troubleshoot Windows' client access problems, don't forget to check out Microsoft's online support Web site at **www.microsoft.com/support**. A common problem for Windows 98 and NT 4 with Service Pack 3 and higher clients is that passwords are sent encrypted so you either need to configure *Samba* to accept encrypted passwords or change your Windows registry to send passwords in plain text. To configure *Samba*, add `encrypt password=yes` under the global section of the `smb.conf` file. Then you need to run `smbpasswd user-name` to add username to *Samba's* encrypted database. To change the Windows Registry to enable plain text password, execute the registry files found in `/usr/doc/samba-2.0.5/docs`. These files have `.reg` extensions. Copy them over to your Windows computer and execute them.

There is an excellent troubleshooting document at `/usr/doc/samba-2.0.5/docs/textdocs/diagnosis.txt` that was authored by Andrew Tridgell, the original creator of *Samba*.

Hints

The following hints are based on the hints document located at `/usr/doc/samba-2.0.5/docs/textdocs/hints.txt`.

- Use *SWAT* to assist you in configuring `smb.conf`.
- Use *smbtestparm* to validate `smb.conf` for syntax or logical errors.
- Use Windows Wordpad to read UNIX text files to avoid formatting problems.
- To avoid username mismatch between the usernames on your Windows client and those on the Openlinux server, use the `username` map option in `smb.conf`.

For More Information

You can find additional *Samba* documentation on your OpenLinux system:

```
/usr/docs/samba-2.0.5/docs

/usr/docs/samba-2.0.5/textdocs
```

You can obtain online information from the following Web sites:

URL	Resource Name
www.samba.org	The official home page for *Samba*
lists.samba.org	Mailing lists archive
comp.protocol.smb	USENET newsgroup about SMB

Chapter 4: Using NFS and LPRng for UNIX File and Printer Sharing

Overview of NFS

Overview of LPRng

Configuring NFS Filesharing

Using COAS to Mount Your NFS Directory

Troubleshooting NFS

Configuring LPRng Printer Sharing

Starting and Stopping LPRng

Today, there are thousands of Linux file and print servers. The ability to share is essential. Data sharing in a local networked environment is typically done by sharing a set of disks over the network; NFS(*Network File System*) allows this to occur. LPRng is the method of printing under OpenLinux. Unlike some operating systems, the entire process of printing is visible to the end user. This visibility allows for significant customization so that the users' and system administrators' needs are fulfilled. While by no means exhaustive, this chapter will examine the specifics of these essential network services.

Files Referenced in this Chapter

File	Purpose
/dev/nfsd	file present if NFS is compiled into kernel
/etc/exports	file that allows NFS export configuration
/etc/hosts.allow	file responsible for allowing access to host
/etc/rc.d/rc.d/init.d	file which contains information about which *rpc* programs need to be restarted
/etc/fstab	file responsible for mounting file systems at boot
/etc/printcap	file containing all information related to your printer

Overview of NFS

Using NFS to share files is similar to using NetWare volumes, Samba shares, and so on. NFS has become the standard method of sharing data in Linux as well as in all the varieties of BSD UNIX, Solaris, Irix, etc. The concept of having a mutual set of disks has been a part of UNIX from its origin.

Overview of LPRng

LPRng is an enhanced version of the printing system used by BSD UNIX for OpenLinux. As with BSD UNIX and OpenLinux, a set of similar binaries is at the heart of the printing system. These files perform queuing, filtering, prioritizing, printing, accounting, and so on. As with other UNIX operating systems, the translation of the document into PostScript is a vital part of the printing process. The steps that are involved in printing and the customizations that are allowed are all part of LPRng in OpenLinux.

Configuring NFS Filesharing

The first part of configuring an NFS server is to determine the client-server relationship. This means you need to decide what the client wants and needs and how the server can deliver those files. In the case of NFS, you decide who your clients are, what they want to share with others, and what they want to place in a central repository but not share with others. When configuring a server, you decide what access to your various files and directories you want to give the users. Although it's a good idea to determine all this information before you begin the configuration process, you can continue making an NFS server without this data. After determining the client-server relationship, you need to create an export.

Creating an Export

The first step in creating an export is to ensure that NFS services are compiled into your kernel. You can determine this on the basis of whether you have the file `/dev/nfsd`. In OpenLinux, the default kernel has NFS compiled in, so unless you rebuilt your kernel, you don't have to worry. If somebody recompiled your kernel or you don't know how to add NFS into the kernel and recompile it, see the troubleshooting section later in this chapter. After you have checked that you have NFS capabilities, you can begin the process of creating an export. You can do so either by manually editing the configuration files or by using a GUI to help edit the files.

It is beneficial for users to understand what a tool is actually doing, so we will begin by guiding you through the process of creating an export manually. After you have gone through the manual configuration process and you understand more about the underlying concepts that are involved in creating an export, we will go over the process of creating an export with a GUI.

Manually Creating an Export

To begin the process of creating an export, export only the `/home` directory. While it is possible to export any directory, seeing how this is done will help you understand the process in its simplest form. The `/home` directory contains the files that are most important to users. Few users regularly backup and it is easy for you to do the backup process for them.

A few other directories you may consider exporting as a System Administrator would be `/usr` and `/var/spool/mail`. If you don't understand why you would want to export `/var/spool/mail`, remember that many people consider the loss of an e-mail message tragic. You may want to export the `/usr` directory so the clients can share the software. This is very helpful in cases where licensing is an issue, and it gives all the users the same set of programs to run. Exporting the `/usr` directory does have some potential complications. For example, some of your users could have different hardware configurations, which will create problems after you export `/usr/X11R6`. There are several ways you can get around these problems, but the solutions may cause more work than they're worth. To find out, try exporting the `/usr` directory to a select few clients and see what you have to go through.

To export the `/home` directory, we need to begin the process of preparing the system for it. Start by editing the `/etc/exports` file. Below are three separate examples that illustrate some of the different possibilities.

```
/home     *.foo.com(rw,insecure)
/home     192.168.1.1-192.168.1.50(ro,noaccess)
/home     192.168.5(rw,secure)
/home     192.168.7.1(rw,secure) 192.168.7.3,192(rw,secure) 168.7.23(rw,secure)
```

On the left is the directory we want to export. The code on the right indicates where it is being exported to: a domain, a single host, or a range of IP addresses. The code in parentheses begins with either `ro` or `rw`, which means read only and read write, respectively. This code is followed by the options `insecure`, `noaccess`, and `secure`. The terms `secure` and `insecure` relate only to the ports that can be assigned to NFS. The port numbers for `insecure` can be above 1024, and they must be below 1024 for `secure`. In a sense, the option `noaccess chroots` the users. Users cannot go above or below in the directory specified, so they are no longer free to roam the filesystem. There are several other options you can use, and you can find them in `man 5 exports`.

After you set up the exports file, ensure that */sbin/portmap* is running. Do this by typing `rpcinfo -p (hostname)`. If you want NFS to load on startup, make sure that *portmap* is loaded before it in your SYS V Initialization steps. After doing so, specify which domains can access *portmap* in your `hosts.allow` file. To prevent anyone outside your domain from accessing *portmap*, add the following lines to your `/etc/host.allow` file:

```
portmap: .foo.com : allow

portmap: ALL : deny
```

By adding these lines, users who aren't in foo.com cannot use *portmap*. You could have used IP addresses as well. Put the lines in this order is because the daemon goes from top to bottom; if your file looked like the following, you would have denied even yourself:

```
portmap: ALL : deny

portmap: .foo.com : allow
```

Now restart *portmap,* because it is already running by default in OpenLinux:

```
killall rpc*
```

You must kill every *rpc* program because they are all dependent on */usr/sbin/rpc.portmap*.

To check what *rpc* programs you need to restart, go to `/etc/rc.d/ init.d` and see what *r* programs were started. For each one, type:

```
./r(foo) start
```

To make sure *nfs* works, go to `/etc/rc.d/init.d/` and type:

```
./nfs start
```

Because it started without any problems, you can now make a symbolic link to `/etc/rc.d/init.d/nfs` so that *nfs* starts on boot by typing:

```
ln -s /etc/rc.d/init.d/nfs /etc/rc.d/rc3.d/S(some number after "network"
"init" and "netmount" and before "dhcpd")nfs
```

For example:

```
ln -s /etc/rc.d/init.d/nfs /etc/rc.d/rc3.d/S22nfs
```

If something went amiss when you tried starting *nfs*, go to the troubleshooting section at the end of this chapter.

Manually Mounting an Export

Now that you have created your export, you want your users to be able to mount it. Just as you had to edit a configuration file to create an export, you must edit another file to mount an export. The optimal file to edit in this case is `/etc/fstab`. In `/etc/fstab` there are six columns (although they don't always look like columns). Only the first four columns are relevant to this chapter. This file is readable to any user, but is only writeable as root.

The first column contains the device you are going to mount. There are several different types of devices that can appear in this column, including NFS servers.

```
/dev/sda1

/dev/hdb

foo:/home/foo
```

The last line is the name of the NFS server, which qualifies as a device, and the exported root directory. In `fstab`, you can select any fully qualified domain server.

CAUTION

> Using an NFS server outside your LAN would be quite slow even with a T1 or greater bandwidth connection.

The second column indicates where the device is to be mounted with respect to your local file system. Now take a look at both the first and second columns of `/etc/fstab`:

```
/dev/sda1      /

/dev/hdb      /mnt/cdrom

nil.foo.edu:      /home
```

You can see how the devices are mounted into the local file system, which allows access. In this scenario, the users are importing their `home` directories.

The third column of `fstab` indicates the file system type:

```
/dev/sda1      /      ext2

/dev/hdb      /mnt/cdrom      iso9660

nil.foo.edu:      /home      NFS
```

In Linux, there is a large list of file systems that can be read or written to.

In the fourth column, you can define additional options relating to the file system. With NFS devices, this is the heart of its configuration at a user's end. The following are the basic options you can place in the fourth column.

- `rsize=x` The number of bytes that the NFS server will read before transmission. Depending on network speed, traffic, server load, and client performance, this number can vary greatly. In most environments, it is safe to set this at 8KB or 16KB. This number must be converted directly to bytes, so `rsize` of 16KB would be written as `rsize=16384`.
- `wsize=x` If `rsize` is the number of bytes read at a time, `wsize` naturally is the number of bytes written at a time. Because most clients read and write to an NFS server equally, it is wise to set the `wsize` to be the same as the `rsize`.
- `timeo=x` This is the number of tenths of a second the client waits for a response from the server before retransmission. If the server does not respond in the first interval, the client doubles the interval until a maximum of 60

seconds is reached. The default is 7, and unless you have a very busy network, there typically isn't a reason to change this setting.

- `retrans=x` This is the number of times that you, as the client, allow your system to retransmit before your system gives the error message `server not responding`.

There are several additional options that you can give in the fourth column but they are typically not used. If you want further information on these options, enter `man 5 nfs` at the command line.

Using COAS to Mount Your NFS Directory

If you don't want to hand-edit a file, there is a graphical tool you can use to do all this configuration and mount your NFS directory. This tool is called *COAS* (Caldera Open Administration Tool), and it comes with every OpenLinux system. You can find an icon for it on the Kpanel.

Click on the *COAS* icon, and then choose System, Filesystem. The File System window will appear, displaying a list of mounted file systems and the corresponding mount points, as seen in Figure 4-1. Here you are given the option to mount or unmount file systems.

To mount a NFS file system, select Mount NFS from the Action menu. The File System Options window appears as seen in Figure 4-2. If you click on OK, the Mount File System window will appear.

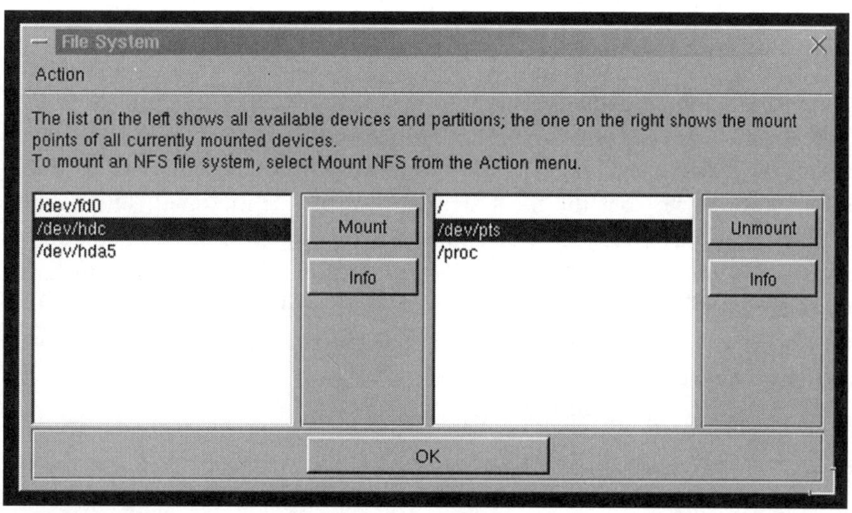

Figure 4-1 *The File System window*

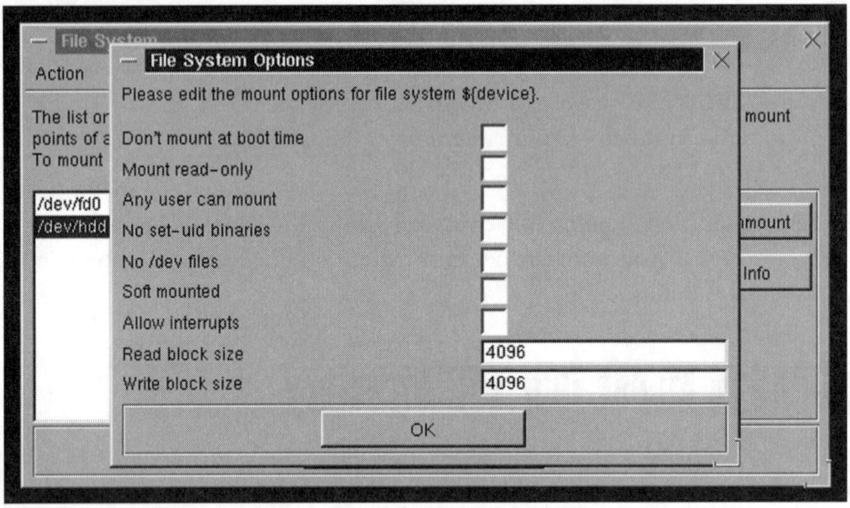

Figure 4-2 *The File System Options window*

The Mount File System window asks you where the file system you would like to mount is. Enter in the Device field the NFS server and the directory on the NFS server to which you want to import. Enter the mount point for the device on your system in the Directory field.

Finally, you can change any of the settings for the mounted file system just as you could in the fourth column of the `fstab` file. To do this, press the defaults,nolock button. The File System Options window will reappear. Here you have several options for mounting the file system. When mounting an NFS file system you should select "No set-uid binaries", as no programs are given root privileges. Additionally, you should select "No /dev files" because in most cases the administrator isn't exporting the `root` directory. The "Soft mounted" option alerts the user if a program experiences a major timeout while trying to execute, mount, write, or read from the NFS import. Leaving this option unselected will hard mount the file system, meaning that the program will report timeouts to the console. Major, default timeouts will retry forever whether the file system is hard or soft mounted. The "Allow Interrupts" option is only available when an imported filesystem is hard mounted. In the case of a major timeout, it will send the program making the request an interrupt, which causes an open file to close. The "Read block size" and "Write block size" fields allow you to specify the number of kilobytes that will be read or written by the server at a time, from the requestor.

After making your selections, click on OK to return to the Mount File System window. The last button asks if you want to add the file system entry to the `fstab` file. By adding it to `fstab` it will load on boot so that you do not have to go through this process again (at least until something needs to be changed).

Manually Mounting Your Import

If you decided to continue without the GUI, you need to learn how to mount your import. This is a fairly simple process but because it only occurs automatically at boot (if you want it to), you need a non-automatic way. If you mount the import from boot, or if you mount it without a reboot, the NFS server still must go through the verification and port allocation for the user. First, you need to either be the root user, su to root, or be a user with privileges to implement the changes that were modified in the `fstab` file.

Since most Linux users dread the reboot, they implement these changes without rebooting. If you wish to mount the `/home` directory type the following as root:

```
mount /home
```

As long as the user who is currently logged in has the rights to access this mount, it will be mounted. If the user doesn't have the rights to import `foo:/home`, he would not be able to mount the directory even if he used the `su` command, due to *nfs* permissions.

> **NOTE**
>
> You will not be able to mount the directory until you have added the corresponding entry into the `etc/fstab` file either manually or with the aid of COAS.

Starting or Stopping NFS

For one reason or another on either a server or a client system, you might need to stop NFS. This procedure is done differently on servers and client systems. For example, if you want your server to go into `init 1`, the process of shutting down *nfs* is done automatically. If you are planning to shut down your NFS server at a given time, it is always wise to e-mail everybody who will be affected so they are aware of this fact and can save their data and stop using NFS applications.

The first step to stopping *nfs* has already been mentioned; if it is possible, contact all of the users prior to this action. Then, shut down the *nfs* daemon by going to the `/etc/rc.d/init.d/` directory, and typing `./nfs stop`. This stops the *nfs* daemon. If for some reason, after a long period of time, the command line still says it is stopping NFS, you have to follow more drastic procedures because the *nfs* daemon is hung. You can send it a kill signal: `kill -s 9 nfsd`. If it still doesn't stop, you can stop *portmap*, or kill *portmap* if necessary, and in most cases you should be able to kill the *nfs* daemon without changing init levels, or rebooting.

You start *nfs* on your server by first ensuring that the daemon is scripted in `/etc/rc.d/init.d/`. After you check whether *nfs* is scripted, run `/usr/sbin/rpc.portmap`.

This begins the process of allowing ports to be mapped on demand. Next, you can start the *nfs* daemon. If you have a script in `/etc/rc.d/init.d/`, go to that directory and type `./nfs start`. You then see on the output `starting nfs` in the terminal.

Starting *nfs* on a client system is simply the process of mounting the NFS export on your system. As we mentioned previously, you can do this using *COAS* or from a command line. You can stop *nfs* on a client server by unmounting the import, which can also be done within *COAS* or from a command line by typing `umount /home`, where `/home` is the imported directory.

Troubleshooting NFS

Troubleshooting NFS can be a complex and challenging task for the adminstrator. Hopefully, one of the following scenarios will apply to the symptoms of your NFS woes. In each of the following scenarios, it is assumed that both the server and client have full network connectivity. A good test of this is to have the client ping the server or have the server ping the client. We have also assumed that all other relevant servers are functioning properly (DNS, DHCP, and so on).

Scenario 1

You are able to create an export, but *nfs* fails. This is most likely caused by either not running *portmap* or not having *nfs* compiled in the kernel. For instructions on recompiling your kernel see the Appendix.

Scenario 2

You are running *nfsd*, and when users try to log on, they get an *rpc* error. This is caused by not having *portmap* running, or because *portmap* died. You need to (re)start *portmap* or kill and then restart it if it is still running. You should then restart *nfsd* this by going to the `/etc/rc.d/init.d/` directory and typing `./nfs restart`.

Scenario 3

You try to mount your NFS import and you receive the warning `permission denied`. This occurs when you are logged in as someone without the ability to connect to the NFS export, or your system is denied in the `/etc/exports` file. This denial could also be caused by domain issues, or IP address issues.

Scenario 4

You try to mount your import but the mount fails without an error message. Check your kernel and, if applicable, recompile as mentioned above.

Configuring LPRng Printer Sharing

There are many reasons why you might want to share a printer, such as efficiency, lower cost, and increased employee communication. Many printers are ready to be networked just by being connected to an Ethernet and given an appropriate queue. Other printers require a bit more work but they can still be just as effective.

In Linux, the underlying concepts of printer sharing are a part of the operating system. To understand printing and printer sharing, you need to understand how something is printed in Linux.

The age old question of "which comes first?" is an apt illustration for the printing process under Linux. Does the application want to print first or does the system want to receive a print job? Let's begin by saying that the application is what initiates the printing process. If an application decides that it wants to print a document, another application that runs in the background then takes over the process of printing. The application *lpr* is used only to send print jobs to the printer. If you do not want to use another application, such as *Emacs*, to print from, you can print directly from a command line. If you wanted to print your security log `/var/log/secure`, you would type:

```
cat /var/log/secure | lpr -Plp
```

`P` stands for printer and `lp` stands for the print queue to which you want to send the print job. Although you can attempt to print from a command line by typing this command without setting up a printer, your job will be sent to a print queue and never get printed without a printer definition.

Creating a Printer Definition

To set up a printer, you begin by editing the configuration file `/etc/printcap`. This file contains all of the information regarding your printer that you need to define. Let's look at a sample `/etc/printcap` file. We will divide this file into sections for easier discussion, as it also shows a non-PostScript local printer and a remote printer.

PostScript Printer

```
##PRINTTOOL## LOCAL bj200 360x360 letter {}
ps:\
        :sd=/var/spool/lpd/ps:\
        :mx#0:\
        :lp=/dev/lp0:\
        :if=/var/spool/lpd/ps/filter:\
        :sh:
```

Line 1 indicates that the local printer is a bj200 that prints at 360x360 resolutions on letter sized paper.

Line 2 indicates the name of the queue.

Line 3 indicates where the spooler is (where queued jobs go).

Line 4 indicates the maximum size of a print job. 0 means no limit. There are few times when you need to limit the size of a print job.

Line 5 indicates the printer location as a device; here it is the first parallel port.

Line 6 indicates the location of the filter which handles all PostScript print jobs.

Line 7 indicates that banner pages should not be printed; remove this line if you want them.

Non-PostScript Printer

```
##PRINTTOOL## LOCAL
lp:\
        :sd=/var/spool/lpd/lp:\
        :mx#0:\
        :lp=/dev/lp0:\
        :sh:
```

Line 1 indicates that this is a local printer.

Line 2 indicates the name of the print queue.

Line 3 indicates the location of the queued print jobs.

Line 4 indicates the maximum print job size.

Line 5 indicates the location of the printer as a device.

Line 6 indicates that banner pages should not be printed.

Remote Printer

```
##PRINTTOOL## REMOTE
lp|ps:\
        :sd=/var/spool/lpd/lp:\
        :mx#0:\
        :rm=razimon.foo.net:\
        :rp=fir:
```

Line 1 indicates that this is a remote/networked printer.

Line 2 indicates that the printer accepts both PostScript and non-PostScript jobs.

Line 3 indicates where the jobs are queued before they are sent to the printer/print server.

Line 4 indicates the name of the print server.

Line 5 indicates the name of the remote printer.

There are several more options you can add to the `/etc/printcap` file to give additional configuration abilities. Basically, if you can think of something that you want to configure on the printer, the option is there. To find out more about these options, refer to **man 5 printcap**.

Now I can hear you say "How do I know how to set my printer, which isn't a PostScript printer and it isn't a bj200 like in your example?" Well, you can find out the various definitions and names that GhostScript uses, or you can use some of the tools OpenLinux provides for you. The following section goes through the process of setting up a printer using *COAS*.

Using COAS for Printer Configuration

You begin by selecting *COAS*, Peripherals, Printer from the Kpanel. Select Add from the Printer menu of the Printer configuration window, as seen in Figure 4-3.

Now select your printer from the Select printer model window, as seen in Figure 4-4.

After you have selected the printer, you need to give it a logical name, as shown in Figure 4-5. You can call it anything you like, even if it is a network printer. This is only for your reference when you print.

You can add both a network printer and a remote printer to a client, but as a system administrator you should add a shared printer. To do this, you set up your printer as if it is a local printer, as shown in the Printer attributes window seen in Figure 4-6.

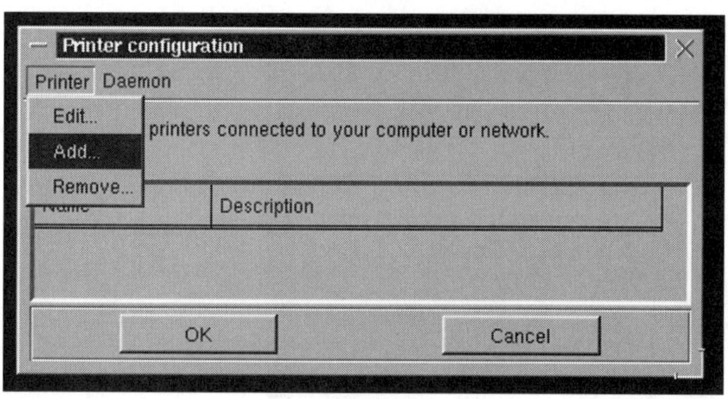

Figure 4-3 *Printer configuration*

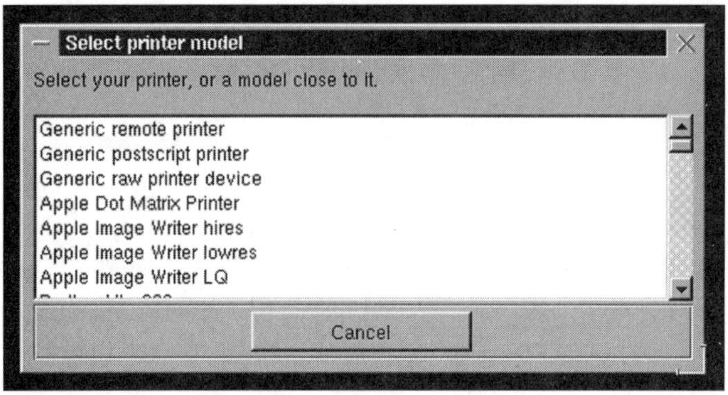

Figure 4-4 *Select printer model*

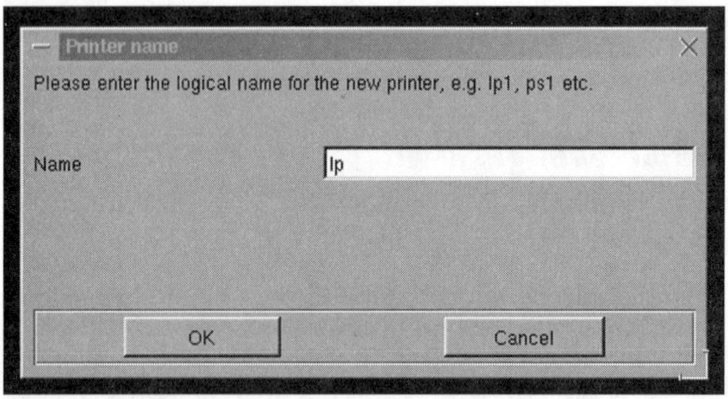

Figure 4-5 *Naming your printer*

After entering the basic settings here, click on OK to return to the Printer configuration window.

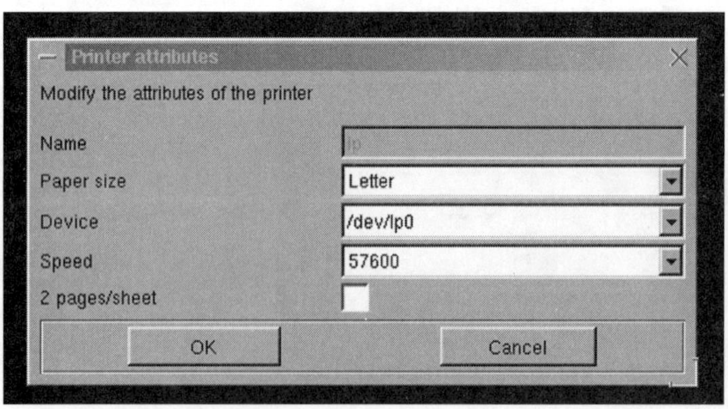

Figure 4-6 *Printer Attributes*

For the fine tuning that you must do to configure a network printer, select Edit from the Printer menu. At this point, a second and more advanced Printer attributes window will appear, as seen in Figure 4-7. Although you have already named your printer, you can give it other logical names. This allows you to have a different local name from the name that your networked printer clients. In the description field, you can give a more in-depth description. This can be beneficial in *Samba* or when you have several networks and printers, so that you can remember the location, age, special hardware, and so on of the printer. In the Type field you can select the type of your printer, whether it is an HP 4000, a generic raw printer, or otherwise. Next, you can set the default resolution and paper size. After doing that, you have the device point that the printer is on, along with the speed (the polling speed, or the speed the port can negotiate with the printer).

CAUTION

> If your port can only negotiate a baud rate of 57,600 and you set it to a higher rate, it won't increase the printing speed, and it might negatively affect the print quality.

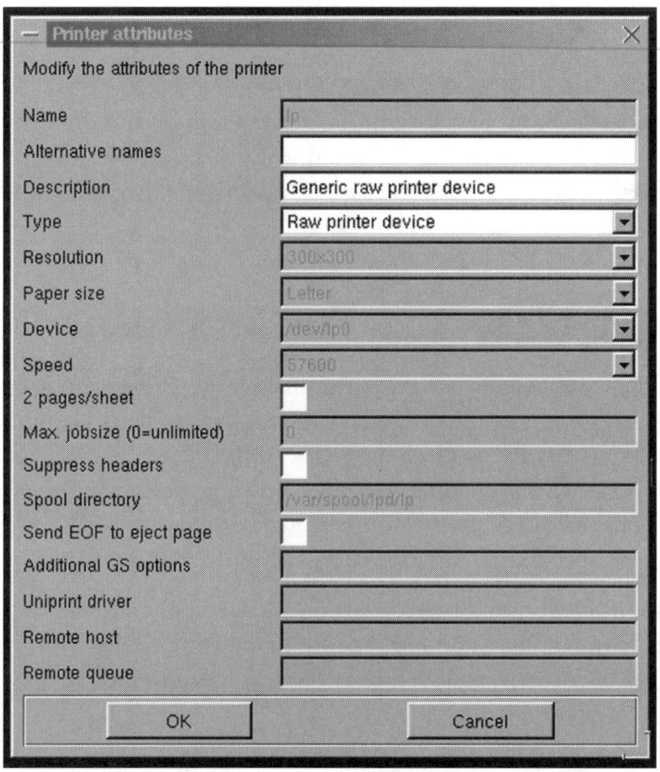

Figure 4-7 *Network Printer Attributes*

At this point, you identify whether the printer can print on both sides of the page, and what the maximum job size will be. (Limiting the job size isn't the only method that can be used to allow people to receive their print jobs quickly; you can also use job size- based queuing). You then have the option to suppress headers (banner pages), and the spool directory. This allows you to further customize your system. The next option allows you to send the EOF signal to identify the end of a page. You should use this only if your printer requires it, or your printer will eject a blank page.

You are now allowed to pass any additional options that you want to GhostScript. There is good documentation on GS that tells you of the options that are available to you.

Finally, you will need to identify the remote host (print server) and the remote queue (print queue on the print server), which is also known as the printer's name on the print server.

Creating a Print Queue

Now that you have configured your printer, you will want to make the print queues. One of the advantages of LPRng over LPR is the program *checkpc*, which automatically sets up this information. At a command line, you need to type:

```
checkpc -f
```

This sets up your print queues and your permissions. You can modify the permissions by editing the `/etc/lpd.perms` file. For further information on this file, you can type **man 5 printcap**. The file `lpd.perms` is fairly easy to understand because it is commented very well.

Starting and Stopping LPRng

As an administrator, you may occasionally need to interrupt printing services on your network. Starting LPRng is easy after it is configured: all you have to do is load the daemon *lpd* and you have started LPRng. Although this starts LPRng, you might want to do an analysis of what is going on. To do this you can go to `/var/spool/lpd/(ps or lp)` and check your status and logs, or you can simply use the following software that is specifically designed to assist you with this analysis.

- *Lp* A program responsible for sending requests to the daemon. You can run the program from a command line and take various parameters, such as: priority-level, number of copies, debug verbosity level, and so on. Find further details on *lp* by typing **man 1 lp**.
- *Lpc* This program allows you to stop or start either a single printer or multiple printers. This is preferred over stopping the daemon because

stopping the daemon stops the capability to queue as well. With *lpc* as an administrator, you can redirect print jobs, change their places in the queue, reprint a job, and so on. You can find further details by typing **man 1 lpc.**

- *Lpd* This is the print daemon, and thus it is what all of the other programs interact with when they are getting their printer information or sending commands to the printer. You can find further details by typing **man 8 lpd**.
- *Lpq* This program allows you to examine the print queue so you can see what jobs are in the queue and when to run *lpc.*
- *Lpr* This program is used to send print jobs: it places them in the queue, and advises you when a printer hasn't been defined, is offline, and so on.
- *Lpraccnt* This program listens for the print jobs coming in on their typical port 3000 (but can be reconfigured) and sends the information to standard output.
- *Lprm* This is the ultimate program that is involved in starting and stopping printing because it has complete power to kill a print job in midstream or to simply remove it from the queue.
- *Lpstat* This program checks the status of a specified printer to see if it is functioning or not. By using this program along with *cron*, you will be notified if something is amiss with the printer.

Troubleshooting LPRng

Unfortunately, you might run into problems with LPRng. There are four main types of problems that occur in LPRng (assuming it is setup properly): users cannot print, print jobs are lost, printers fail, and text is garbled or missing.

- **User cannot print:** This situation often appears as if the job goes to `/dev/null`. Begin by ensuring that they have permission to print. You can check this in `/etc/lpd.perms`.
- **Print job is lost:** Using *lp* in debug mode with verbosity will help you see many of the errors since it monitors the process of *lpr* until it is placed in the queue. After it is in the queue, you can use it to get further details about the job in the queue.
- **Printer fails:** You can use the utility *lpstat* to tell you when a problem occurs. In many cases, you will know before the clients contact you.
- **Garbled or missing text:** After you ensure that it isn't your printer (out of toner, and so on), the error lies either in the `/etc/printcap` file or the `/etc/lpd.conf` file. Typically, this latter file does not need to be modified, but you can check it. The file is well commented so it is easy to understand.

For More Information

URL	Resource Name
http://www.patoche.org/LTT/	Linux Tips & Tricks
http://www.picante.com/~gtaylor/pht/	The Linux Printing HOWTO
http://www.linuxdoc.org	Linux Documentation Project

PART III
Configuring Internet Services on OpenLinux

5 Configuring DNS and bind

6 Configuring the Apache Web Server

7 Configuring SMTP E-mail with sendmail and procmail

8 Configuring FTP Servers with WU-FTPD

9 Configuring UseNet News with innd

10 Configuring Radius with Livingston's radiusd

11 Building a Firewall with ipchains

12 Configuring the squid Proxy Server

13 Configuring Telnet, SSH, and DHCP Services

Chapter 5: Configuring DNS and bind

DNS Overview

Configuring DNS

Troubleshooting bind

bind, the generic name of the DNS server that comes with OpenLinux, originated as a project at the University of California at Berkeley several years ago. It has passed through many hands since, and now resides in the hands of the Internet Software Consortium, which maintains the current version, Version 8. Although the previous version (Version 4) is still in use in many places, only Version 8 ships with Caldera OpenLinux 2.3.

NOTE

> You will often see references in this chapter to *named*, short for NAME Daemon, which is the actual *bind* program.

Files Referenced in this Chapter

The following files are used by OpenLinux's implementation of *bind*:

File	Purpose
`/etc/named.conf`	The named configuration file
`/var/named/root.hints`	The root DNS cache file
`/var/named/pz`	A directory of primary zone files
`/var/named/sz`	A directory of secondary zone files

The following files, although not used by *bind*, are relevant to name resolution:

File	Purpose
`/etc/hosts`	The hosts file contains IP addresses for hostnames in a simple text file
`/etc/nsswitch.conf`	The Name Service Switch configuration file tells OpenLinux whether to query the hosts file, DNS, or NIS to resolve hostnames
`/etc/resolv.conf`	The Name Resolver configuration file tells OpenLinux how to perform DNS queries

DNS Overview

Name resolution is the process of taking a *hostname* and producing its corresponding *IP address*. OpenLinux supports three different methods of name resolution: the `/etc/hosts` file, DNS, and NIS (an older protocol typically used only on UNIX systems). This chapter focuses on DNS (*Domain Name System)* and its interaction with the `/etc/hosts` file. If you are already familiar with DNS basics, feel free to proceed to the next section.

DNS looks up a name so it can tell computers on the Internet that, for example, my Web server www.cheek.com and my ftp server ftp.cheek.com are actually 208.12.12.134, and so on. In addition, *Reverse DNS* does the opposite—it takes an IP address, such as 208.12.12.134, and converts it back into the hostname www.cheek.com. The process of connecting to a DNS server, giving it a hostname, and requesting the corresponding IP address is called a *DNS lookup*, or *DNS query*. Similarly, requesting a hostname from a DNS server when giving it an IP address is called a *Reverse DNS lookup*.

NOTE

Not only does DNS provide IP address and hostname lookups, it can also give detailed information about a host, specify many IP addresses for a single host, provide distributed name resolution, and more. This chapter deals only with setting up a basic DNS server that provides IP address and hostname lookups.

Some computers on the Internet act as DNS servers, meaning they respond to these DNS requests; many computers do not, however, and need to know the address of a DNS server that will respond to these requests for them. Having your own DNS server speeds DNS lookups from machines on your network, enables you to handle DNS requests from other machines (if your company is an ISP, this might involve handling Internet connection requests), and allows you full control over any domain names you own. For example, I have DNS servers running on my machines to provide DNS services for computers in my office and to handle DNS requests for my own domain as well as my clients' domains.

By default, OpenLinux uses the local `/etc/hosts` file and, optionally, other DNS or NIS servers for name resolution. When a DNS server is installed and configured on OpenLinux, it needs to be told to use itself for name resolution also. To configure a DNS server and have it work, the machine needs an IP address and a functional IP stack. Ideally, it should contain at least one network card. (Chapter 2, Configuring OpenLinux's Basic Network, discusses how to configure basic IP networking on OpenLinux.)

How DNS Works

DNS is organized in a hierarchy, just as hostnames are. Consider the fictional hostname www.linuxkb.cheek.com. When a DNS lookup is requested for this hostname, a query is sent to find .com, then cheek.com, then linuxkb.cheek.com, and then www.linuxkb.cheek.com. The DNS server with information about .com might not be the same server that knows cheek.com, which might not be the same server that knows linuxkb.cheek.com, and so on. In this respect, DNS is arranged like a tree, with a root, branches, and leaves (see Figure 5-1).

The *root* is where DNS lookups start. DNS servers that contain information about the root are called *root servers*. On the Internet, the root servers are a.root-servers.net, b.root-servers.net, c.root-servers.net, and so on, up to m.root-servers.net. These servers maintain information about *top level domains,* such as .com and .net. The servers that handle .com then know where to find cheek.com; the servers that handle cheek.com know where to find linuxkb.cheek.com, and so on. A DNS lookup walks this tree from the root through the branches until it finds the server that knows about the hostname for which it is looking. When it finds that server, it queries the server for the needed information.

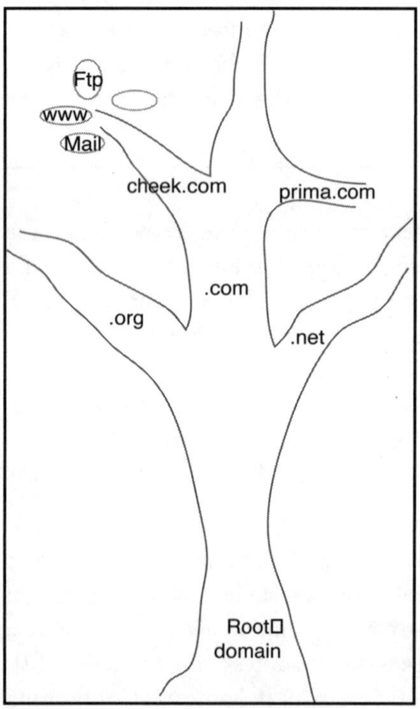

Figure 5-1 *DNS is logically organized like a tree, with a root, branches, and leaves. The root domain corresponds to the root of a tree, top level domains are branches from the root, and domain names are branches from them. Hosts are analogous to leaves on the tree.*

An important concept with DNS is the *root domain*. All domain names have an implied period at the end of their names, which stands for the root domain. For example, cheek.com really is cheek.com., although only computers actually use the trailing period. This period is significant in DNS, though, because it means that a particular domain starts from the root domain, and not some other domain. This becomes important as you configure the DNS server.

> Even though the root domain exists on all domains (using .com. instead of just .com, for example), typically it is just implied. I will continue to refer to domains by the standard notation, for example .com, except when distinguishing between the two.
>
> NOTE

You are probably familiar with some of the more common top level domains, such as .com, .net, and .org. Many more exist; one special domain is the in-addr.arpa domain. The in-addr.arpa *(INverse ADDRess.ARPAnet)* domain is a domain that handles all reverse DNS lookups. To perform a reverse DNS lookup, a computer performs a normal query in the in-addr.arpa domain. The IP addresses to look up become the hostname of the in-addr.arpa domain, although their order is reversed. The address 208.12.12.134 is queried as 134.12.12.208.in-addr.arpa; more technically, the host 134 is queried from the subdomain 12.12.208.in-addr.arpa. A DNS server queried this way returns the corresponding hostname (such as www.cheek.com).

DNS also specifies which machines in a domain handle its e-mail. A domain can have dozens, hundreds, or even thousands of hosts in it, but typically mail sent to those domains is collected on a small number of machines, perhaps on only one. A special DNS entry is used to specify which hosts collect mail for domains and subdomains.

Configuring DNS

Even if your organization does not have a valid, registered Internet domain name, *bind* will function, but it works much better if you do have one. This section walks you through setting up a DNS server for the fictional domain.com domain, with hosts ns.domain.com at IP address 192.168.1.1, mail.domain.com at IP address 192.168.1.2, and www.domain.com at IP address 192.168.1.3 (see Figure 5-2). The ns.domain.com server is a primary DNS server for the domain.com domain, and a secondary backup DNS server for the domain2.com domain. domain2.com's primary DNS server is ns.domain2.com at IP address 192.168.2.1.

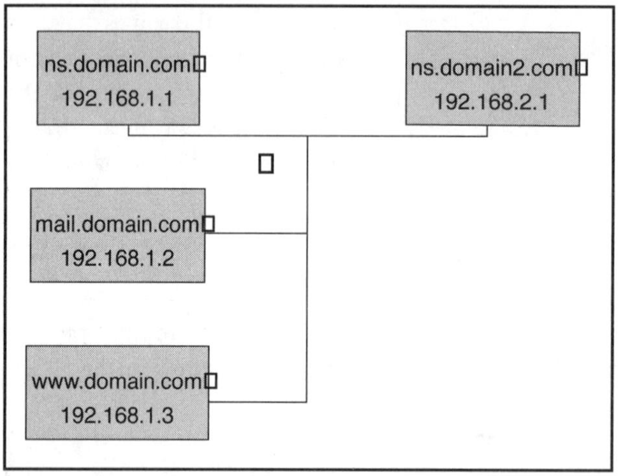

Figure 5-2 *This is the fictional domain.com network used in this chapter.*

NOTE

It's a good idea to substitute your own domain name, hostnames, and IP addresses for the ones used in the examples.

Creating the bind Configuration Files

If *bind* is to run, it needs to know the following information (which is stored in the file `/etc/named.conf`).

- What directory to use for its files (OpenLinux uses `/var/named`)
- Where to find the root server listing file (OpenLinux uses `/var/named/root.hints`)
- Where to find the zone authority files (OpenLinux uses `/var/named/pz` and `/var/named/sz`)

Basic Configuration

Create the file `/etc/named.conf` exactly as shown in Listing 5-1, substituting your domain for domain.com and your in-addr.arpa subdomain for 1.168.192.in-addr.arpa. This file is also included on the CD-ROM under `/files/bookfiles/chapter5/named.conf`.

Listing 5-1 The basic configuration file /etc/named.conf

```
// /etc/named.conf

options {
  directory "/var/named"; // everything goes in /var/named
};

zone "." { // the root zone
  type hint;
  file "root.hints";
};

zone "0.0.127.in-addr.arpa" { // the reverse loopback zone
  notify no;
  type master;
  file "pz/127.0.0";
};

zone "domain.com" { // domain.com master zone
  notify no;
  type master;
  file "pz/domain.com";
};

zone "1.168.192.in-addr.arpa" { // the reverse 192.168.1 zone
  notify no;
  type master;
  file "pz/192.168.1";
};

zone "domain2.com" { // domain2.com slave zone
  notify no;
  type slave;
  file "sz/domain2.com";
  masters {192.168.2.1; };
};
```

> **NOTE**
>
> Five zones (the root zone and four below it) were defined in Listing 5-1. A zone is a domain or subdomain that has (or can have) hosts within it. The subtle difference between a zone and a domain is that a zone encompasses only those hosts directly underneath it; for instance, the host www.cheek.com is part of the cheek.com domain, the .com domain, and the root domain, but only part of the cheek.com zone.

As you can see, each section of the file has data contained inside curly braces. The `directory` line inside the `options` section tells *bind* that we want all files to go inside the `/var/named` directory. The remaining five `zone` sections tell *bind* that we want our DNS server to contain information about five zones innately: the root zone (.), the 0.0.127.in-addr.arpa zone (which is the reverse zone for 127.0.0.1, the loopback interface), the domain.com zone, the 1.168.192.in-addr.arpa zone (the reverse zone for 192.168.1.*x*), and the domain2.com zone.

The root zone and the 0.0.127.in-addr.arpa zone are required. After that, there can be as few or as many zones as you want. Don't define any other zones if you just want to configure a DNS server that holds no information for domains on its own; this can be useful if you just want *bind* to cache information it receives from other DNS servers.

The `type` line tells *bind* how to handle the file it finds in each section. A `hint` type identifies a file that contains a list of root servers. A `master` type means that *bind* is to be *authoritative* for that zone as a master DNS server. (Master servers are primary DNS servers, which hold their information on their own hard drives.)

The `slave` type tells *bind* to be authoritative as a slave DNS server. (Slave servers are secondary to master servers, meaning that the slave server just copies locally whatever information its associated master server holds.) The `masters` line tells *bind* which server is the primary, master server for these slave zones.

When a DNS server is authoritative for a zone, it means that it knows innately about that zone, and can be counted on always to have correct information for that zone. When a DNS query comes into a DNS server, the server can respond directly with information if the request was made for a zone for which it is authoritative. In this case, the DNS server queried does not need to contact the root server and walk the tree-like DNS structure to get its information—it can respond on its own. On the Internet, the InterNIC requires that at least two DNS servers have authoritative information for each domain registered through its service. In practice, this is a good minimum.

Creating the Root Cache

To give *bind* good data, you need to populate the files you told it to use. Create the directory `/var/named` if it doesn't exist, and then create the `/var/named/root.hints` file as shown in Listing 5-2. This file is also on the CD-ROM under `/files/book-files/chapter5/root.hints`.

Listing 5-2 The root zone hints file /var/named/root.hints

```
;; /var/named/root.hints
.    NS   A.ROOT-SERVERS.NET.
.    NS   B.ROOT-SERVERS.NET.
.    NS   C.ROOT-SERVERS.NET.
.    NS   D.ROOT-SERVERS.NET.
.    NS   E.ROOT-SERVERS.NET.
.    NS   F.ROOT-SERVERS.NET.
.    NS   G.ROOT-SERVERS.NET
.    NS   H.ROOT-SERVERS.NET.
.    NS   I.ROOT-SERVERS.NET.
.    NS   J.ROOT-SERVERS.NET.
.    NS   K.ROOT-SERVERS.NET.
.    NS   L.ROOT-SERVERS.NET.
.    NS   M.ROOT-SERVERS.NET.

A.ROOT-SERVERS.NET.     A   198.41.0.4
B.ROOT-SERVERS.NET.     A   128.9.0.107
C.ROOT-SERVERS.NET.     A   192.33.4.12
D.ROOT-SERVERS.NET.     A   128.8.10.90
E.ROOT-SERVERS.NET.     A   192.203.230.10
F.ROOT-SERVERS.NET.     A   192.5.5.241
G.ROOT-SERVERS.NET.     A   192.112.36.4
H.ROOT-SERVERS.NET.     A   128.63.2.53
I.ROOT-SERVERS.NET.     A   192.36.148.17
J.ROOT-SERVERS.NET.     A   198.41.0.10
K.ROOT-SERVERS.NET.     A   193.0.14.129
L.ROOT-SERVERS.NET.     A   198.32.64.12
M.ROOT-SERVERS.NET.  A   202.12.27.33
```

This /var/named/root.hints file tells *bind* which servers are authoritative for the root domain. *bind* uses this when it needs to check on a zone for which it is not authoritative. Notice that the domain names and hostnames used in this zone file end in a period, indicating that they are part of the root domain.

Creating the 127.0.0 Zone Authority

Create the /var/named/pz/127.0.0 file as follows, changing domain.com to your domain name (see Listing 5-3). This file is also available on the CD-ROM under /files/bookfiles/chapter5/127.0.0.

Listing 5-3 The 127.0.0 zone authority file /var/named/pz/127.0.0

```
; /var/named/pz/127.0.0
$TTL 1D
@     IN   SOA    domain.com. hostmaster.domain.com. (
           1      ; Serial
           8H     ; Refresh
           2H     ; Retry
           1W     ; Expire
           1D)    ; Minimum TTL
           NS     ns.domain.com.
1          PTR    localhost.
```

This file provides the reverse DNS information for the 127.0.0 zone. Note that the hostnames and domains, even localhost, listed here also end with a period. Each line has a Resource Record (*RR*), which is the technical term for a DNS entry. Typically, RRs are listed one per line, the exception here being the Start Of Authority (*SOA*) resource record (which has its own line plus five more, with data in parentheses).

The RRs in this file are the SOA, Name Server (*NS*), and PoinTeR (*PTR*). The SOA record gives the zone to which this file corresponds, as well as other information about how to propagate the record on a network. The NS record tells which hosts act as DNS servers for that zone. There is only one DNS server for this domain, but many domains have two or more DNS servers, each with its own NS record.

The PTR record simply gives the name of the host associated with its IP address. Only one host can be specified for each IP address, so if you have multiple hostnames with the same IP address, you must choose only one hostname to enter into this record. PTR records are valid only in zone files that are used to hold reverse DNS information.

Creating the domain.com Zone Authority

The next zone file referenced in the `/etc/named.conf` file is `/var/named/pz/domain.com` (see Listing 5-4). If you use a different domain, change the filename to correspond with the domain name. This file is available on the CD-ROM under `/files/bookfiles/chapter5/domain.com`.

Listing 5-4 The domain.com authority file /var/named/pz/domain.com

```
; /var/named/pz/domain.com
$TTL 1D
@     IN      SOA    domain.com. hostmaster.domain.com. (
              199906031   ; Serial
              8H                      ; Refresh
              2H                      ; Retry
              1W                      ; Expire
              1D)                     ; Minimum TTL
              NS                      ns.domain.com.   ; Name server
              MX          100         mail.domain.com. ; Mail exchanger
localhost     A                       127.0.0.1
ns            A                       192.168.1.1
mail          A                       192.168.1.2
www           A                       192.168.1.3
```

This file gives DNS information for the domain.com domain and introduces a couple of new RRs—the *A* RR and the *MX* RR. *A* stands for *Address* in this case, and it gives the IP address for the hostname specified on the same line. Address records are the ones that actually correlate hostnames to IP addresses for DNS lookups.

> **NOTE**
>
> A word on A records versus PTR records. Both Address records and Pointer records correlate hostnames and IP addresses, but they do not do the same thing. Address records are used in DNS lookups to specify which IP address is used for a specific host. A host can have more than one IP address specified for it, in which case *bind* randomly picks one when asked. Pointer records are used in reverse DNS lookups, and specify which hostname is used for a specific IP address. This correlation must be one-to-one; specifying multiple hosts for the same IP address is not allowed here.

MX stands for mail exchanger, and is used to specify which host collects mail for the domain. The number before the hostname (100, in this case) is its priority. Multiple mail exchangers can be specified for a particular zone, each with different priorities. When e-mail is sent to a zone, the host with the lowest MX priority is tried first; if that host cannot be contacted, the host with the next lowest priority is contacted, and so on. Multiple MX records are used to ensure that e-mail is not lost if one host goes down.

There are a few other things that are important about this file. First, the serial number should always be a concatenation of the current year, the month, the day of the month, and a number representing the revision number of the file on that date. The serial number I used, 199906031, represents the first change on June 3, 1999. For the second change of the day, I would instead use 199906032, and so on. Use whatever number is correct for the current date.

CAUTION

> Always update the serial number when you edit a zone file! Forgetting to do so might keep your changes from being recognized by DNS servers.

Second, the hostmaster.domain.com. on the SOA line is not a hostname, even though it looks like one—it is in fact an e-mail address, one for the person responsible for that particular zone. *hostmaster* is used as a standard e-mail address, although it can easily be any other e-mail address. This e-mail address generally is an alias pointing to a real person.

Creating the 192.168.1 Zone Authority

The next file you need to create is `/var/named/pz/192.168.1` (see Listing 5-5). You should change the IP addresses, filename, and domain name to reflect your actual situation. The IP addresses are listed one by one with their corresponding hostnames. This file is available on the CD-ROM under `/files/bookfiles/chapter5/192.168.1`.

Creating the domain2.com Zone Authority

In my example network, the OpenLinux server ns.domain.com is acting as a secondary DNS server for the domain2.com domain. The `/etc/named.conf` file has specified `/var/named/sz/domain2.com` as the file to contain the DNS information for this zone, and has also specified that the master server for domain2.com is at IP address 192.168.2.1.

A nice side effect of having a slave zone, such as this one, is that you don't need to create the file; *bind* creates the file when it starts, and it is updated on a regular basis. If the master server cannot be contacted and a file by that name exists on the hard drive, the information in that file is used. (If no file exists and the master server cannot be contacted, *bind* gives an error message and does not provide DNS services for that zone.)

Listing 5-5 The 192.168.1 zone authority file /var/named/pz/192.168.1

```
; /var/named/pz/192.168.1
$TTL 1D
@     IN     SOA          domain.com. hostmaster.domain.com. (
             199906031    ; Serial
             8H           ; Refresh
             2H           ; Retry
             1W           ; Expire
             1D)          ; Minimum TTL
             NS           ns.domain.com.
1            PTR          ns.domain.com.
2            PTR          mail.domain.com.
3            PTR          www.domain.com.
```

Adding New Hosts to Your DNS Records

DNS records need to be kept current with the actual hostnames and IP addresses of the machines on your network. When new computers come online, be sure to add an appropriate line to both your domain.com authority file (`/var/named/pz/domain.com`) and the 192.168.1 authority file (`/var/named/pz/192.168.1`) so that they reflect your current network configuration. Similarly, when you remove hosts from your network, you must also remove the applicable lines from these files. As always, remember to update your serial numbers on these files and restart the named server.

Configuring Your Own Host to Use Its DNS Server

We've waded through a lot of technical information, and it's good to be done with that; the rest of this chapter won't be as heavy. Now that you've entered all the necessary information into the *bind* configuration files, you might be tempted to start performing DNS queries, pinging hostnames, and so on. *Don't do this yet!* You still need to configure your machine to use its own DNS server, and you need to start the *named* daemon. Proper DNS resolution won't occur until these steps are taken.

Your OpenLinux server probably is configured either to use a different DNS server at this point, or to use none at all. Your machine needs to be told that it now operates a DNS server. Both the name resolver and the name service switch file need to be edited.

Configuring the Name Resolver

The `/etc/resolv.conf` file tells OpenLinux how DNS name resolution should be performed. A sample file is given in Listing 5-6.

Listing 5-6 The name resolution configuration file /etc/resolv.conf

```
# /etc/resolv.conf
domain domain.com
search domain.com
nameserver 127.0.0.1
```

The `domain` line specifies the domain your OpenLinux machine is in. The `search` line tells OpenLinux to append the specified domain when no domain is given; with this line, www is resolved as www.domain.com. The `nameserver` line tells OpenLinux that when it needs to perform a DNS lookup, it should use the nameserver at 127.0.0.1 (which is itself). Substitute your domain for domain.com here, but *never* put a hostname in the `nameserver` line—always use an IP address.

CAUTION

> Using a hostname instead of an IP address on the nameserver line can cause all DNS resolution to fail from this machine.

The Name Service Switch File /etc/nsswitch.conf

The `/etc/nsswitch.conf` file tells OpenLinux which service to use for which type of lookup. Hostname resolution is specified on the line starting with `hosts:`. This line should read:

```
hosts:          files dns
```

This means check the `/etc/hosts` file for name resolution first, then check DNS if no match is found in the `/etc/hosts` file.

NOTE

> OpenLinux 1.x used the file `/etc/host.conf` instead of `/etc/nsswitch.conf`. The format of the `/etc/host.conf` file is not the same as `/etc/nsswitch.conf` file.

Starting and Stopping bind

Next, *bind* must be started. *bind* comes with a program called *ndc* to start and stop the daemon. Its invocation is simple. To start *bind*, use

```
ndc start
```

To stop *bind*, use

```
ndc stop
```

Because you configured everything, you can try starting *bind* now. A successful startup shows you the following:

```
Name Server Started
```

If everything went well, check the name server using the host command:

```
host www.domain.com
```

If everything goes well, you should see this:

```
www.domain.com has address 192.168.1.3
```

If that's the case, congratulations! You now have a working DNS server! The last step is to make it load automatically when the server starts; you can do this with the *COAS* tool, described in Chapter 2, "Configuring OpenLinux's Basic Network" (under the heading "Starting and Stopping rc Network Services"). If you get something other than this, you should first check the files you created earlier in the chapter to ensure that they are exactly as shown in this book (with the exceptions of hostnames, domain names, and IP addresses, if you used your own instead of mine). If you don't find any problems there, try the troubleshooting tips in the next section.

Troubleshooting bind

There are several tools available to troubleshoot a DNS server that is not working the way you want it to work. Typical symptoms of a poorly functioning DNS server include:

- Name resolution fails.
- Slow connection or no connection to common services, such as FTP, Web, or Telnet.
- The server pauses 30 to 90 seconds when loading common services at bootup, such as *sendmail* or Apache.
- A host responds to pings by IP address but not by hostname.

One key thing to remember is that these might not be DNS server issues, but might just be name resolution problems. A DNS lookup is only the last step in name resolution, and the breakdown could be anywhere. In particular, name resolution can fail when either the `/etc/hosts`, `/etc/nsswitch.conf`, or `/etc/resolv.conf` files are corrupt or missing, or even when the computer in question is unplugged from the network or from a power source. These issues can halt name resolution and have nothing to do with a bad DNS server. Check these files to see if they are misconfigured before you start to troubleshoot *bind*; note, though, that they must be properly configured on the machine requesting name resolution, which is not necessarily the machine providing DNS services.

Another common issue is getting complaints that people "can't find your Web site": if they enter your Web site's URL into their browser, they find that your site doesn't show. This is potentially a DNS issue, but not necessarily. Even if it is a DNS issue, it might not be your DNS server; it could be their DNS server misbehaving, or a server along the path between theirs and yours. For this specific issue, I suggest troubleshooting DNS last.

Basic troubleshooting steps include checking whether the IP protocol stack is working properly, whether there is physical connectivity to the network, and so on. After checking those areas for problems, use the tools and concepts introduced in this section to troubleshoot the *bind* DNS server. Typically, the fix is just to edit one of the configuration files and restart the DNS server, but that is not always the case. After you read these tips, use your judgment to determine what to do.

Checking the Status of bind

If network connectivity is fine and you suspect that the DNS server is causing the problem, first check the status of *bind*. Issuing the command `ndc status` will tell you if *bind* is running:

```
ndc status

22240 ?        00:00:00 named
```

This tells you that the *bind* DNS server, *named*, is running as process 22240. A more verbose way of getting statistics is to use the command `ndc stats`, which causes the file `/var/named/named.stats` to be written. Its output is best checked with the command `head /var/named/named.stats` (see Listing 5-7).

```
ndc stats

head /var/named/named.stats

Dumping Statistics
```

Listing 5-7 Output from the command head /var/named/named.stats

```
+++ Statistics Dump +++ (928545110) Fri Jun  4 18:11:50 1999
8636                time since boot (secs)
8636                time since reset (secs)
0                   Unknown query types
83                  A queries
1                   SOA queries
16                  MX queries
1                   ANY queries
++ Name Server Statistics ++
(Legend)
```

My name server has processed 101 queries in the past two hours and twenty-some minutes. All the queries were recognized; most were queries for an address, a few were queries for my mail exchanger, one was for the Start Of Authority record, and the *ANY* request meant "send me all records." If these numbers are zero, or do not increase over time, that could mean there is a problem with your DNS server.

The last `ndc` command we mention here is `ndc dumpdb`. Issuing this command tells *bind* to list all records for zones in which it is authoritative; it outputs the file `/var/named/named_dump.db`, which appears similar to a concatenation of all zone files listed in your `/etc/named.conf` file. This is a good way to check whether *bind* is serving the data you think it should be serving.

Checking the System Log

When *bind* starts (or restarts), it writes debugging information to the system log `/var/log/messages`. Checking this file after an `ndc start` or `ndc restart` command can yield valuable debugging information. Check the last few entries in the system log by issuing the command `tail/var/log/messages`. Its output is shown in Listing 5-8.

```
ndc start

Name Server Started

tail /var/log/messages
```

Listing 5-8 Output from the command tail /var/log/messages

```
Jun  4 18:34:04 saltlake named[22664]: starting.  named 8.1.1 Sat Apr  3
   17:44:53 MST 1999 ^Iroot@knob.calderasystems.com:/build/BUILD/bind-
   8.1.1/src/bin/named
Jun  4 18:34:04 saltlake named[22664]: cache zone "" (IN) loaded (serial 0)
Jun  4 18:34:04 saltlake named[22664]: master zone "0.0.127.in-addr.arpa" (IN)
   loaded (serial 1)
Jun  4 18:34:04 saltlake named[22664]: master zone "domain.com" (IN) loaded
   (serial 199906031)
Jun  4 18:34:04 saltlake named[22664]: listening [127.0.0.1].53 (lo)
Jun  4 18:34:04 saltlake named[22664]: listening [208.12.12.157].53 (eth0)
Jun  4 18:34:04 saltlake named[22664]: Forwarding source address is
   [0.0.0.0].1234
Jun  4 18:34:04 saltlake named[22665]: Ready to answer queries.
```

This shows you which version of *bind* you have, which zone files it loaded, and on what ports it is listening. This is the best place to check for errors when *bind* is starting.

bind also logs statistics to the system log every hour by default. These come in the form of *NSTATS* and *XSTATS* messages. They look like a miniature version of the `named.stats` file, with statistics about how many DNS requests have been made. If they do not show up every hour, something might be wrong with your DNS server. These can also be checked by using the command `tail /var/log/messages`.

The host and dig Commands

`host` and `dig` both provide quick and easy ways to perform DNS queries from the command line. `host` is typically used to check just a single host or IP address, while `dig` (*Domain Information Groper*) is generally used to get information about an entire domain.

Using the host Command

In its simplest invocation, `host` is used with either a hostname or IP address as its single parameter. One neat thing about `host` is that it will convert an IP address into its corresponding in-addr.arpa hostname automatically, saving keystrokes and eliminating the need to remember to enter the numbers in reverse order.

```
host www.domain.com

www.domain.com has address 192.168.1.3
```

```
host 192.168.1.3

3.1.168.192.IN-ADDR.ARPA domain name pointer www.domain.com
```

If you ask `host` about an entire domain, it responds with further information:

```
host domain.com

domain.com mail is handled (pri 100) by mail.domain.com
```

`host` takes the DNS server to query as a second argument. When you're troubleshooting specific DNS problems, it is usually a good idea to tell `host` which server to query; if not told which DNS server to query, `host` picks one, which might not be the one you want to verify.

Using the dig Command

`dig` is a more complete command, and by default will tell you every record of a specific type in a zone. It takes both the type and the zone as parameters. (The type can be omitted to show all *A* records in the zone.) To show all the *NS* records for domain.com, type:

```
dig ns domain.com
```

`dig` uses the current first DNS server specified in your `/etc/resolv.conf` file, unless told to use a different one. Specifying a DNS server to use can be beneficial here. You can do that by entering an @ symbol, followed by the name of the DNS server to use, as the first parameter:

```
dig @ns.domain.com mx domain.com
```

When used without any parameters, `dig` queries the default server for the root zone's authority files. This information can be used to create a current version of the `root.hints` file `/var/named/root.hints`.

TIP

Because typing `dig` by itself gets the current root zone authority records, a useful way to refresh the `/var/named/root.hints` file is by redirecting the output, when `dig` is called in this manner, to the `root.hints` file. The root servers change over time, so it is wise to update the `root.hints` file every few months.

To do this, use the following command:

```
dig > /var/named/root.hints
```

Then, restart the DNS server.

Both host and dig are useful tools in checking DNS zone information. It's easy and fun to practice these tools on other domains on the Internet, to get a feel for how they work.

The nslookup Command

nslookup differs from both dig and host in that it is a full-featured, interactive DNS querying tool, not just a quick and easy one. Normal usage with nslookup is to call it by name without any parameters on the command line, and then set those options from its own command line (which nslookup presents for you). An example follows:

```
nslookup
Default Server:  localhost
Address:  127.0.0.1
> server ns.domain.com
Default Server:  ns.domain.com
Address:  192.168.1.1

> set type=any
> domain.com
Server:  ns.domain.com
Address:  192.168.1.1

domain.com
                    origin = domain.com
                    mail addr = hostmaster.domain.com
                    serial = 199906031
                    refresh = 28800 (8H)
                    retry   = 7200 (2H)
                    expire  = 604800 (1W)
                    minimum ttl = 86400 (1D)
domain.com          nameserver = ns.domain.com
domain.com          preference = 100, mail exchanger = mail.domain.com
domain.com          nameserver = ns.domain.com
ns.domain.com       internet address = 192.168.1.1
mail.domain.com     internet address = 192.168.1.2
> exit
```

In this example, I invoked nslookup, changed the DNS server it would use to ns.domain.com, told it to query any type of resource records, and had it list pertinent information about the domain.com zone. Then I exited the nslookup command.

Certain commands, such as `set`, `server`, `exit`, and so on, are recognized by `nslookup`; all others are deemed zones that need querying. Typing the zone to query gives you basic information about the zone, but much more is available if you use the `ls` command. `ls` takes the zone as a parameter. `ls` by itself gives a lot of information, but `ls -a` gives more information than just `ls`. `ls -d` gives as much information about a zone as is available.

`nslookup` has more options available than I have space to list here. Fortunately, it has a help command (invoked with a single `?` at its command prompt) which lists its commands and options in a compact form. `nslookup` is a good tool to use when there is a lot of detail needed about a DNS server's zone information and you want to spend some time getting information about it. I use it as my backup use-if-everything-else-fails DNS tool.

For More Information

More information on DNS and the bind server can be found in several places on the Web. Here are a few of my favorite URLs:

URL	Resource Name
http://www.isc.org/products/BIND/	Internet Software Consortium's *bind* Home Page
http://linuxkb.cheek.com/page.php?dns	Linux Knowledge Base DNS Information
http://www.linuxdoc.org/HOWTO/DNS-HOWTO.html	Linux Documentation Project—How to Set Up a DNS Server
http://www.dns.net/dnsrd/	The DNS Resources Directory

Chapter 6: Configuring the Apache Web Server

Apache Enhancements from Other Sources

Configuring Apache

Enabling Server Side Includes

Security Considerations

Web Statistics Analyzers for Use with Apache

As of this writing, Apache is the world's most popular Web server (according to surveys from Web statistics companies, such as Netcraft). Apache was based on the httpd Web server from the NCSA (*National Center for Supercomputing Applications*), at the University of Illinois at Urbana-Champaign. Apache has now preempted that project; NCSA's httpd server is no longer being developed or enhanced. Apache still carries the name *httpd*, though; in OpenLinux, the Apache program filename is *httpd-apache*.

Apache can handle the standard Web requests, such as static HTML pages, CGI (*Common Gateway Interface*) content, and SSI (*Server Side Includes*). More and more Web sites have database interaction and are being built with server-side scripting languages, such as ASP (*Active Server Pages*) or PHP (*P Hypertext Preprocessor*). Apache supports extension through modules that can either be built in or loaded dynamically; these extensions can perform database lookups, speed CGI processing and more. (Most of the time, if Apache can't do this in the base package, someone has built a module to add that capability.)

Files Referenced in this Chapter

The following table lists the files used by the Apache Web server. (Additionally, a personal document root is in the `public_html` directory inside each user's home directory.)

File	Purpose
`/etc/httpd/apache/conf`	Apache configuration files directory
`/etc/httpd/apache/conf/httpd.conf`	Apache's basic configuration file
`/etc/httpd/apache/conf/srm.conf`	Apache's server resource management configuration file
`/etc/httpd/apache/conf/access.conf`	Apache's access configuration file
`/etc/httpd/apache/logs`	Apache's log directory, symbolically linked to `/var/log/httpd/apache`
`/var/log/httpd/apache/access_log`	Apache's access log
`/var/log/httpd/apache/error_log`	Apache's error log
`/var/run/httpd.pid`	Apache's process ID file
`/home/httpd`	Apache's http daemon home directory
`/home/httpd/html`	Apache's document root
`/home/httpd/cgi-bin`	Apache's CGI directory

Apache Enhancements from Other Sources

One limitation of Apache is its lack of support for SSL (*Secure Sockets Layer*) which is required for secure Web transactions. SSL is available in 56 bit and 128 bit encryption (over 56 bit encryption is non-exportable). The algorithm used for the encryption in SSL is patented as well, making it even more difficult for there to be a legally usable open source implementation. Currently, Raven and Stronghold are two Apache based servers that are commercially available. There is also the open source Apache-SSL. However, this is not legal to use within the United States due to the encryption patent.

A less limiting but perhaps more frustrating limitation of Apache is the method of configuration. Apache utlilizes text configuration files (as do many Linux programs). Making any changes to Apache requires hand-editing these configuration files. There are front end programs that edit the configuration files for you, which provides you with an easy interface, but none are bundled with OpenLinux.

Configuring Apache

The Apache that ships with OpenLinux supports HTML, CGI, and SSI content. The Basic Apache Configuration section lists the values that need changing for any type of Web site, or at least those that I suggest you change from their default values as a matter of course. These values apply to a typical Apache configuration for a small Web site where most content is static, such as for a small business Web site or a small corporate intranet.

Basic Apache Configuration

A basic Apache Web server setup serves static HTML pages with occasional CGI content. Configuring Apache for this is fairly simple, because these are base defaults for most Web sites. Standard HTML files can be placed inside the `/home/httpd/html` directory and given either an .html or .htm extension.

CGI scripts can be placed inside the `/home/httpd/cgi-bin` directory, where Apache will consider them to be cgi scripts. CGI scripts can be placed outside the `cgi-bin` directory provided the necessary changes are made to the configuration files. Usually if this is done, it is set up so that files ending in .cgi, and .pl are considered cgi programs. World execute permission (chmod a+x) must be set in order for scripts to run.

By default, Apache looks for the index.html file when a Web browser asks for a URL without a filename. If it can't find index.html, it looks for index.htm. If it can't find index.htm, it returns an error to the browser, stating that the directory index was forbidden.

Since Apache runs as the nobody user and group (by default), all HTML files need to be owned by httpd or world readable for Apache to read them.

There are three steps to configuring Apache for basic Web site serving: configure basic server settings, configure the server's request management, and configure access rights for the Web site. Each of these corresponds to a different file in the `/etc/httpd/apache/conf` directory.

> NOTE
>
> The version of Apache that ships with OpenLinux 2.3 uses three separate configuration files, as shown in this book—`/etc/httpd/apache/conf/httpd.conf`, `/etc/httpd/apache/conf/srm.conf`, and `/etc/httpd/apache/conf/access.conf`. Newer versions of Apache use just one file, `/etc/httpd/apache/conf/httpd.conf`, which contains all directives previously found in the three files.

Basic Server Configuration

Basic configuration is contained in the `/etc/httpd/apache/conf/httpd.conf` file. Each line controls a specific setting for Apache, such as the port number and IP address(es) to which it listens, where and what types of information to log, and so on. Caldera has set most of them to reasonable default values, but there are a few lines that need changing. Edit the file and look for the following lines:

```
ServerAdmin root
```

- This is the e-mail address of the Apache server administrator. Change this to your e-mail address.

```
CustomLog /var/log/httpd/apache/access_log common
```

```
#CustomLog /var/log/httpd/apache/access_log combined
```

- The two forms of this command each tell Apache what information to log and where to log it. I suggest adding a hash mark (#) to the first line and removing it from the second to tell Apache to use the combined log format instead of the common format. The combined log format logs the same information as the common format, such as date, time, URL requested, status of the request, and so on. It also logs the user agent (Web browser) of the person accessing the site, as well as the URL of the Web page that brought the user to this page. Both of these items are worth logging for statistical tracking purposes.

```
ServerName localhost
```

- Change `localhost` to the fully-qualified domain name of this machine. Typically, this will be something like **www.domain.com**.

Configuring Server Request Management

According to the /etc/httpd/apache/conf/srm.conf file, server request management consists of defining "how requests are serviced, and how results should be formatted." Edit this file, and look for these lines:

```
DirectoryIndex index.html
```

- This tells Apache which file to look for when it is not given a filename on the URL. Each filename Apache should check needs to be listed here, in the order they should be checked. Change this to:

```
DirectoryIndex index.html index.htm
```

- Now Apache will look for index.htm after first checking for index.html. OpenLinux, like other Linux (and UNIX) systems, typically uses index.html for the default DirectoryIndex, but Microsoft products sometimes want to use default.htm or some other name. If you want other filenames to be checked, such as default.htm or home.htm, you can add them here.

```
#AddHandler cgi-script .cgi
```

- Remove the hash mark here to enable Apache to use CGI programs from within the /home/httpd/html document root. All files ending with a .cgi extension here will be treated as CGI scripts. Remember that these CGI files must be given world execute permissions. Adding .pl here (AddHandler cgi-script .cgi .pl) will allow perl scripts to be treated as cgi (without having to use the .cgi extension on them).

Configuring Global Access

Access rights are determined by the /etc/httpd/apache/conf/access.conf file. Access rights determine which machines can access certain files, what directories have CGI scripts, whether to show file contents when there is no index.html file, and more.

These are set on a directory-by-directory basis. OpenLinux restricts much by default; this is good from a security standpoint, but makes it necessary to update this file often.

For security when you do not control the content, consider running independent server processes uniquely configured for each virtual domain, or by using the suexec feature of apache. See the section called "Security Considerations" later in this chapter.

Here's what to change in this file for a basic server setup. Underneath the <Directory /home/httpd/html> line, look for the following:

```
# Options Indexes FollowSymLinks
```

```
Options None
```

- Uncomment the first line by removing the hash mark, and comment the second line by adding the hash mark in front of it. Turning on the *Indexes* option tells Apache to give a file listing when a directory is requested and there is no `index.html` file (or other DirectoryIndex file) in that directory. The *FollowSymLinks* option tells Apache that it is all right to process a file request for a symbolically linked file. If you have *sym-linked* files or directories here, Apache will return an error when these files are requested and the *FollowSymLinks* option is not enabled.

```
AllowOverride None
```

- You can control access configuration with a file named `.htaccess`, located inside each document directory, if this line is changed from *None* to *All*. This is beneficial if you want users who have permission to create files inside the document root to specify their own settings—they do not need to edit the global `access.conf` file, or have you do it for them. Allowing this access can make your users more self-sufficient.

Advanced Apache Configuration

If all you want to do is set up a basic Web server, the instructions in the preceding section told you all you need to know; you can skip to the next section, "Starting and Stopping Apache," to get Apache to work with your new settings. If you want to learn how to do more advanced administration, however, this section provides you with more detail about some Apache settings and some of Apache's more powerful capabilities. Some of these capabilities, which are examined in the next few subsections, are

- Adding Support for Server Side Includes
- Adding Virtual Hosts
- Editing Apache's MIME Types
- Performance Tuning
- Enabling Web-Based Server Status Reports

Adding Support for Server Side Includes

Server Side Includes (SSI) is a method of producing dynamic content without CGI. SSI lets you embed the output from programs, the current date and time, server variables, and other information directly into HTML documents, without you needing to write a program. Edit the `/etc/httpd/apache/conf/srm.conf` file, and look for the following lines:

```
#AddType text/html .shtml
```

```
#AddHandler server-parsed .shtml
```

By uncommenting these lines, you can have Apache treat every file with a .shtml extension as a *server-parsed* file, or one that potentially contains server side includes. The standard extension for these files is .shtml, for server-parsed HTML, but you can change this to be a different extension if you wish; simply change .shtml in both of the preceding lines to a different extension.

Adding IP-Based Virtual Hosts

Virtual hosting is taking one Web server and having it serve many different Web sites. One Web site is the default Web site, and the other sites are called *virtual hosts*. Administering one Apache server serving many different Web sites is much easier than administering several different Apache servers, as you can probably imagine. Apache can support as many virtual hosts as your system can handle—many people have configured hundreds of virtual hosts on a single Apache server, although I have never personally configured more than a dozen or so on a single machine. OpenLinux should easily be able to handle hundreds, if not thousands, of virtual hosts on a high-powered machine.

There are two ways virtual hosting can work. With IP-based virtual hosting, each Web site has its own IP address, and therefore has complete control over services at that IP address. With name-based virtual hosting, many different sites can share the same IP address but do not get exclusive access to that IP address. While IP-based virtual hosting gives more control, it can eat up IP addresses quickly if you host many different sites. Name-based virtual hosting requires the Web browser to specify which Web site it is accessing (older browsers do not have this capability). Name-based virtual hosting also prevents a browser from connecting directly to an IP address—a hostname must be specified in the URL. Whether to host a Web site as a name-based or as an IP-based virtual host is a complex decision.

SideBar

Which is Better, IP-Based or Name-Based Virtual Hosts?

Neither is better. With IP-based virtual hosts, you have a bit more control (such as use of BindAddress) over the server. All web browsers are compatible with IP-based virtual hosts. Unfortunately, using an IP address for each Web site can consume IP addresses very rapidly if you're hosting many sites.

Name-based virtual hosts allow you to use the same IP address for many different sites, and therefore do not use up extra addresses. They require a current Web browser, however; older browsers cannot access the proper content on a name-based virtual Web site.

Adding an IP-based virtual host requires taking a few distinct steps:

- Determine the new IP address, new hostname, new document root, and new CGI directory of the Web site.
- Configure OpenLinux to use the new IP address.
- Bind the Apache server to the new IP address.
- Create a new virtual host definition, and populate the virtual host definition with configuration settings.
- Create the new document root and CGI directories, and populate them with files.
- Configure DNS for the new hostname, if necessary.

I will give an example from one of my virtual hosts, zd.cheek.com. This Web site is an IP-based virtual host using IP address 208.12.12.131, with a document root of `/home/vhosts/zd/html` and a CGI directory of `/home/vhosts/zd/cgi-bin`. My OpenLinux machine used for this, seattle.cheek.com, has a single Ethernet interface using IP address 208.12.12.130 as its standard IP address.

This machine was already using its standard IP address to serve the Web site seattle.cheek.com, so I needed to assign a second address for the new virtual host. I aliased the second address, 208.12.12.131, to the same Ethernet interface using OpenLinux's IP aliasing. (Chapter 1, "Configuring OpenLinux's Basic Network," explains how to assign multiple IP addresses to a single interface using IP aliasing.)

To create a new virtual host definition, I added several lines to the end of this file. These lines are the same configuration lines that Apache uses throughout its configuration files, encapsulated by a `<VirtualHost>` command.

```
<VirtualHost 208.12.12.131>

ServerName zd.cheek.com

ServerAdmin webmaster@cheek.com

DocumentRoot /home/vhosts/zd/html

ScriptAlias /cgi-bin/ /home/vhosts/zd/cgi-bin/

ErrorLog logs/zd.errors

CustomLog logs/zd.access combined

<Directory /home/vhosts/zd/html>

Options FollowSymlinks

</Directory>

</VirtualHost>
```

As you can see, the `<VirtualHost>` command encapsulates the entire definition, much like HTML tags do. The `<VirtualHost>` command takes as a parameter the IP address of the new Web site. The ServerName is the hostname of the new Web server, and the ServerAdmin is the e-mail address of the person responsible for the server. In this case, I wanted any correspondence to go to the Webmaster e-mail account.

The `DocumentRoot` names the document root of the Web site (the directory where the HTML files are stored). The ScriptAlias command tells Apache that all URL paths starting with `/cgi-bin/` are CGI scripts that reside in the `/home/vhosts/zd/cgi-bin` directory. Notice that the directory name here ends with a trailing slash (/)—without that slash, CGI scripts will fail. I added ErrorLog and CustomLog commands, so that the logs from this virtual host will be separate from the normal Apache Web logs; had I not done so, these log entries would be mixed in with the normal log entries from my main Web site. Finally, the Directory and Options lines tell Apache that for this Web site and in that directory, I want Apache to follow symbolic links when it looks for files—this site uses symbolic links, so I wanted to tell Apache explicitly to follow those.

After creating the directories for the HTML and CGI content and configuring DNS (explained in Chapter 4, "Configuring DNS and bind"), Apache will be ready to serve your new Web site. If Apache is already running, you will need to restart it. The section "Restarting Apache After a Configuration Change," later in this chapter, discusses how to do this. The new Web site should be browseable by both hostname and IP address.

Adding Name-Based Virtual Hosts

Adding a name-based virtual host is almost the same as adding an IP-based virtual host. IP aliasing is not typically needed , as one advantage of name-based hosting is not requiring extra IP addresses. Because no extra IP addresses are used, Apache does not need to be told to bind to any more addresses. The steps for adding a name-based virtual host, then, are as follows:

- Determine the existing IP address, new hostname, new document root, and new CGI directory of the Web site.
- Create a new virtual host definition, adding a NameVirtualHost directive, and populate the virtual host definition with configuration settings.
- Create the new document root and CGI directories, and populate them with files.
- Configure DNS for the new hostname (always necessary).

Had my zd.cheek.com Web site been a name-based virtual host, not much would have changed in the configuration file. I would only have added the `<VirtualHost>` definition, with the following line before the `<VirtualHost>` command:

```
NameVirtualHost 208.12.12.131
```

This line instructs Apache to allow multiple Web sites to be assigned to the same IP address, and determines which Web site to use based on the hostname given by the Web browser. If the NameVirtualHost command is not specified before configuring a name-based virtual host, Apache will not allow an IP address to be used for more than one Web site. Only one NameVirtualHost command needs to be given for each IP address assigned to name-based virtual hosts; if I had 10 different Web sites using 208.12.12.131, I would only need one NameVirtualHost command. Because I had already created the virtual host, all I needed to do was create the new directories `/home/vhosts/zd/html` and `/home/vhosts/zd/cgi-bin`, and populate those with HTML and CGI files.

After creating the directories for the HTML and CGI content, a new DNS for the hostname would need to be added. Because name-based virtual hosts require a hostname, adding a DNS entry is an important step. After this is done, Apache will be ready to serve your new Web site. If Apache is already running, you will need to restart it. The new Web site should be browseable by hostname, but not by IP address.

Editing Apache's MIME Types

As a Web server administrator, you may occasionally need to edit Apache's *MIME* (Multipurpose Internet Mail Extensions) types. MIME types tell the Web browser what type of file is being sent to it: an HTML or text file, an image, an audio or video file, and so on. Apache reads the `/etc/httpd/apache/conf/mime.types` file to determine the proper MIME type for a file with a given extension. Here are a few examples of MIME types:

MIME Type	Apache's Corresponding File Extension(s)
text/html	.html .htm
audio/x-wav	.wav
image/gif	.gif

MIME types are registered with the Internet Assigned Numbers Authority; any additions to the `mime.types` file should be for types already registered with them. As the administrator, you decide what file extensions to associate with a MIME type. The `mime.types` file gives a MIME type, one per line, followed by the file extension(s) associated with its type. For example, the line below associates all files with .jpeg, .jpg, and .jpe extensions with the image/jpeg type (but notice that the extensions here are not preceded by a period).

```
image/jpeg                    jpeg jpg jpe
```

Manipulating MIME types becomes important as new types are added, and even more important as different file types use the same extension. For instance, the extension .rpm is used by RealNetwork's RealPlayer Module and also by OpenLinux's Red Hat Package Manager. Apache's `mime.types` file considers .rpm files as RealPlayer Modules by default:

```
audio/x-pn-realaudio-plugin  rpm
```

When someone tries to get a Red Hat Package with a browser, their RealNetwork Player may pop up and try to play the package as a sound file. This line can be commented out, with a hash mark at the beginning, to make Apache stop considering .rpm files as RealPlayer Modules.

Enabling Web-Based Server Status Reports

Apache has the ability to provide brief statistical reports for a Web browser. These are disabled by default. To enable them, edit the `/etc/httpd/apache/conf/access.conf` file, and look for the following lines:

```
#<Location /server-status>
#SetHandler server-status
#order deny,allow
#deny from all
#allow from .your_domain.com
#</Location>
```

To enable the server status report, uncomment these lines and change `.your_domain.com` to be your domain name; this tells Apache to allow viewing of this report only from computers in your domain. To view the report, open a Web browser and go to **www.your_domain.com/server-status/**, substituting your Web server hostname for www.your_domain.com. The statistics in the report will show how many servers are running and what each of them is doing, such as reading a request, responding to a request, idling, and so on. The report is terse by default, but can be made more verbose (as shown in Figure 6-1) if you add the following command after the previous `</Location>` line:

```
ExtendedStatus On
```

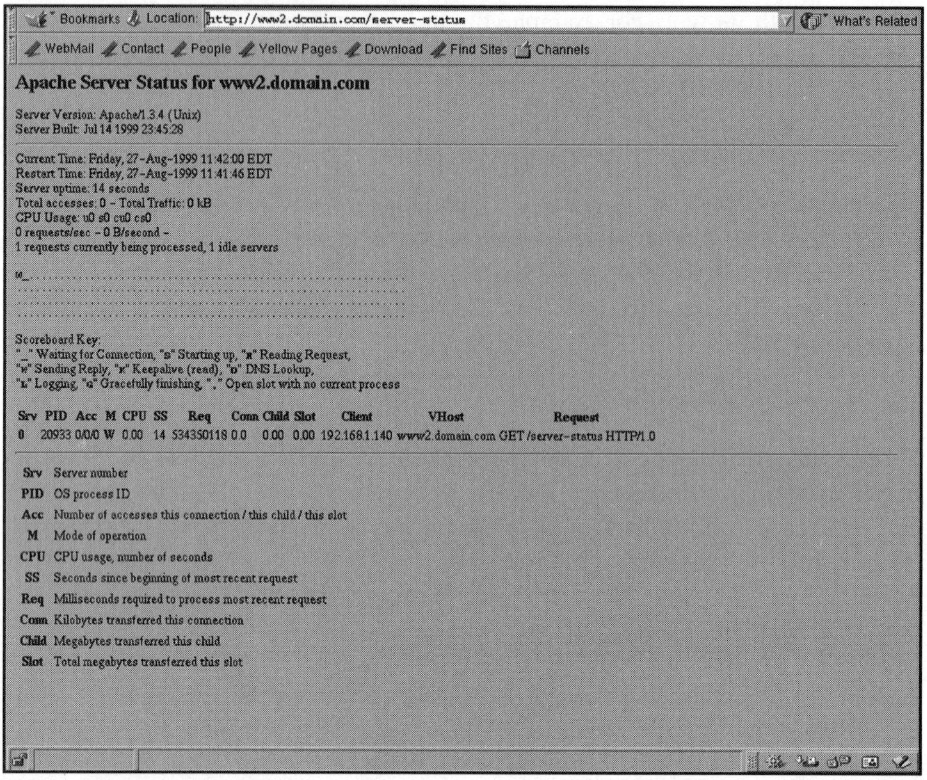

Figure 6-1 *An extended Apache server report not only shows what each server is doing, but also gives extended information about each connection currently made to the Apache servers.*

If you would prefer authentication by username/password rather than the domain name or IP address the request came from, you can comment out (part of the block you just uncommented):

```
order deny,allow
deny from all
allow from .your_domain.com
```

and add before the `</Limit>` line:

```
AuthType Basic
AuthName server-status
AuthUserFile /etc/httpd/apache/conf/server-status.passwd
Require valid-user
```

Then you create the server-status.passwd file, by running:

```
/home/httpd/bin/htpasswd -c /etc/httpd/apache/conf/server-status.passwd admin
```

This will then prompt you for a password and create the file. When you connect to server-status with this configuration you will need to use the username admin, and the password you set. You could also combine this with the order, deny, and allow lines, to require you connect from where you define, and know the username/password.

Enabling Server Side Includes

In order to support server side includes (server parsed HTML), you need to uncomment the following lines in `srm.conf`:

```
#AddType text/html .shtml

#AddHandler server-parsed .shtml
```

In addition, in the `access.conf` file, you need to add `Options Includes` to the appropriate `<Directory>` section. To add SSI to the entire HTML area, change:

```
Options None
```

to

```
Options Includes
```

in the `<Directory /home/httpd/html>` section of `/etc/httpd/apache/conf/access.conf`.

Apache supports the following SSI commands via the comment tag (`<!—#command options —>`):

`config errmsg`	Controls what message is sent back to the client if an error occurs while parsing the document.
`config timefmt`	Specifies a time format to use when displaying dates. Uses standard strftime library parameters.
`config sizefmt`	Determines formatting to be used when displaying file sizes.
`include virtual`	Includes a file relative to the DocumentRoot.
`include file`	Includes a file relative to the current directory.
`echo var`	Echoes the value of the specified environment variable.
`fsize virtual`	Prints the size of the specified file relative to the DocumentRoot.
`fsize file`	Prints the size of the specified file relative to the current directory.

`flastmod virtual`	Prints last modification date of the specified file relative to the DocumentRoot.
`flastmod file`	Prints last modification date of the specified file relative to the current directory.
`exec cmd`	Executes the specified command string using `/bin/sh`.
`exec cgi`	Executes given the virtual path to a cgi scriptAlias.
`if expr`	If conditional expression.
`elif expr`	"Else if" conditional expression.
`else`	Else part of if conditional.
`endif`	End of if conditional.

After enabling SSI, you can test several of the SSI commands with the following example. Place the following files in the `/home/httpd/html` directory:

```
header.html:

<HTML>
<HEAD>
<TITLE>Server Side Includes Test</TITLE>
</HEAD>
<BODY>

footer.html:

<BR>
<HR>
All pages served by Apache on OpenLinux !
<HR>
<BR>
</BODY>
</HTML>

test.shtml:

<!–#include virtual="/header.html" –>
<!–#if expr="$REMOTE_ADDR= /$SERVER_ADDR/" –>
Wouldn't you rather enjoy surfing somewhere else ?<BR><BR>
<!–#else –>
Welcome <!–#echo var="REMOTE_ADDR" –>!!<BR><BR>
```

```
<!-#endif ->
The local date/time is: <!-#exec cmd="/bin/date" -><BR>
<!-#include file="footer.html" \>
```

When you load `http://localhost/test.shtml`, you will see the following:

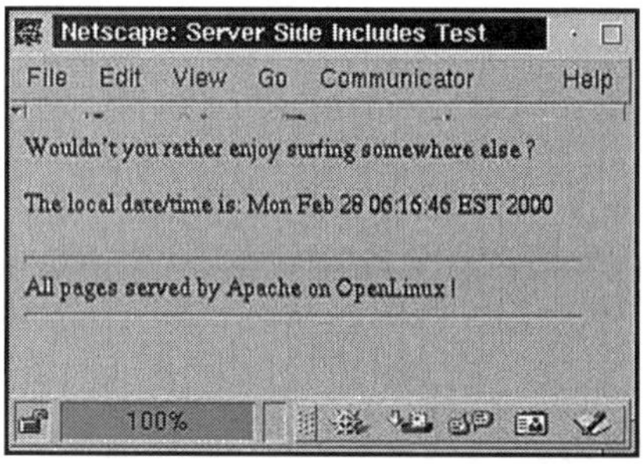

When you load it from a host other than yourself (or place the `test.shtml` on an IP-Based virtual host and access it from yourself):

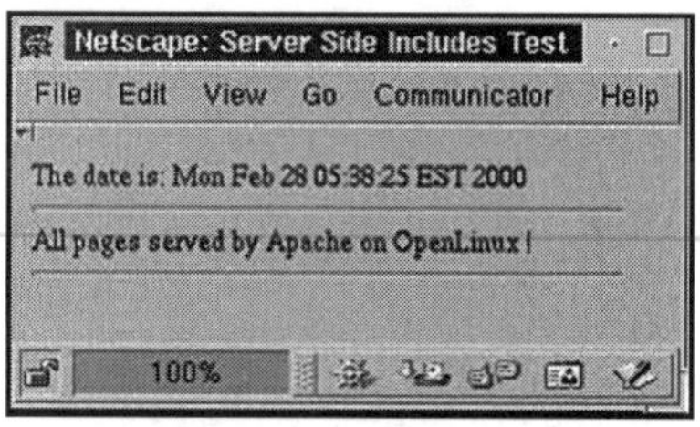

Starting and Stopping Apache

Each time an Apache setting is changed, the server must be restarted. In addition, the Apache server must be told to start automatically when OpenLinux starts. Sometimes Apache needs to be started or stopped by hand, perhaps to test a configuration or check for errors.

Enabling or Disabling Automatic Apache Startup

COAS will allow you to enable and disable Apache's automatic startup when the system restarts. From the System Administration option, choose Enable/disable system services, and look for the Web Server line. To enable Apache at system boot, check the box next to it. To disable Apache at system boot, uncheck this box. *COAS* is explained in more detail in Chapter 1, "Configuring OpenLinux's Basic Network."

Starting and Stopping Apache by Hand

OpenLinux includes scripts to start and stop Apache. These scripts can be run by hand to start and stop Apache on the fly.

```
/etc/rc.d/init.d/httpd start
```

This command starts the Apache server, if stopped. If it is already running, nothing will happen. If no error messages show on the console, the server started correctly.

```
/etc/rc.d/init.d/httpd stop
```

Similar to the first command, this command stops Apache if it is started. If it is already stopped, nothing will happen.

Restarting Apache After a Configuration Change

Apache won't know to change its behavior after a configuration file change unless it is told to restart itself. To restart Apache, we need its process ID. Apache stores its process ID in the file `/var/run/httpd.pid`. Find this process ID by using the `cat` command:

```
cat /var/run/httpd.pid

7078
```

The current process ID can be any number. (On my system, it was 7078.) Use the appropriate number in the following command, which sends a signal to Apache to reread its configuration files and is cleaner and more efficient than stopping and starting the server manually.

```
kill -HUP 7078
```

Performance Tuning

The default Apache options with a new OpenLinux installation are set for low-volume Web sites with light traffic. In most cases, these settings will work for high-volume sites, but they will reduce performance considerably. Here are some settings to play with to increase performance, all of which can be found in the `/etc/httpd/apache/conf/httpd.conf` file:

```
MaxKeepAliveRequests 100
```

`MaxKeepAliveRequests` sets the number of requests that Apache will allow with a persistent connection. Persistent connections are quicker that normal connections, because the Web browser and Apache do not need to establish a socket connection for each request. Increasing this number will help speed up connections from a single user who views many pages in succession.

```
KeepAliveTimeout 15
```

`KeepAliveTimeout` is the number of seconds Apache will wait during the same persistent connection for the next request. Increasing this number can help performance, but increasing it too much can leave too many sockets open, waiting for connections. Use your discretion on this; however, I do not recommend setting this above 60.

```
MinSpareServers 1
```

Apache starts many incarnations of itself to help balance the load when many Web requests are made at the same time. It keeps some extra servers around for quick bursts of Web hits, and then kills some off when too many are around. `MinSpareServers` is how many extra servers to keep around, at minimum; if there are fewer than these, more are started. I suggest increasing this number significantly if you have a fair or heavy amount of Web traffic. If you have a medium-traffic site, use at least 5; if you have lots of traffic, you might want a much larger number here.

```
MaxSpareServers 2
```

If there are more spare servers than `MaxSpareServers`, some are killed off. Again, I suggest increasing this number significantly if you have a fair or heavy amount of Web traffic. If you have a medium-traffic site, use at least 10.

```
MaxClients 15
```

`MaxClients` is the total number of server incarnations that can ever be active at once. Apache will never start more servers than this number, so if your sites get more traffic at once than this, your viewers will not be able to connect to your Web sites. Fifteen is a low default value; I suggest at least 50 for this value.

```
MaxRequestsPerChild 30
```

`MaxRequestsPerChild` is the number of requests a single server incarnationwill handle before being killed. Apache kills its server incarnations after 30 requests with the default value. If you run a very busy server, this can be a performance bottleneck and you should set this value higher. You should not exceed 1000 with this value, as if apache, or the system libraries have a memory leak, your httpd processes could consume lots of memory.

You can use the server-status feature to help you adjust your tuning parameters. For instance, you could check your server-status output and have output with `ExtendedStatus` On. A rule of thumb you can use is to make sure MinSpareServers is at least the requests/second rounded up to the nearest integer. If you know your server's peak time, you can send it a `kill -HUP`, and collect data for some number of minutes during a peak load. Then you could use that value for requests/sec as a minimum amount for MaxSpareServers. If you do the same during a quiet period, you may want to average these figures and set StartServers to that average. After making any changes, watch your server status to see how your changes have affected the server.

Security Considerations

If all anyone ever wanted to do with a webserver was to serve static HTML documents, security would be simple. However, people want to create dynamic web pages, integrate with databases, customize the content based on the viewer (or browser), etc. In order to do this, features like cgi and server side includes need to be enabled. The problem is then that cgi programs run as the user specified in the server's User directive (by default nobody).

Let's look at one problem with the standard cgi model. Domain 1 creates a form which gets information from a site visitor, and writes information to a guestbook file. Another script then can read the file and display it in a formatted manner. Under the current model, at least the guestbook file must be world writable, and if you need to create a file in a directory, the directory needs to be world writable. Obviously, anyone could then modify the file or delete it at the least. Ideally, it would be nice for each Web site to run cgi programs as the user that owns the Web site (1 for each virtual domain). With that scenario, files and directories would not need to be world writable.

One way to accomplish this is to start a server process for each domain hosted, with each one having its own configuration files. You would then use the BindAddress directive to Bind each particular server to the IP address for that virtual domain (you must use IP-Based virtual hosts for this technique). Here are the config files I used (they have had many defaults and extras removed to keep them small for demonstration purposes):

```
httpd_1.conf:


ResourceConfig /etc/httpd/apache/conf/srm_1.conf
AccessConfig /etc/httpd/apache/conf/access_1.conf
User user_1
Group users
ServerRoot /etc/httpd/apache
BindAddress 127.0.0.1
ErrorLog /var/log/httpd/apache/error_log_1
TransferLog /var/log/httpd/apache/access_log_1
LogLevel warn
LogFormat "%h %l %u %t \"%r\" %>s %b" common
CustomLog /var/log/httpd/apache/access_log_1 common
```

```
PidFile /var/run/httpd_1.pid
ScoreBoardFile /var/log/httpd/apache/apache_status_1
ServerName localhost
UseCanonicalName on

srm_1.conf:

DocumentRoot /home/httpd_1/html
DirectoryIndex index.html
DefaultType text/plain
ScriptAlias /cgi-bin/ /home/httpd_1/cgi-bin/

access_1.conf:

<Directory />
Options None
AllowOverride None
</Directory>
<Directory /home/httpd_1/html>
Options None
AllowOverride None
order allow,deny
allow from all
</Directory>
<Directory /home/httpd_1/cgi-bin>
AllowOverride None
Options ExecCGI
</Directory>

httpd_2.conf:

ResourceConfig /etc/httpd/apache/conf/srm_2.conf
AccessConfig /etc/httpd/apache/conf/access_2.conf
User user_2
Group users
ServerRoot /etc/httpd/apache
BindAddress 127.0.0.2
ErrorLog /var/log/httpd/apache/error_log_2
TransferLog /var/log/httpd/apache/access_log_2
LogLevel warn
```

```
LogFormat "%h %l %u %t \"%r\" %>s %b" common
CustomLog /var/log/httpd/apache/access_log_2 common
PidFile /var/run/httpd_2.pid
ScoreBoardFile /var/log/httpd/apache/apache_status_2
ServerName localhost
UseCanonicalName on

srm_2.conf:

DocumentRoot /home/httpd_2/html
DirectoryIndex index.html
DefaultType text/plain
ScriptAlias /cgi-bin/ /home/httpd_2/cgi-bin/

access_2.conf:

<Directory />
Options None
AllowOverride None
</Directory>
<Directory /home/httpd_2/html>
Options None
AllowOverride None
order allow,deny
allow from all
</Directory>
<Directory /home/httpd_2/cgi-bin>
AllowOverride None
Options ExecCGI
</Directory>
```

Then create the `/home/httpd_1` and `/home/httpd_2` directory hierarchies. I then placed the following simple cgi script in both `/home/httpd_1/cgi-bin` and `/home/httpd_2/cgi-bin`:

```
#!/bin/tcsh
echo "Content-Type: text/plain"
echo ""
/usr/bin/id
```

Then I started the two servers:

```
httpd.apache -f /etc/httpd/apache/conf/httpd_1.conf
httpd.apache -f /etc/httpd/apache/conf/httpd_2.conf
```

I then verified my configuration by going to `http://10.0.0.1` and `http://10.0.0.2`. It indicated that it was running as `user_1` for `10.0.0.1`, and `user_2` for `10.0.0.2`.

If you use this configuration, you will want to modify the `/etc/rc.d/init.d/httpd` script, or replace it with one of your own. The existing httpd script is designed to start one *httpd* process for the system, not multiple ones.

For some servers, this is one way to go about handling cgi security issues. This is also a great way to have php scripting run as the virtual domain's owner. Both files and cgi programs are accessed as the user you configure for each virtual domain.

However, this method is somewhat wasteful of system resources. If you configure 200 sites, you will have hundreds of processes running. For small numbers of virtual domains and for specific situations this is a powerful method of giving flexibility to Web developers without the compromise of security for flexibility.

Apache has another feature that is better on resources and gives the same security with cgi programs. This feature is called the suEXEC feature. As shipped with OpenLinux, the suexec feature is not available. In order to use this feature, you will need to recompile Apache from its sources. It is beyond the scope of this book to cover all the steps involved in that process. If your going to many servers (100 or more) and want cgi programs to run as the virtual domain owner, check out the references section for a link to Apache's documentation on the suexec feature.

Troubleshooting Apache

During a Web server restart, Apache will complain to the console if it finds an option it doesn't like in its configuration files. Fatal errors will keep the Web server from starting at all; non-fatal errors will allow Apache to start, albeit with limited functionality. Watch for these errors when you start or restart Apache. When it cannot find a file or directory it needs, for example, Apache will complain with an error similar to the following:

```
fopen: No such file or directory
httpd: could not open error log file /var/log/ahttpd/apache/error_log.
```

As you can see, I mistyped the filename of the error log file above. This error kept Apache from starting.

```
httpd: [Mon Aug  2 11:01:30 1999] [error] Cannot resolve host name
   host.some_domain.com -- ignoring!
Warning: DocumentRoot [/www/docs/host.some_domain.com] does not exist
```

This one, though, is a non-fatal error. Apache could not resolve my mistyped VirtualHost directive because I gave it a bogus hostname. It was, however, able to process the default Web server, and started its normal Web serving properly. Other errors will show up in the server logs—typically, these are non-fatal errors (the Web server is running), but they can alert you to problems that may affect your viewers.

There are a few ways of troubleshooting Apache, whether the errors are fatal or not. Most of the time, the error message specifically references the line or configuration directive that it didn't like. In checking Apache, you can see whether the server has been started at all, what process ID it is running under as its main process, and what the error and access logs are showing.

If you are unsure about how Apache was compiled/configured, you can do an `httpd.apache -V` on the command line to find out. Here is the output from the `httpd.apache` bundled with OpenLinux 2.3:

```
Server version: Apache/1.3.4 (Unix)
Server built:   Aug 10 1999 19:17:10
Server's Module Magic Number: 19990108:0
Server compiled with....
 -D HAVE_MMAP
 -D HAVE_SHMGET
 -D USE_SHMGET_SCOREBOARD
 -D USE_MMAP_FILES
 -D USE_FLOCK_SERIALIZED_ACCEPT
 -D HTTPD_ROOT="/usr/local/apache"
 -D SUEXEC_BIN="/usr/local/apache/sbin/suexec"
 -D DEFAULT_PIDLOG="logs/httpd.pid"
 -D DEFAULT_SCOREBOARD="logs/apache_runtime_status"
 -D DEFAULT_LOCKFILE="logs/accept.lock"
 -D DEFAULT_XFERLOG="logs/access_log"
 -D DEFAULT_ERRORLOG="logs/error_log"
 -D TYPES_CONFIG_FILE="conf/mime.types"
 -D SERVER_CONFIG_FILE="conf/httpd.conf"
 -D ACCESS_CONFIG_FILE="conf/access.conf"
 -D RESOURCE_CONFIG_FILE="conf/srm.conf"
```

Checking Whether Apache Started

Because Apache writes its process ID to the `/var/run/httpd.pid` file, an easy way to check if Apache is running is to see if this file exists. Use the `cat` command to view the file. Here is an example that shows Apache running under process ID 7078.

```
cat /var/run/httpd.pid
```

```
7078
```

If it were not running, your output would instead look something like this:

```
cat: /var/run/httpd.pid: No such file or directory
```

This method is not bulletproof, however; after a system crash, Apache can exit without removing its `/httpd.pid` file. For more accurate results, use the `ps ax` command:

```
ps ax | grep [h]ttpd

...

26490 ?        S      0:00 httpd -f /etc/httpd/apache/conf/httpd.conf

26492 ?        S      0:00 httpd -f /etc/httpd/apache/conf/httpd.conf

26493 ?        S      0:00 httpd -f /etc/httpd/apache/conf/httpd.conf

26494 ?        S      0:00 httpd -f /etc/httpd/apache/conf/httpd.conf

...
```

Four Apache server processes are running, under process IDs 26490, 26492, 26493, and 26494. The actual number of servers started on your system will depend on how you have the MinSpareServers, MaxSpareServers, and StartServers settings configured in your `/etc/httpd/apache/conf/httpd.conf` file.

Checking the Server Logs

Apache's server logs are by default named `/var/log/httpd/apache/access_log` and `/var/log/httpd/apache/error_log`. `access_log` gives the details of each request for a file, whether successful or not; `error_log` gives missing or bad file requests, and a lot of other system messages. These logs provide information about how the server is running and whether it is doing what you expect it to do.

These files can grow to be large, so it is generally not a good idea to view the entire file. The `tail` command can be used to show just the last few lines of these files. The `tail` command needs the name of the filename to view; without any further options, it will show the last 10 lines of the file.

```
tail /var/log/httpd/apache/access_log

httpd: [Sat Jul 31 18:43:43 1999] [warn] child process 7392 did not exit, sending
another SIGHUP
```

```
httpd: [Sat Jul 31 18:43:43 1999] [warn] child process 7393 did not exit, sending
    another SIGHUP

httpd: [Sat Jul 31 18:43:45 1999] [notice] SIGHUP received.  Attempting to restart

httpd: [Sat Jul 31 18:43:45 1999] [notice] Apache/1.3.4 (Unix) configured — resuming
normal operations

httpd: [Mon Aug  2 10:54:21 1999] [notice] caught SIGTERM, shutting down

httpd: [Mon Aug  2 11:01:30 1999] [error] Cannot resolve host name
    host.some_domain.com -- ignoring!

Warning: DocumentRoot [/www/docs/host.some_domain.com] does not exist

httpd: [Mon Aug  2 11:01:30 1999] [notice] Apache/1.3.4 (Unix) configured — resuming
   normal operations

httpd: [Mon Aug  2 11:20:34 1999] [notice] caught SIGTERM, shutting down

httpd: [Mon Aug  2 11:26:24 1999] [notice] Apache/1.3.4 (Unix) configured — resuming
    normal operations
```

These last 10 lines are spread over three different days. Notice that Apache writes a successful startup message to the error log when it starts correctly. Checking the error log is another good way to see if it did start at all.

Normally, `tail` gives the last 10 lines and then exits. To check a log and have `tail` print all subsequently written lines until it is stopped, use `tail -f FILENAME` (follow). It will then continue printing new lines written to the log until stopped with a Ctrl+C keypress. If you want more than the last 10 lines, you can use `tail -n 20 FILENAME` (which will give twenty lines). Any number can be substituted for 20 here.

Checking the access logs will also yield interesting information about who is visiting the site and what is being viewed. These logs are detailed; log analyzers such as Analog and WebTrends will provide overviews of the logs, but viewing the logs themselves is the best way to get the details. Each line looks similar to this:

```
208.12.12.130 - - [02/Aug/1999:11:57:57 -0700] “GET /images/kb-88x31-blue.gif
HTTP/1.0” 200 1038 “http://saltlake.cheek.com/” “Mozilla/4.61C-Caldera [en] (X11;
I; Linux 2.2.9 i686)”
```

This says that the machine with IP address 208.12.12.130 requested the `/images/kb-88x31-blue.gif` file roughly at noon on August 2. The server gave it a status of 200, which means “OK,” and transferred 1038 bytes to the Web browser. This browser was a Netscape 4.61, Caldera edition browser, running on a Linux Pentium II machine with kernel version 2.2.9, using X11. This was my machine, requesting a file from my Web server. Had I requested a file that didn't exist, I would have gotten this in the access log:

```
208.12.12.130 - - [02/Aug/1999:12:06:39 -0700] "GET /badfile.html HTTP/1.0" 404 206
"-" "Mozilla/4.61C-Caldera [en] (X11; I; Linux 2.2.9 i686)"
```

Because badfile.html didn't exist, Apache returned with a 404 error, which in this context means that the file does not exist (although generally the code would just mean that it was not found). It took 206 bytes to tell me that the file didn't exist. The "-" means that there was no referring Web page; I typed in the URL by hand. These errors are also logged in the error log:

```
httpd: [Mon Aug  2 12:06:39 1999] [error] [client 208.12.12.130] File does not
exist: /usr/lkb-install/html/badfile.html
```

This line doesn't give me as much detail, but it is nice enough to give me the full pathname on the file system of the file Apache tried to retrieve. It's much easier to check this file for this reason. Apache logs a failed file request twice because most log analyzers do not check the error log, only the access log.

It can be difficult to wade through an entire log file when looking for something specific. The `grep` command will return only those lines with a specified keyword in them. To look at the access log lines from `aol.com`, try:

```
grep aol.com /var/log/httpd/apache/access_log
```

Only lines with the text "aol.com" would be shown. Because America Online is a popular service, you might still have hundreds or thousands of lines shown from this command. To show only the last 10 lines of output, combine the `grep` command with a pipe character (|) and the `tail` command:

```
grep aol.com /var/log/httpd/apache/access_log | tail
```

Now only the last 10 aol.com accesses are shown. If you wanted to just search the last 10 accesses for aol.com addresses, you could combine these commands in the reverse order:

```
tail /var/log/httpd/apache/access_log | grep aol.com
```

TIP

> **grep** has many more search abilities for text files like these Apache logs. You can learn about the advanced searching capabilities of this command by typing **man grep** to view its manual page.

Troubleshooting with lynx

The lynx Web browser is a quick and easy browser that works well for simple Web site troubleshooting. Because it is text-based, it does not require the overhead of X11. lynx can be used to force a query to a specific Web site, so you can then check the access and error logs for Apache's response to that query. lynx can be given the URL on the command line, such as:

```
lynx http://localhost/
```

This renders the **localhost** Web page on a text screen. If you would rather see the source, you can use the `-source` option:

```
lynx -source http://localhost/
```

If you don't care about viewing the Web page and just want to force a request, redirect the output to `/dev/null`:

```
lynx -source http://localhost/ > /dev/null
```

This forces a request and throws away the output. Don't forget to use `-source` when redirecting the output, so that lynx will exit when done.

Web Statistics Analyzers for Use with Apache

An important part of maintaining a Web site is getting statistical reports on how much traffic the site is generating, where it is coming from, what errors are being received, and so on. Apache does not come with any statistical programs, but there are two programs I recommend for this purpose. The first is Analog, a freeware program, which takes an Apache log file and produces reports based on the information in the log file. A much more advanced program for generating Web usage statistics is WebTrends, which is commercial software. (Unfortunately, they don't produce the Logfile Analyzer for Linux; they offer only the much more expensive Enterprise Reporting Server, which generates real-time reports of great depth and detail.)

For More Information

More information on the Apache Web server can be found at several places on the Internet. Here are a few of my favorite URLs:

URL	Resource Name
http://www.apache.org	Apache Software Foundation Web Site
http://linuxkb.cheek.com/page.php?apache	Linux Knowledge Base Apache Information
http://www.apache-ssl.com	Apache SSL Software Site
http://hoohoo.ncsa.uiuc.edu/docs/tutorials/includes.html	Server Side Includes Documentation
http://hoohoo.ncsa.uiuc.edu/cgi/	Common Gateway Interface Documentation
ftp://ftp.iana.org/in-notes/iana/assignments/media-types/	Internet Media Type Registry
http://www.statslab.cam.ac.uk/~sret1/analog/	Analog Log Analyzer for Linux
http://www.Webtrends.com	WebTrends Enterprise Reporting Server for Linux
http://www.apache.org/docs/	Apache User's Guide
http://www.apache.org/docs/suexec.html	Apache suEXEC Support
http://www.php3.org	PHP3 Home Page
http://boutell.com/wusage/	Wusage Usage Statistics Analyzer
http://apache.org/dist/binaries/linux/	Apache binary distributions for Linux

Chapter 7: Configuring SMTP E-mail with sendmail and procmail

SMTP E-mail Overview

Configuring sendmail and procmail

Troubleshooting sendmail

Troubleshooting procmail

OpenLinux bundles the program *sendmail* to transfer e-mail via SMTP (the *Simple Mail Transfer Protocol*), a protocol responsible for passing e-mail from one computer to another, and ultimately transporting it to a user's mailbox. Outgoing mail is sent to the proper mail server and incoming mail is routed to the proper inbox for later retrieval by *sendmail*. Caldera has integrated another program, *procmail*, into the process of delivering incoming mail to a user. This chapter discusses *sendmail* and *procmail* as they work together.

Files Referenced in this Chapter

The following files are used by OpenLinux's *sendmail* and *procmail* packages:

File	Purpose
`/etc/sendmail.cf`	*sendmail's* basic configuration file
`/etc/sendmail.cw`	A list of hosts and domains for which *sendmail* receives mail
`/etc/aliases`	A list of system-wide e-mail aliases
`/etc/mail/virtuserstable`	A list of virtual user mappings
`/etc/mail/virtuserstable.db`	A hashed database list of virtual user mappings
`/etc/mail/relay-domains`	A list of hosts for which *sendmail* will relay mail.
`/etc/mail/access`	Access control list for *sendmail*
`/etc/mail/access.db`	Hash database access control list for *sendmail*
`/usr/share/sendmail/cf/cf/generic-col2.2.mc`	This file is used to generate a new `/etc/sendmail.cf` file
`/etc/procmailrc`	*procmail's* global recipe file
`/var/spool/mail`	Incoming mail is stored in this directory
`/var/spool/mqueue`	Outgoing mail is stored in this directory

NOTE

In each user's home directory, *sendmail* looks for a `.forward` file. Additionally, *procmail* looks for a `.procmailrc` file in each user's home directory.

SMTP E-mail Overview

E-mail on the Internet is handled by several different protocols. When an e-mail is sent, typically the message is transferred from the user's mail program to the outgoing mail server, and then on to the destination mail server (and through any servers in between) via SMTP. There the message waits for the user to read it via a different protocol, such as POP3 or IMAP (see Figure 7-1).

Just as different protocols are used to take e-mail from user to user, different programs are involved at each step in the path. Besides the various programs used to read and send mail, such as Netscape Mail or Microsoft Outlook, two programs typically have a hand in the transfer process. One handles the SMTP transfer, and one handles the POP3 or IMAP transfer.

NOTE

Wondering what the significant differences are between POP3 and IMAP? POP3 is the successor to POP2, an older protocol no longer used. POP3 has some security holes, and by automatically forwarding all mail to the user's MUA it assumes that each user only uses one computer, which makes it difficult for roaming users. IMAP lets users roam between computers much more easily, by storing all mail on the server. This lets the server keep track of which messages have been read and which are new.

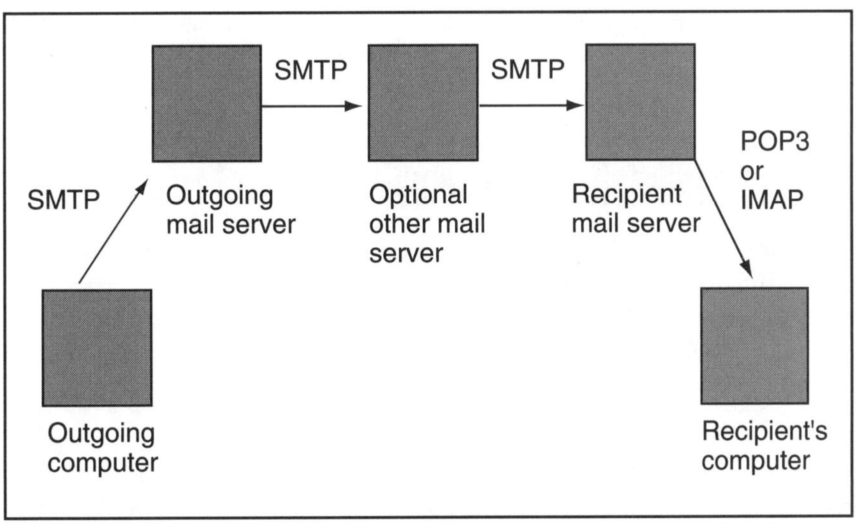

Figure 7-1 *E-mail is transferred from a user's mail program to the outgoing mail server, and then on to the destination mail server via SMTP, where it then waits for the user to read it via POP3 or IMAP.*

One MDA, One MTA

Caldera has integrated *procmail* into the process of delivering incoming mail to a user. *procmail* acts as a filter on the incoming mail. It can do lots of neat things, like route mail into different folders, send automatic replies to e-mail, filter based on content, and execute a program when mail arrives, all while delivering the mail to the inbox. As opposed to *procmail*, which is an MDA (*Mail Delivery Agent*), *sendmail* is an MTA (*Mail Transfer Agent*). Therefore, *sendmail* hands the incoming mail it receives to *procmail* for mailbox delivery.

Other MTAs versus sendmail

Linux commonly uses Mail Transfer Agents other than *sendmail*. Other programs, such as *smail* and *qmail*, are drop-in replacements for *sendmail*. These programs are smaller and easier to work with, although not as robust or configurable. Because of their smaller size, proponents say that they are less susceptible to security holes and are faster on the mail delivery.

Another MTA, *fetchmail*, is not a replacement for *sendmail*. *fetchmail* is used to transport mail from one server to another via POP3, instead of via SMTP. This is useful when a mail server is not reachable using the SMTP store-and-forward technique, in which the server with the mail initiates the transportation. For instance, many small workgroups will share a single IP address via a process called Network Address Translation (IP Masquerading, in Linux terminology). A Linux mail server sitting on the private side of this configuration would not be reachable from the public Internet side, and could not receive SMTP mail connections. The server could, however, initiate POP3 connections to the mail server which has the mail, and retrieve each message locally.

Configuring sendmail and procmail

The basic configuration file for *sendmail*, `/etc/sendmail.cf`, is enormous and complex. It's so complex that it is usually generated by *m4*, a program specifically written to generate complex configuration files. In *m4*, a simple configuration file and a lot of rulesets are taken, and a complex configuration file is produced.

Fortunately, Caldera has already done this for you, and has produced a working `/etc/sendmail.cf` file from *m4*. The defaults in this file will work fine if you just want to send outgoing mail. If you want to receive e-mail with *sendmail*, however, it will need some tweaking. We've broken this tweaking process down into two sections, Basic *sendmail* Configuration and Advanced *sendmail* Configuration. If you go through the steps in the basic section, you will have a functional *sendmail* for incoming mail. These steps are

- Configuring Acceptable Mail Hosts
- Creating User Aliases
- Controlling E-mail Forwarding

The Advanced *sendmail* Configuration section deals with fine-tuning a working *sendmail* setup. There are many aspects of *sendmail* that can be tuned to a fine detail, far too many to cover in a single chapter. In that section, we discuss the aspects that I have most often been asked to configure. These steps, while optional, can be beneficial additions to your OpenLinux system.

- Configuring Virtual Users
- Controlling Mail Relaying
- Controlling Spam E-mail

After *sendmail* receives mail properly, it takes each message and hands it to *procmail* to deliver to the user's inbox. Normally, *procmail* does only that. However, it has the ability to do many other things with each message, on a system-wide or user-by-user basis. The *procmail* Configuration section explains how to utilize some of these beneficial features, including:

- Moving User Mail to a Different Directory
- Separating E-mail into Folders
- Deleting Unwanted E-mail Automatically
- Creating Automatic Reply Messages
- Advanced Filtering

Basic sendmail Configuration

Using *sendmail*, outgoing mail will transfer properly without configuration. However, to receive any mail, it will need to be configured. This section details the minimum number of steps necessary to get a functioning mail server from a default OpenLinux installation. We recommend making these changes even if you only want to send outgoing mail.

Configuring Acceptable Mail Hosts

In order to function properly, *sendmail* needs to know the hosts and domains for which it will be receiving mail. This is everything after the @ sign in the e-mail address. Typically it is just the Internet domain name (such as domain.com), although it can be a sub-domain (seattle.domain.com) or a hostname (mypc.domain.com). Any and all domains, sub-domains, and hostnames where you or anyone else will be receiving mail need to be enumerated. On my mail server, saltlake.cheek.com, I use the following:

- cheek.com
- mail.cheek.com
- saltlake.cheek.com

In my DNS records I have aliased mail.cheek.com to saltlake.cheek.com, and have made my saltlake machine the default mail exchanger for the entire domain. So mail sent to joseph@cheek.com, joseph@mail.cheek.com, and joseph@saltlake.cheek.com will get sent to my primary mail server, saltlake. Any mail sent to a different machine, such as seattle.cheek.com, will get sent directly to my seattle machine.

If you will be sending internal (in-house) e-mail to this machine, perhaps from one employee to another, it is also a good idea to include just the local part of the hostname, such as mail or saltlake, so that mail to joseph@mail, for instance, will be accepted. Any mail *sendmail* receives destined for one of the machines on this list will be delivered locally; any mail sent to a different machine will be forwarded (or perhaps discarded, if mail relaying is turned off).

Another set of domain names to add to the list are any virtual hosts whose mail you will host. If your company is an ISP, or you have multiple domain names, add those to this list, so that *sendmail* knows to receive mail for them also.

These hostnames and domain names need to be listed, one per line, in the file `/etc/sendmail.cw`. The list for my machine is shown in Listing 7-1; because I host virtual domains, I list them below as `domain1.com`, `domain2.com`, and `domain3.com`. (Note that any changes to the `/etc/sendmail.cw` file require restart of the *sendmail* mail server to take effect.)

Listing 7-1 An example /etc/sendmail.cw file

```
# sendmail.cw - include all aliases for your machine here.
cheek.com
saltlake
saltlake.cheek.com
mail
mail.cheek.com

domain1.com
domain2.com
domain3.com
```

Creating User Aliases

Each user account automatically has an e-mail account, and *sendmail* will deliver mail to all users created on the server; my cheek.com mail server will route mail addressed to joseph@cheek.com to the *joseph* account. Normally, mail sent to an address that is not a user on the system will bounce back to the sender with an undeliverable message. Mail aliases will allow a single user account to receive mail at multiple addresses. Each address other than its own is aliased to the user account.

Because I have a user account named *joseph* on my mail server, mail to joseph@cheek.com goes to my *joseph* mailbox by default. When I wanted to create a mail address of info@cheek.com, and have mail sent to it appear in my mailbox, I determined that I just needed to alias *info* to *joseph*.

The `/etc/aliases` file contains these e-mail aliases. The format is the alias, a colon, some whitespace, and then the actual user account. Here is an example for info@cheek.com:

```
info: joseph
```

A more complicated example would be if I had two employees, Dan and John, who worked for me as a salesman and technical support representative, respectively. After I create the user accounts *dan* and *john*, I could alias sales@cheek.com and support@cheek.com to them. When an e-mail message addressed to info@cheek.com comes in, I could have it sent to all three of us. This would require an `/etc/aliases` file like this:

```
sales: dan

support: john

info: joseph, dan, john
```

An alias can expand to more than one user, as in the *info* example above. This allows for simple mailing lists to be created. Complex mailing lists can be better handled by programs such as *majordomo*, but this works for simple lists.

Mail can also be sent to a program or a file using the aliases file. To send to a program, use a pipe (|) character immediately followed by the full pathname of a program, instead of the user account. Both the text and headers of each mail message sent to the aliased account will be piped to the specified program. This is good for autoresponders; the following line, when placed in the `/etc/aliases` file, will pipe all mail sent to autoresponder@cheek.com to the program `/usr/local/bin/autoreply`:

```
autoresponder: |/usr/local/bin/autoreply
```

The /usr/local/bin/autoreply program would have to exist, and would probably be written to extract the From: address and to send a mail message back to that address.

Similarly, mail can be placed in a file by using the full pathname of the file instead of the user account. Suppose that you want to log all incoming mail sent to info@cheek.com in the file /var/log/info_mail_log. Use the following:

```
info: /var/log/info_mail/log
```

CAUTION

> Be sure to use the full pathname of the file, as the first slash character tells sendmail that mail sent to this alias is sent to a file, and not a user account.

After the /etc/aliases file has been changed, the program *newaliases* must be run to tell *sendmail* that new aliases exist.

CAUTION

> Mail aliased with the /etc/aliases file is done so with daemon user and group permissions. If mail is sent to a file, it must be writable from the user and group daemon; if mail is piped to a program, that program must be executable from the user and group daemon.

Controlling E-mail Forwarding

Just as the system administrator can use the /etc/aliases file to create mail-forwarding aliases for any account on the system, each user can control mail forwarding for his or her own mail account. This is controlled by a file named .forward (pronounced *dot-forward*), located in the user's home directory. It's good to use the .forward file when the user has accounts on many different computers and wishes all mail to be forwarded to one machine. (I use .forward files on my seattle and sanfrancisco machines to forward e-mail to my main mailbox on my saltlake machine.)

The specifics of the .forward file are similar to those for the /etc/aliases file: a name is treated as an e-mail alias, text beginning with the pipe character (|) is treated as a program to which the message is piped, and text beginning with a slash character (/) is treated as a file in which to save the message. The difference is that these do not need the original username and a colon before the forwarding text. To make this more clear, let me give some examples. If I wanted to forward mail from my *joseph* account to my wife Liza's account, I would place the following in my .forward file:

```
liza
```

To forward mail to my account on the seattle machine, I could use:

```
joseph@seattle
```

To save all mail in the file `/home/joseph/mymail`, and not in the inbox, I would use:

```
/home/joseph/mymail
```

You can forward to more than one address at once with *sendmail*. To save all mail in `/home/joseph/mymail` and also leave a copy in my inbox, I would use:

```
/home/joseph/mymail, joseph
```

Mail can just as easily be sent to a different account altogether, by using the full e-mail address in the `.forward` file:

```
me@other.email.account.com
```

CAUTION

> Mail forwarded through a `.forward` file is done so with user and group permissions corresponding to the user account that owns the `.forward` file. In the cases presented above, the user is joseph and the group is users. If mail is sent to a file, it must be writable from that user and group; if mail is piped to a program, the program must be executable by that user and group.

Advanced sendmail Configuration

After you configure *sendmail* with the basic functions in the previous section, you might want to get more control over how *sendmail* deals with e-mail. Whereas the basic functions are mandatory for an incoming mail server, these are completely optional. You must first have configured the basic functions, however, before proceeding to this section.

Configuring Virtual Users

Virtual users exist on any system with virtual hosts. As I explained in the "Configuring Acceptable Mail Hosts" section, *sendmail* will accept mail for any virtual hosts on your OpenLinux system, if told to do so. By default, *sendmail* does not distinguish between e-mail accounts for your system and e-mail accounts for virtual hosts; if you are hosting domain1.com and domain2.com on your domain.com machine, *sendmail* considers bob@domain.com, bob@domain1.com, and bob@domain2.com as the same user *bob*. This doesn't become a problem unless these three different e-mail addresses belong to three different users, who want their own mail in their own inboxes.

Unfortunately, the default /etc/sendmail.cf file in OpenLinux 2.3 doesn't support virtual users, so you will need to add support for virtual users in this file. To do this, edit the /usr/share/sendmail/cf/cf/generic-col2.2.mc file. Look for the lines that add support for a mailer table:

```
dnl # We provide a mailertable to fine-tune routing.
dnl #
FEATURE(mailertable, `hash /etc/sendmail/mailertable')
```

Below that line, add another for the virtual user table:

```
FEATURE(virtusertable, `hash /etc/sendmail/virtusertable')
```

CAUTION

> Regenerating the /etc/sendmail.cf file will cause any changes you have made to this file to be lost! This can cause all mail services to quit working. Proceed only after making a backup copy of the /etc/sendmail.cf file.

The next step is to regenerate the /etc/sendmail.cf file. This process will overwrite the existing one, so if you have made any changes to that file, make a backup copy! Generate the new file by executing the following command, and then restart *sendmail* to put the changes into effect.

```
m4 /usr/share/sendmail/cf/m4/cf.m4 /usr/share/sendmail/cf/cf/generic-
col2.2.mc > /etc/sendmail.cf
```

Keep in mind that this completely regenerates the /etc/sendmail.cf file, and it will need to be edited again with all of the changes you may have made earlier. This allows virtual users to be specified in the /etc/sendmail/virtusertable file. By editing this file, you can specify that mail sent to bob@domain.com be sent to one place, bob@domain1.com be sent somewhere else, and bob@domain2.com be sent to a third place. Create the /etc/sendmail/virtusertable file as in Listing 7-2. Be sure to use tabs, not spaces, to separate the left and right columns.

Listing 7-2 A sample /etc/sendmail/virtusertable

```
# makemap hash /etc/sendmail/virtusertable < /etc/sendmail/virtusertable
bob@domain.com      bobjohnson
bob@domain1.com     bobsmith
bob@domain2.com     bobturner
```

This file tells *sendmail* that incoming mail addressed to bob@domain.com gets put in the *bobjohnson* inbox, mail to bob@domain1.com gets put in the *bobsmith* mailbox, and mail to bob@domain2.com gets delivered to the *bobturner* inbox. All of these e-mail accounts must exist on your system.

Notice the commented-out `makemap` command at the top of the listing. This command must be run after each change to the `virtusertable` file. Execute it now—this rebuilds the virtual user table database `/etc/sendmail/virtusertable.db`, and is akin to running the `newaliases` command after each change to the `/etc/aliases` file. Since this data is looked up on demand from *sendmail*, you do not need to restart *sendmail* after you make changes to the `/etc/sendmail/virtusertable` file.

In the examples above, all mail was delivered to local mailboxes. It could just as easily be delivered to other mailboxes on other mail servers. If Bob Turner had a personal e-mail account somewhere else, we could have used:

```
bob@domain2.com      bobturner@some.other.server.com
```

The virtual user table also provides a *catch-all* mail delivery directive. Consider Listing 7-3:

Listing 7-3 A catch-all example in the /etc/sendmail/virtusertable file

```
# makemap hash /etc/sendmail/virtusertable < /etc/sendmail/virtusertable
bob@domain.com       bobjohnson
jeff@domain.com      jeffbaker
@domain.com          johnbrown
```

As you can see, Bob Johnson gets mail sent to his e-mail address, Jeff Baker gets mail sent to his address, and John Brown gets mail addressed to anyone else at domain.com. This is good to use when a single person is the main e-mail contact for a domain, which often happens with small businesses. Make sure that the catch-all listing is at the end of the listings for its domain, or else it may pre-empt other listings.

Controlling Mail Relaying

OpenLinux won't send mail from every address to every address by default—the mail must either originate or get delivered on its own server to be processed. *sendmail* used to deliver mail from any server to any server; this is called mail relaying, and is now considered a security hole, partly in that many people will use mail relays to send unsolicited e-mail (spam mail). When spam e-mail is sent from a different computer than it originated from, it is harder to trace.

When *sendmail* sees mail going through it that neither originates nor terminates at its server, it refuses to send the mail, giving a `<550 Relaying Denied>` message. Often, legitimate mail is sent, however, that neither originates nor terminates on the OpenLinux server. A good example is mail originating from an employee's desktop computer using their favorite mail program, such as Netscape Mail or Microsoft Outlook. These mail messages technically originate from their own computer, not the server, and may be bound for anyplace on the Internet. These computers need to be able to send mail anywhere, without receiving the `<550 Relaying Denied>` message.

The `/etc/mail/relay-domains` file contains a list of hosts for which relaying is allowed. These must be either fully qualified domain names or IP addresses. No wildcards are allowed, so if you need to give access to your 200 employees, you will need 200 lines of hosts, one per line. Because my saltlake.cheek.com machine acts as a mail server for my workgroup, my file looks like this:

```
# /etc/mail/relay-domains - include all hosts that clients send mail from here
seattle.cheek.com
sanfrancisco.cheek.com
laptop.cheek.com
```

I have four computers in this workgroup: saltlake.cheek.com, seattle.cheek.com, sanfrancisco.cheek.com, and laptop.cheek.com. There is a line for each machine here, with the exception of saltlake, because mail originating from saltlake is automatically accepted. Keep in mind that these must be fully qualified domain names, not aliases—I could not just enter seattle, sanfrancisco, and laptop and expect it to work correctly. The .cheek.com is significant here. After a change to this file, *sendmail* must be restarted. See the section "Starting and Stopping *sendmail* and *procmail*" later in this chapter for details.

TIP

> According to *sendmail* documentation, this list of hosts can be either fully qualified domain names or IP addresses. I have had problems with IP addresses in this list, so if I need to enter an IP address for which there is no DNS hostname, I generally create a fake entry to add to the `/etc/hosts` file for that machine, and add that fake name to the `/etc/mail/relay-domains` file.

If the `/etc/mail` directory does not exist, it must be created first with the `mkdir` command. You must restart *sendmail* after any changes to the `/etc/mail/relay-domains` file.

Controlling Spam E-mail

You might, like me, receive far too many e-mail messages along the lines of "make money quick," "buy our products," "sell your products here," and so on. All mail sent through *sendmail* to users on your system, whether they are legitimate or unsolicited messages (junk mail), is accepted. To limit the amount of spam mail sent to users on your system, *sendmail* can be configured to filter out some of these messages based on their source—a set of IP addresses, domain names, or e-mail addresses.

To configure this filter, the *access database* feature of *sendmail* must be enabled. This entails changing the `/usr/share/sendmail/cf/cf/generic-col2.2.mc` file, just as in the preceding "Configuring Virtual Users" section. The following line must be added to that file:

```
FEATURE(access_db)
```

This will enable support for the `/etc/mail/access` file, which is a database of IP addresses, domain names, and e-mail addresses to accept or reject. You can refer back to the "Configuring Virtual Users" subsection to review the process of editing the `/usr/share/sendmail/cf/cf/generic-col2.2.mc` file and generating a new `/etc/sendmail.cf` file if you need to. Here, I discuss what to do after the new `sendmail.cf` file is generated. After the `sendmail.cf` file is regenerated, create the `/etc/mail/access` file as demonstrated in Listing 7-4:

Listing 7-4 A sample /etc/mail/access file

```
# makemap hash /etc/mail/access < /etc/mail/access
spammer.com          550 Go away
192.168              REJECT
192.168.1            OK
friend@       550 Go away
```

The left column is a domain name, IP address subnet, or partial e-mail address to accept or reject. The right column is an error code and text message, or a standard procedural message, such as *REJECT* or *OK*. Separate these columns with tabs, not spaces.

Because there are a few different ways to handle mail here, I explain what these lines mean. The first line tells *sendmail* to reject any mail coming from spammer.com with a "`550 Go away`" error message. `550` is a code meaning the mail was not accepted; the text can be anything you want it to be. The next two lines tell *sendmail* to reject all mail from the 192.168 subnet, except for mail coming from the 192.168.1 subnet.

Instead of using a customized error message, just *REJECT* or *OK* is used. In these cases, *sendmail* issues an appropriate generic response. Finally, the last line tells *sendmail* to reject any mail coming from an e-mail address starting with *friend@* (many times, junk e-mail will be sent with a from address such as this).

One significant aspect of this file is that when more than one line matches an e-mail message, the *last* line matched is the one that is used. In the example above, mail from a 192.168.1.1 host would match both the second and third line of the access file; because the second line rejects it but the third line makes it ok, that mail would be accepted.

To effectively fight spam with these files, you must keep the `/etc/mail/access` file updated with particulars for your system. Each time junk e-mail is sent to one of your users, you must examine the text message and retune this file to block it out next time. After each change to the `etc/mail/access` file, including creating it in the first place, you must create a database from this file. To do so, use the following command:

```
makemap hash /etc/mail/access < /etc/mail/access
```

This database is checked against each message that *sendmail* receives, so you do not need to restart *sendmail* after each change to this file. However, you must restart *sendmail* after you regenerate the `/etc/sendmail.cf` file. Unfortunately, these changes do not filter e-mail based on content; content filtering is more easily done by *procmail*, on a user-by-user basis. This process is explained later, in the "Deleting Unwanted E-mail Automatically" section.

Configuring procmail

Up to this point in the chapter, I have generally ignored *procmail*. One of the benefits of *procmail* is that it works invisibly if it is not configured. Configuration can be global, with defaults for all mailboxes, or user-by-user. *procmail* will take the incoming mail from *sendmail* and deliver it to the correct mailbox, optionally performing processing based on the content of the message. For example, I use *procmail* to separate into different folders the mail sent directly to me, to my e-mail aliases, and to mailing lists that I am on.

All of *procmail's* filtering information is stored in a recipe file; the global recipe file is `/etc/procmailrc`. In each user's home directory is a local `.procmailrc` recipe file. These files contain a list of filters stating what *procmail* should look for in each message, and what it should do if it finds a match.

Because *procmail* is separate from *sendmail*, and is a filter, it is not run as a daemon and does not need to be shutdown or restarted when a `procmailrc` file changes.

Separating E-mail into Folders

Perhaps the most common use for *procmail* is to separate mail into different folders. Normally, all incoming mail is stored in a single place—the user's inbox. *procmail* can look at the From: or To: headers, the Subject: line, the body of the message, or many other places to determine what should happen to a message. Let me give an example of a `procmailrc` file I use, and then explain how it works. Create the `.procmailrc` file shown in Listing 7-5 in your home directory on the OpenLinux mail server:

Listing 7-5 A typical .procmailrc file

```
:0:
* ^TOlinux-list@ssc.com
linux-list

:0:
* ^TOjoseph@cheek.com
my-mail

:0:
* ^TOinfo@cheek.com
info-mail
```

> **NOTE:** For purposes of e-mail, a folder is a collection of mail stored in a single file. This is different from the file system notion of a folder, which is a directory that stores multiple files.

Each of these simple rules is three lines long. The first line of each rule—a colon, a zero, and another colon—tells *procmail* that a new recipe is starting, and to use a default lockfile. The next line, starting with the asterisk, is the filter condition. These filters check for specific e-mail addresses in the To: line, such as `linux-list@ssc.com`, `joseph@cheek.com`, or `info@cheek.com`. The last line tells *procmail* what to do with each message that matches the filter condition; in these cases, the mail is sent to folder `linux-list`, `my-mail`, or `info-mail`, respectively. Any mail that is not matched by one of these conditions is delivered to the user's inbox.

These recipes are checked, one by one, from the first at the top of the `procmailrc` file to the last at the end of the same file. If recipes are in both the `/etc/procmailrc` file and the user's `.procmailrc` file, the system file is checked first. Mail is not delivered to the inbox unless it does not match a single recipe from either file. When a message matches a filter condition, the specified action is taken, and mail processing stops on that message. This means mail that would match more than one filter condition is only acted on by the first filter whose condition it matches. You can tell *procmail* to continue processing a mail message after it matches a filter condition by appending the letter `c` to the new recipe line. This tells *procmail* to generate a copy of the mail that matched the filter, and to continue processing on that copy of the message from that point in the `procmailrc` file. With the `procmailrc` file above, if mail was sent to both `joseph@cheek.com` and `info@cheek.com`, it would match the `joseph@cheek.com` filter and end up in the `my-mail` folder. If I wanted it to be delivered to both the `my-mail` and the `info-mail` folders, I could have used this:

```
:0:c
* ^TOjoseph@cheek.com
my-mail

:0:
* ^TOinfo@cheek.com
info-mail
```

The `c` at the end of the first line tells *procmail* to generate a copy of the message and continue processing. The mail would have then been matched by the next filter condition, matching `info@cheek.com`, and been delivered to the `info-mail` folder also. Had the mail not been also sent to `info@cheek.com`, the message copy would not match the last filter condition, and it would have then been delivered to my inbox. Then I would have had a copy of that message in both the `my-mail` folder and the inbox.

Each recipe condition is a regular expression, such as would be matched with the `egrep` command. Above, the caret (`^`) tells *procmail* to match only at the beginning of the line. *TO* is a macro that expands to all forms of To: headers, such as `To:`, `Cc:`, etc. If you only wanted matches on the To: line, you could replace *TO* with To:. Unfortunately, the *TO* macro cannot match mail sent to users as a `Bcc:`, as no header line is generated for a blind carbon copy. Obviously, a Bcc: filter condition would not match either.

NOTE

> Regular expressions are powerful and complex—they can be used to match many aspects of an e-mail message—but explanation of them in any depth is beyond the scope of this book. For more information, I suggest checking the egrep man page.

Moving User Mail to a Different Directory

Separating e-mail is great when it is read on the local filesystem or via the IMAP protocol. POP3 does not provide for multiple mail folders, so any mail sent to a place other than the inbox cannot be read by a POP3 reader. When these messages are routed to different folders, however, they are stored by default in the user's home directory. These can clutter up the home directory over time. I suggest moving mail folders into their own directory, such as a mail subdirectory from the user's home directory.

Mail folder locations are determined by the `MAILDIR` variable. The easiest place to set this is in the `procmailrc` file itself, before the recipe filters. Add this to the beginning of your `procmailrc` file:

```
MAILDIR=$HOME/mail
```

Now all mail to folders will be delivered in the mail subdirectory of your home directory. The mail subdirectory must exist, and you must have write permissions to that directory (*procmail* must be able to create files in it, and write to files already created inside it). This variable does not affect the location of the inbox, which is stored in the `/var/spool/mail` directory. You might want to add this to the `/etc/procmailrc` file if you want each user's filtered mail to be stored in their mail subdirectory. Keep in mind, though, that the mail directory must then exist *for each user on the system*.

CAUTION

> Note that *procmail* will deliver mail to any folder where it has filesystem permissions to do so. If told to deliver mail to a file to which it does not have write permissions, the mail will be lost! Always make sure that you have write permissions to your mail folders. Many system administrators insert a generic rule at the beginning of their `procmailrc` files when testing major `procmailrc` changes:
>
> ```
> :0:c
> *
> all-mail-goes-here
> ```
>
> This will save all mail in the all-mail-goes-here folder (if *procmail* can write to it), and continue processing with a copy of the message. All mail will be matched by this blank rule, as there is no condition after the asterisk on the second line.

Deleting Unwanted E-mail Automatically

The filtering capabilities of *procmail* make it a good tool to use to get rid of unwanted e-mail. Because mail can be written to any folder, and folders are just files on the filesystem, unwanted mail can be disposed of by placing it in the `/dev/null` folder.

Mail saved in the /dev/null folder effectively gets deleted. Spam e-mail will many times either have a strange From: address or a strange Subject: line; both of these can be filtered. Consider the following recipes:

```
:0:
* ^From:.bogus.email@nodomain.com
/dev/null


:0:
* ^Subject:.[mM]ake.[mM]oney.[qQ]uick
/dev/null
```

The first deletes any e-mail from the address bogus.email@nodomain.com. The second deletes any mail with a "make money quick" subject header, whether the header is capitalized or not. Because these filter conditions are regular expressions, they can get fairly advanced. Regular expressions will not be discussed here, but a basic rule is to use periods instead of spaces; a period matches any character, whereas spaces terminate a regular expression.

Creating Automatic Reply Messages

Not only can mail be sent to mail folders or deleted, it can also be sent to a program for processing. Sometimes you or your users might want to create automatic replies to mail received, such as a tailored "out of office" message or an autoreply program. The most effective way to do this is by processing the received mail through another program. The *formail* program will generate a mail header based on the information it receives from a mail message. It can generate the proper headers for a reply to a message, and then *sendmail* can send the newly generated reply back to the user. This requires a more advanced *procmail* recipe, such as:

```
:0:
* ^Subject:.*autoreply
| (formail -r ; echo "This is your reply.") | sendmail -t
```

This example takes any mail with the word "autoreply" in the subject (the ".*" in the recipe condition means any combination of characters) and pipes it to *formail*, *echo*, and *sendmail* for processing. *formail* generates the reply headers, *echo* gives the body of the mail message, and then *sendmail* sends the message back to the originator.

Advanced Filtering

Many more advanced options exist with *procmail*. Mail can be forwarded with an action beginning with the bang (!) character, such as this example, in which all mail with a subject of "Important Message" is forwarded to a pager's e-mail address:

```
:0:
* ^Subject:.Important.Message
! pageme@domain.com
```

Recipes can have multiple filter conditions or can contain more recipes. Actions can contain many different programs hooked together by pipes, semicolons, curly braces, and parentheses. The *procmail* `man` pages give examples of these and more.

Starting and Stopping sendmail and procmail

The easiest way to start or stop *sendmail* is with the same scripts that OpenLinux uses when it boots up or shuts down. As `root`, type the following to stop *sendmail*:

```
/etc/rc.d/init.d/mta stop
```

To start *sendmail*, type:

```
/etc/rc.d/init.d/mta start
```

Because *procmail* is a filter and does not run as a daemon, it need not ever be stopped or started. Knowing when to restart *sendmail* or to run a particular command is useful knowledge, but not always obvious. Many times, you can instruct a daemon to restart by sending it a particular signal, such as the HUP signal. However, this will not work with *sendmail*, due to the way OpenLinux starts it. Here are some suggestions.

- If you have changed the `/etc/aliases` file, *sendmail* does not need to be restarted. Run the command `newaliases` instead.
- If you have changed a file that needs a database to be rebuilt with the `makemap` command, *sendmail* does not need to be restarted. Run the appropriate `makemap` command instead.
- If you have changed a core *sendmail* file, such as `/etc/sendmail.cf` or `/etc/sendmail.cw`, *sendmail* must be restarted. Use the `/etc/rc.d/init.d/mta restart` command.
- If you changed a `procmailrc` file, nothing needs to be restarted. These files are always read on demand.

Troubleshooting sendmail

As you can probably tell, *sendmail* is an enormous program with an equally enormous number of configuration options. The information in this chapter will help you get it working correctly, but even so there will be times when it just does not do what you expect it to do. Troubleshooting *sendmail* is one of the fine arts of OpenLinux administration. This section will give you some of the basic tools you need to do this.

Most of the time, *sendmail* will send outgoing mail correctly; even a plain vanilla `sendmail.cf` file with no customization should allow outgoing mail to be sent. Many of the issues you will face will be with incoming mail—perhaps it comes in and gets routed incorrectly, perhaps it comes in and gets sent back out, perhaps *sendmail* rejects it, or perhaps it never comes in at all. From a user's standpoint, it just doesn't get to them. Your task will be to determine at what point it was rejected or misrouted.

Checking the Server Logs

When dealing with a *sendmail* issue, always first check the *sendmail* log `/var/log/mail`. This will tell whether *sendmail* received a particular message, and what it did with it. A normal exchange looks like this:

```
Sep  7 13:07:59 saltlake sendmail[22982]: NAA22982: from=<owner-linux-list@ssc.com>,
size=3339, class=-60, pri=141339, nrcpts=1, msgid=<NDBBIGLOAKEFGNCPIBAPMEGLCAAA.
joseph@cheek.com>, proto=ESMTP, relay=passenger.ssc.com [216.39.159.17]

Sep  7 13:07:59 saltlake sendmail[22983]: NAA22982:to=<joseph@cheek.com>,
delay=00:00:00, xdelay=00:00:00, mailer=local, stat=Sent
```

These two lines tell us that at 1:07 PM, local time, *sendmail* received a message from `owner-linux-list@ssc.com` on the machine `passenger.ssc.com` at IP address 216.39.159.17. It then sent it to me, `joseph@cheek.com`, with 0 seconds of delay. It appears that this mail transaction was successful, because the very last comment is `stat=Sent`. If it had been anything negative, such as `stat=Rejected`, you would be able to tell that the mail was not received correctly.

Each mail transaction has two lines, and they match up with the message transaction ID assigned by *sendmail*. (This message used `NAA22982` to correlate these two lines.) It's good to check these, because the lines might not always be next to each other in the log. Outgoing mail is logged in the same manner:

```
Sep  7 12:51:46 saltlake sendmail[22965]: MAA22965: from=<joseph@cheek.com>,
size=2279, class=0, pri=92279, nrcpts=3, msgid=<NDBBIGLOAKEFGNCPIBAPMEGLCAAA.
joseph@cheek.com>, proto=SMTP, relay=sanfrancisco.cheek.com [208.12.12.156]
```

```
Sep  7 12:51:51 saltlake sendmail[22967]: MAA22965: to=<linux-list@ssc.com>, ctlad-
dr=<joseph@cheek.com> (500/100), delay=00:00:05, xdelay=00:00:01, mailer=esmtp,
relay=passenger.ssc.com. [216.39.159.17], stat=Sent
```

In this case, my e-mail address is the From: address, and `linux-list@ssc.com` is the To: address. Notice the `stat=Sent`, meaning that the mail has been received correctly by their Mail Transfer Agent. Other messages may appear in the log, such as these IMAP announcements:

```
Sep  7 13:29:34 saltlake imapd[23032]: imap service init from 208.12.12.156
Sep  7 13:29:34 saltlake imapd[23032]: Login user=joseph
host=sanfrancisco.cheek.com [208.12.12.156]
Sep  7 13:30:36 saltlake imapd[23032]: Logout user=joseph
host=sanfrancisco.cheek.com [208.12.12.156]
```

These show that I am reading my e-mail via the IMAP protocol as I type this chapter. The log file will tell you whether e-mail is being received or rejected. If you do not see any entries, you might wonder if *sendmail* is running at all; you can check this with the `ps` command.

```
ps ax | grep sendmail
```

You should see:

```
477 ?        S      0:11 sendmail: accepting connections on port 25
```

Here you can see that *sendmail* is running, and waiting for a connection. If it is not running, start it with the `/etc/rc.d/init.d/mta start` command.

Using the finger Command

The `finger` command will tell you if a user has mail, when it was last read, and if mail is forwarded (via a `.forward` file) to a different e-mail account. These are good ways to check the status of a user's mailbox. Here is what mine shows:

```
finger joseph
```

```
Login: joseph                          Name: Joseph Cheek
Directory: /home/joseph                Shell: /bin/bash
On since Tue Sep  7 13:17 (PDT) on ttyp0 from seattle.cheek.com
Mail last read Tue Sep  7 13:40 1999 (PDT)
No Plan.
```

If I had new mail, it would show:

```
New mail received Tue Sep  7 12:45 1999 (PDT)
```

```
Unread since Tue Sep  7 10:34 1999 (PDT)
```

And if I had a `.forward`, it would show:

```
Mail forwarded to joseph@somewhere.else.com
```

Telnetting to Port 25

When it appears that *sendmail* is not routing mail correctly, the best bet you have is to `telnet` to port 25, the SMTP port, and query *sendmail* directly. You will be greeted with a standard *sendmail* welcome message, and then will be able to communicate with *sendmail* as if you were another mail program wishing to send some mail.

```
telnet localhost 25
Trying 127.0.0.1...
Connected to localhost.
Escape character is '^]'.
220 sanfrancisco.cheek.com ESMTP Sendmail 8.9.3/8.9.3; Tue, 7 Sep 1999 14:11:14 -0700
```

There are three different things that are useful to do here: use the `vrfy` command, use the `expn` command, and create an e-mail message by hand.

`vrfy` is short for *verify*, and it means "tell me the user exists." Try this command on yourself. The 250 in the output means that the command succeeded; it gave me my full e-mail address on that OpenLinux server.

```
vrfy joseph
250 <joseph@sanfrancisco.cheek.com>
```

`expn` stands for expand. It is used to expand aliases, mailing lists, and such. It will tell you where the mail will go, if sent to that user. This is a good way to tell whether *sendmail* expects to send the mail to the same addresses where you want the mail to be sent.

```
expn joseph
250 Joseph Cheek <joseph@sanfrancisco.cheek.com>
```

When used on a user with neither aliasing nor forwarding, `expn` does not show much difference from the `vrfy` output. When used on a mailbox with an alias or forwarding, `expn` instead shows the addresses it expands to:

```
expn info
250-<jeff@cheek.com>
250-<dan@cheek.com>
250 <joseph@cheek.com>
```

Creating an e-mail message by hand can be beneficial if you want to be absolutely sure what happens when *sendmail* receives a message. This requires three commands: `mail from`, `rcpt to`, and `data`. The mail needs to be from a user at a valid domain, such as joseph@cheek.com. It also needs to be sent to a valid user on your mail server—in my case, *joseph*. The message body can be anything, terminated by a line with a single period. Try this:

```
mail from: joseph@cheek.com
250 joseph@cheek.com... Sender ok
rcpt to: joseph
250 joseph... Recipient ok
data
354 Enter mail, end with "." on a line by itself
this is an e-mail test.
.
250 OAA31832 Message accepted for delivery
quit
221 sanfrancisco.cheek.com closing connection
Connection closed by foreign host.
```

You just sent an e-mail message with a body of "this is an e-mail test." to user *joseph*. The *quit* command tells *sendmail* you are done and wish to close the connection.

Troubleshooting procmail

Although *procmail* does not provide nearly as much debugging information as *sendmail* does, there are still ways to test it. It is easy to set up a rule to copy all messages to a specific location, generating a pseudo-logfile. You can run *procmail* by hand from the command line, and feed mail messages (complete with headers) either from the keyboard or piped through from a file.

When *procmail* misroutes a message (due to a bad recipe file, perhaps), it is difficult to trace. Many times, the message is lost; in these cases, it's easy to wonder if the message made it at all. Generating a rule at the beginning of the `procmailrc` file to save all messages to a file is wise in these circumstances. Add these three lines to the beginning of your `procmailrc` file:

```
:0:c
*
all-mail-goes-here
```

This will save all mail in the `all-mail-goes-here` folder (if *procmail* can write to it), and continue processing with a copy of the message. All mail will be matched by this blank rule, because there is no condition after the asterisk on the second line. By examining the `all-mail-goes-here` file, you can see the message just as *procmail* sees it. If this file does not exist, you might have a filesystem permissions problem that keeps *procmail* from creating new folders or writing to existing folders.

For More Information

There is plenty of information about *sendmail* and *procmail* on the Web. Here are some good URLs:

URL	Resource Name
http://www.sendmail.org	Sendmail Consortium Web Site
http://linuxkb.cheek.com/page.php?sendmail	Linux Knowledge Base Sendmail Information
http://www.sendmail.com	Sendmail, Inc. Web Site
http://www.procmail.org	Procmail Home Page
http://www.qmail.org	Qmail Home Page
ftp://ftp.planix.com/pub/Smail/	Smail FTP Site
http://www.greatcircle.com/majordomo/	Majordomo Web Site

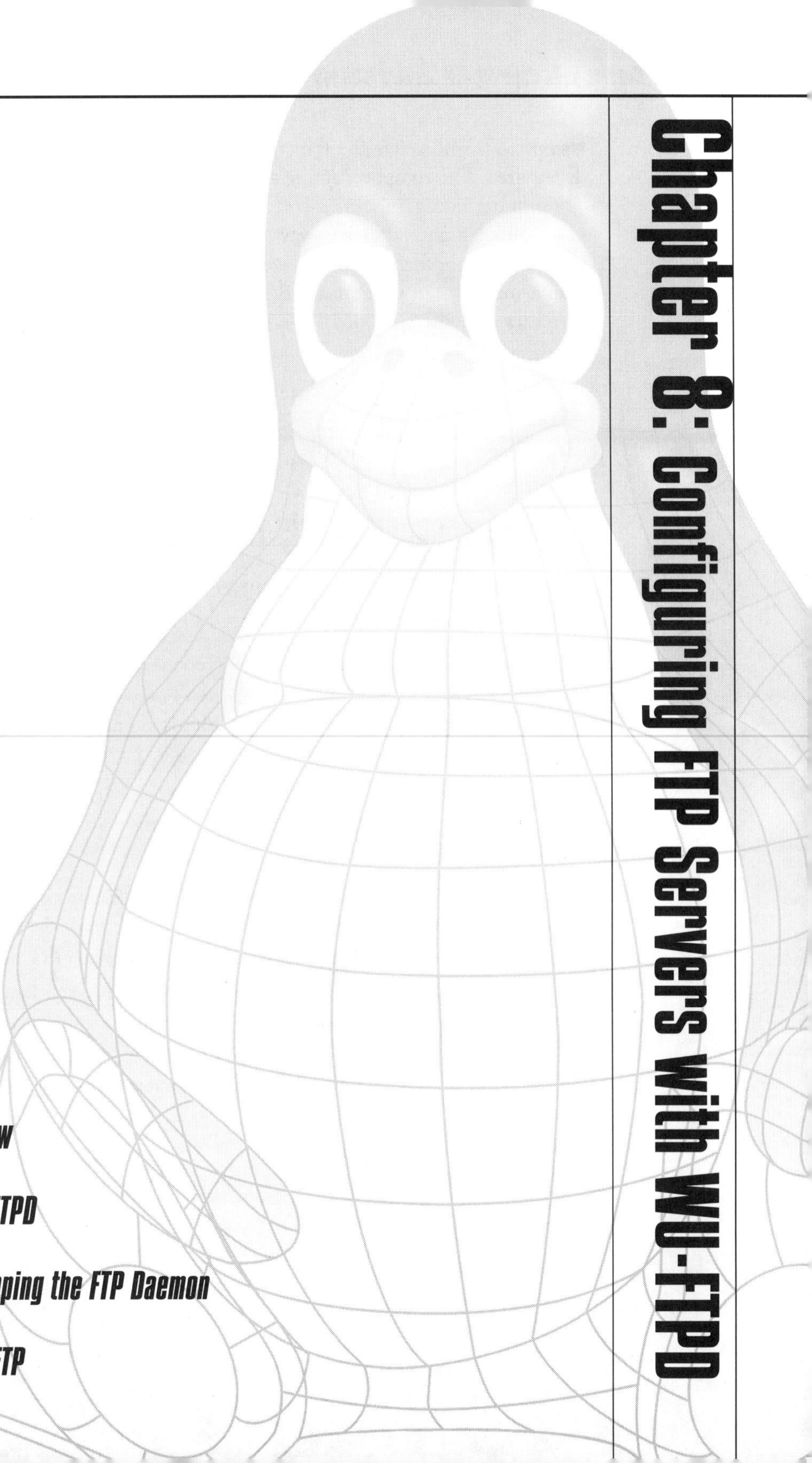

Chapter 8: Configuring FTP Servers with WU-FTPD

WU-FTPD Overview

Configuring WU-FTPD

Starting and Stopping the FTP Daemon

Troubleshooting FTP

To provide interactive file transfers between computers, two pieces of software are required. The computer acting as the server needs a *daemon*, whereas the recipient computer needs only *client* software. FTP (*File Transfer Protocol*) is probably the most popular and effective way to move files (especially large files) from one computer to another computer over the Internet. It's better to FTP a 200MB file than e-mail it as an attachment. Believe me, your mail administrator will hit the roof if you try e-mailing a 200MB file attachment!

It is common to have both the FTP client and the *FTPD*, or FTP daemon, on a single OpenLinux machine; this means that the OpenLinux computer acts as FTP client and server at the same time. The daemon is always lurking in the background until called by an FTP client.

Files Referenced in this Chapter

The following files are used by OpenLinux's implementation of FTP:

File	Purpose
`/etc/inetd.conf`	Defines how FTP connection requests are processed
`/etc/ftpusers`	Defines regular users on your OpenLinux system who cannot use FTP (this is intended as a security precaution)
`/etc/ftpaccess`	Configuration file for WU-FTPD
`/etc/ftpconversions`	A conversion database
`/etc/ftphosts`	Determines access to specified accounts from other hosts
`/usr/bin/ftp`	The standard FTP client
`/usr/bin/ncftp`	A more feature-rich FTP client
`/usr/bin/ftpcount`	Current number of users for each class
`/usr/bin/ftpwho`	The process information for each FTP user
`/usr/sbin/ftpshut`	Shuts down the FTP server at a specified time
`/usr/sbin/in.ftpd`	Name of the FTP daemon
`/var/log/xferlog`	Logs all transfers between FTP clients and the FTP server, for both regular and anonymous users

The following files, although not used by WU-FTPD, are relevant to the FTP server:

File	Purpose
`/etc/services`	Plain ASCII file listing the mapping of Internet services to their port numbers
`/etc/aliases`	Plain ASCII file used for virtual hosting
`/etc/passwd`	Plain ASCII file used to authenticate the user
`/etc/shells`	Plain ASCII file used to verify a valid shell
`/etc/hosts.allow`	Plain ASCII file used to allow specified hosts
`/etc/hosts.deny`	Plain ASCII file used to deny specified hosts

WU-FTPD Overview

WU-FTPD, developed at Washington University, is a replacement for the FTPD that came with older versions of UNIX. WU-FTPD has a number of additional features. Practically all Linux distributions use WU-FTPD, but there are other, similar, packages to choose from. Your OpenLinux installation will perform a standard installation of the WU-FTPD daemon, the FTP client, and all the necessary configuration files.

> **NOTE:** In Greek mythology, a daemon is an attending or guardian spirit between gods and men. In UNIX/Linux, a daemon refers to an unattended program that runs continuously in the background until it is called upon.

Some additional features of WU-FTPD are:

- Logging of all transfers and commands executed
- On-the-fly compression and archiving
- Per-class limits
- Per-directory upload permissions
- Restricted guest accounts
- System-wide and directory messages
- Directory alias and virtual host support
- Cdpath and filename filters

> **NOTE:** Check out the WU-FTPD Web site at **www.wu-ftpd.org** for the latest updates.

FTP Clients

There are many FTP clients from which to choose, including the FTP client called *ftp*. Other FTP clients available in your OpenLinux distribution are *ncftp* and *pftp*. In addition, there are numerous FTP clients written for the X Window system for those who like to point and click. Netscape Communicator, *gFTP*, and *IglooFTP* are some of the more common FTP clients available for the X Window system. Check out **www.linuxberg.com** or **www.freshmeat.net** for the latest alternative FTP clients.

TIP

> To see which version you have installed, just type `ftp localhost` at the Linux command line; the FTP client will display the version number.

Types of FTP Accounts

There are three different types of user accounts available to reach an FTP server: *guest*, *real*, and *anonymous*. The guest account is basically your OpenLinux account; you can use your user account (Linux login account and password) directly on that FTP server—but after logging in, you can access only your home directory. The real account differs from the guest account in that with this account, you have access to the whole file system.

Finally, the anonymous account is to be used if you don't have an account on that FTP server. In fact, the anonymous FTP account is really the OpenLinux account called "`ftp`" (as you can confirm by examining the `/etc/passwd` file, or by using the username `ftp` when accessing the FTP server). This account has no password, so you can use whatever password you want. Typically, your e-mail address is used as the password for the anonymous FTP account; with an anonymous account, you are dropped into the `/home/ftp` directory, which becomes your root directory. This is similar to the guest account, except that anybody can use this anonymous FTP account, on which there is no password protection.

The following is a summary of the three types of FTP accounts.

Account Type	Description
Anonymous	FTP account name is anonymous or ftp. Password can be anything, because there is no password verification. All users of this account can access only FTP directories and files that are public. Most FTP sites offer this account to promote sharing of files for the public.

Guest	The FTP account name is the user's account name on that FTP server; the password is the same as the user's account password. The same username and password are specified in `/etc/passwd` (and therefore you can use them to telnet into the OpenLinux server). By default, all account holders on the OpenLinux server have FTP accounts, because both use `/etc/passwd` to determine access.
Real	Similar to the Guest FTP account, except that users have full rein to navigate the whole file system. Accounts of this type should be granted judiciously, because they can pose a security risk.

Typical FTP Sessions

Now let's take a closer look at the three different types of FTP accounts, and see just how they access the FTP server.

Real or Guest FTP Session

The following is an example session using a real or guest account on the FTP server.

```
[tho@mydomain.com]$ ftp yourdomain.com
Connected to yourdomain.com.
220 yourdomain.com FTP server (Version wu-2.5.0(1)  Sat Apr 3 15:11:49 MST 1999) ready.
Name (yourdomain.com:tho): tho
331 Password required for tho.
Password:
230 User tho logged in.
Remote system type is UNIX.
Using binary mode to transfer files.
ftp>
```

In this session, the username `tho` could have been a real or guest FTP account. In either case, a valid password, as determined by the `/etc/passwd` file, was required to log in.

Anonymous FTP Session

The following example is an FTP session using the anonymous user account.

```
[tho@mydomain.com]$ ftp yourdomain.com
Connected to yourdomain.com.
220 yourdomain.com FTP server (Version wu-2.5.0(1)  Sat Apr 3 15:11:49 MST 1999) ready.
```

```
Name (yourdomain.com:tho): anonymous

331 Guest login ok, send your complete e-mail address as password.
Password:
230 Guest login ok, access restrictions apply.
Remote system type is UNIX.
Using binary mode to transfer files.
ftp>
```

For an anonymous session, the user name is `anonymous`, and you can enter any string of characters (such as your e-mail address) as a password. Most FTP sites are configured to prevent null passwords, so you must enter a string of characters. By default, anonymous FTP via either an FTP client or a Web browser will point you to the FTP root directory, `/home/ftp` (as shown in Figure 8-1).

Opening **ftp://username@your_ftpserver** in your Netscape Web browser will generate a prompt for your username, as you are using the guest or real user account called "username". The username's directory will be displayed. (See Figures 8-2 and 8-3.)

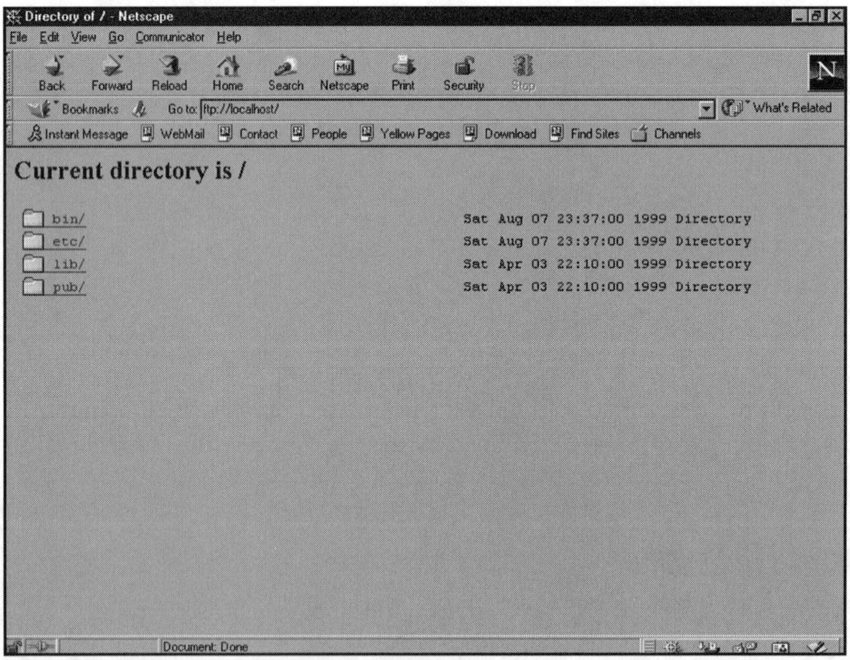

Figure 8-1 *Directory listing for anonymous FTP user*

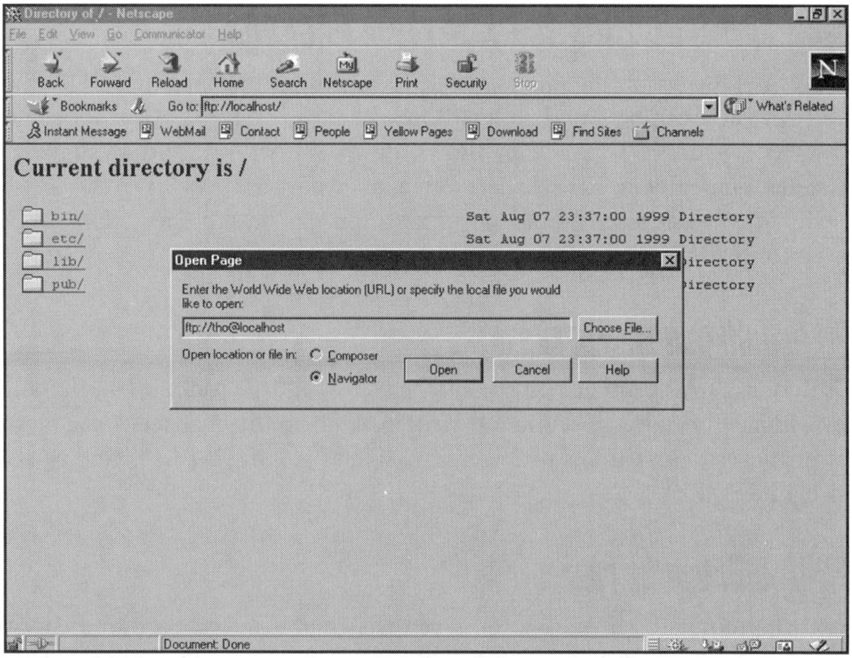

Figure 8-2 *Open FTP Location dialog box*

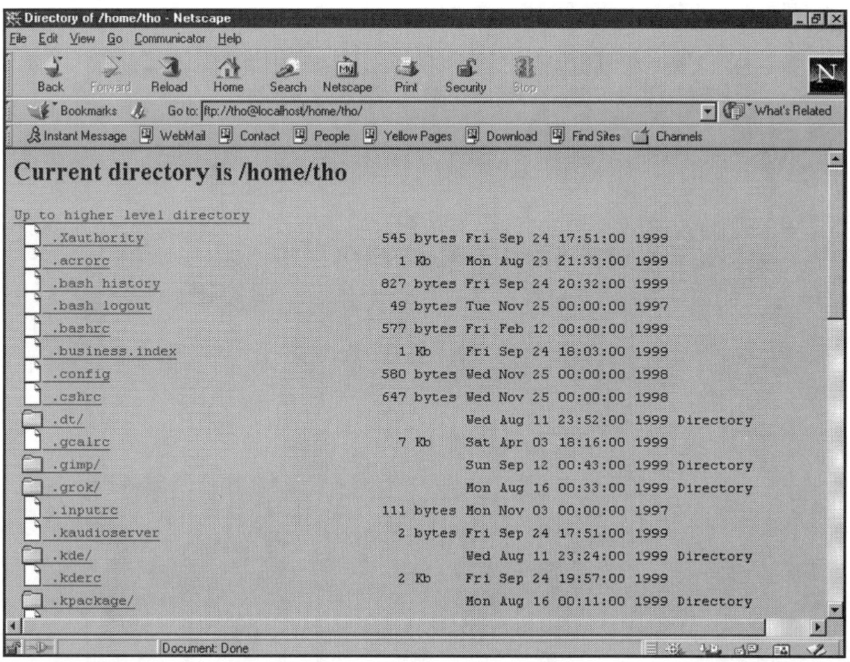

Figure 8-3 *User's FTP listing*

Obtaining and Installing the WU-FTPD Package

Now that you understand the basics, you're ready to install WU-FTPD. The WU-FTPD package can be found on your OpenLinux 2.3 CD-ROM. If for some reason you lose your CD, you can always download it from **http://support.calderasystems.com/caldera;** check here often to make sure you have the latest version, with the latest security and bug fixes. You can install the WU-FTPD package (`rpm` format) in one of two ways: via *kpackage* or *rpm*.

WU-FTPD Installation via kpackage

From KDE, run *kpackage*, or click on the `wu-ftpd-2.5.0-3.rpm` package (the version number might have changed since this was written) from the file manager. (You must have root privileges to install this package.) You should see the *kpackage* window (as shown in Figure 8-4).

WU-FTPD Installation by rpm

From the shell prompt, log in as `root`, or issue the `su` command to get into the root account. Issue the `rpm` command that follows (the version number might differ depending on the version you download).

```
rpm -U wu-ftpd-2.5.0-3.i386.rpm
```

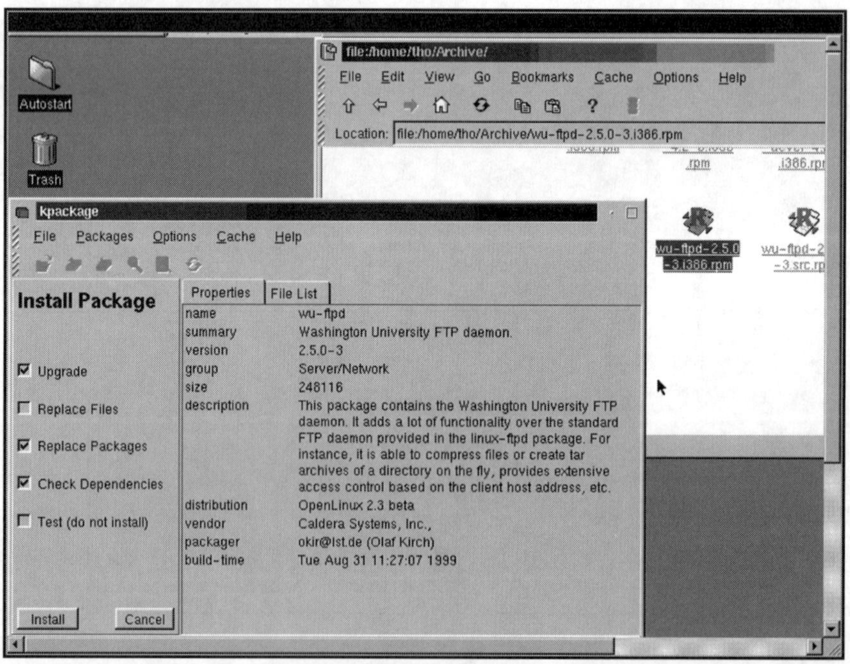

Figure 8-4 *kpackage install package window*

After installation, the following files are created:

- /etc/ftpaccess
- /etc/ftpconversions
- /etc/ftpgroups
- /etc/ftphosts
- /etc/ftpusers
- /etc/logrotate.d/ftpd
- /etc/pam.d/ftp
- /usr/bin/ftpcount
- /usr/bin/ftpshut
- /usr/bin/ftpwho
- /usr/doc/wu-ftpd-2.5.0
- /usr/doc/wu-ftpd-2.5.0/ANNOUNCE-RELEASE
- /usr/doc/wu-ftpd-2.5.0/README
- /usr/doc/wu-ftpd-2.5.0/VIRTUAL.FTP.SUPPORT
- /usr/man/man1/ftpcount.1.gz
- /usr/man/man1/ftpwho.1.gz
- /usr/man/man5/ftpaccess.5.gz
- /usr/man/man5/ftpconversions.5.gz
- /usr/man/man5/ftphosts.5.gz
- /usr/man/man5/xferlog.5.gz
- /usr/man/man8/ftpd.8.gz
- /usr/man/man8/ftpshut.8.gz
- /usr/sbin/in.ftpd
- /usr/sbin/xferstats

Typical WU-FTPD Configuration

Now, let's examine how OpenLinux configures the FTP software. Unfortunately, there is no GUI administration tool for configuring all of WU-FTPD. There is a tool called *linuxconf* that will generate the /etc/ftpaccess file for you, based on a form you fill out. Configuring WU-FTPD requires editing configuration files from the root account. The good news is that OpenLinux does a decent job of setting up WU-FTPD right out of the box. Let's first take a look at the core executable file and configuration files.

CAUTION

> If you plan to place your FTP server on the Internet, carefully consider the associated security issues.

/usr/sbin/in.ftpd

This FTP daemon uses the TCP protocol to transfer files. Configuring *in.ftpd* requires either passing parameters at run time, or modifying the `/etc/ftpaccess` file. The daemon listens at the port number specified in the `/etc/services` file; normally, port # 21 is used for FTP commands, and port # 20 is for FTP data. (WU-FTPD is spawned from `/etc/inetd.conf` at boot time.)

According to the information given in the man page for WU-FTPD, users are authenticated according to these four rules:

1. The username must be in the password database, `/etc/passwd`, or whatever is appropriate for the operating system, and the password must not be null. The client must provide a password before any file operations can be performed. That's why, for an anonymous account, you need to enter a string, such as your e-mail address.
2. The username must not appear in the file `/etc/ftpusers`.
3. The user must have a valid shell, one defined in `/etc/shells`—such as bash.
4. If the user name is anonymous or ftp, an anonymous FTP account (user ftp) must be present in the password file. In this case, the user is allowed to log in by specifying any password; usually the user's e-mail address.

etc/ftpaccess

This is the main configuration file for WU-FTPD. There are many options and parameters to play with. These options can be grouped into the following five categories:

Category	Description
Access	Deals with who can access the FTP server
Informational	Provides greeting messages to the user
Logging	Provides audit trail of who had access and what was done
Permissions	Deals with file and directory permissions
Miscellaneous	Handles anything else

Following is an example of the Access category. It defines a class of users called `all` that is composed of `real`, `guest`, and `anonymous` accounts. The asterisk is a wildcard to accept users from any domains.

```
class   all   real,guest,anonymous   *
```

The next line is an example of the Informational category. It defines the e-mail address for the FTP maintainer; this is displayed when the `%E` message code is included in the message file discussed below.

```
email mailto:root@localhost
```

The next line is another example of the Informational category. It defines how many unsuccessful tries to allow before terminating the FTP connection.

```
loginfails 5
```

The next two lines are further examples of the Informational category. They advise the user to read the file(s) called README *something*, as `README*` is a wildcard for any filename that starts with README. This notification to read occurs once upon login or navigating to another folder.

```
readme   README*    login

readme   README*    cwd=*
```

The next line is another example of the Informational category. It displays the content of the file `welcome.msg` upon user login. This occurs once.

```
message /welcome.msg            login
```

The next line is a final example of the Informational category. It displays the content of the file .`welcome` when the user navigates into a current working folder. This occurs once.

```
message .welcome                cwd=*
```

The next line is an example of the Logging category. It instructs WU-FTPD to log all incoming and outgoing file transfers for anonymous and real FTP users.The log is recorded in `/var/log/xferlog`.

```
log transfers anonymous,real inbound,outbound
```

The next four lines are examples of the Permissions category. They disallow FTP users who belong to guest and anonymous accounts from issuing the commands `chmod`, `delete`, `overwrite`, and `rename`.

```
chmod           no              guest,anonymous
```

```
delete          no              guest,anonymous

overwrite       no              guest,anonymous

rename          no              guest,anonymous
```

The next line is another example of the Permissions category. It instructs WU-FTPD to perform one or more specified levels of password checking for anonymous FTP users. The line is followed by a list of the values of these levels, and the action that WU-FTPD is to take on the basis of these values. See the following table for possible values to use.

```
passwd-check rfc822 warn
```

Values	Action
none	No password checking performed
trivial	Password must contain an @
rfc822	Password must be an rfc822-compliant address (rfc822 describes what are valid e-mail address formats)
warn	Warn the user, but allow them to log in
enforce	Warn the user, and then log them out

The next two lines are an example of the Miscellaneous category. They call for FTP conversion for class `all`, based on the instructions stated in `/etc/ftpconversions`.

```
compress        yes             all

tar             yes             all
```

The last line is another example of the Miscellaneous category. It instructs WU-FTPD to check for the file `/etc/shutmsg` at boot time. If the file exists, new FTP connections will be denied and current FTP connections will be terminated, as specified in the file.

```
shutdown /etc/shutmsg
```

/etc/ftpconversions

This file contains information that details how files are to be converted when being transferred.

CAUTION

It's best to leave `ftpconversions` alone unless you really need to modify the conversion behavior during a file transfer.

Here's an example:

```
:.Z:  :  :/bin/compress -d -c %s:T_REG|T_ASCII:O_UNCOMPRESS:UNCOMPRESS
:   : :.Z:/bin/compress -c %s:T_REG:O_COMPRESS:COMPRESS
:.gz: :  :/bin/gzip -cd %s:T_REG|T_ASCII:O_UNCOMPRESS:GUNZIP
:   : :.gz:/bin/gzip -9 -c %s:T_REG:O_COMPRESS:GZIP
:   : :.tar:/bin/tar -c -f - %s:T_REG|T_DIR:O_TAR:TAR
:   : :.tar.Z:/bin/tar -c -Z -f - %s:T_REG|T_DIR:O_COMPRESS|O_TAR:TAR+COMPRESS
:   : :.tar.gz:/bin/tar -c -z -f - %s:T_REG|T_DIR:O_COMPRESS|O_TAR:TAR+GZIP
```

The first line says to decompress a `.Z` file before transferring, and the second line says to compress before transferring. The remaining lines follow the same rationale for other file formats.

Each line in this file represents a description and action for a conversion. Each line has eight fields separated by colons, as denoted in the following line. Each field references the action to be taken described in the following table.

```
1 : 2 : 3 : 4 : 5 : 6 : 7 : 8
```

Field	Description
1	Strip prefix.
2	Strip postfix.
3	Addon prefix.
4	Addon postfix.
5	External command.
6	Types.
7	Options.
8	Description.

CAUTION

> Currently, field 1 and field 3 are not supported. That's why those fields are blank in the preceding example.

/etc/ftpgroups

This file is used to create groups of users who need enhanced access, as defined by `/etc/group`. After logging in to the FTP server, the user can issue the commands `SITE GROUP group name` and `SITE GPASS password` to become a member of a group specified in `/etc/ftpgroups`.

Here's an example line, followed by a list of descriptions for its contents:

```
test:ENCRYPTED PASSWORD HERE:archive
```

Parameter	Description
`test`	Name of this group
`ENCRYPTED PASSWORD HERE`	Password for this group
`archive`	Group name, based on `etc/group`, which is associated to this group

NOTE

> To generate the encrypted password, simply create a user with a password, and then copy and paste this password from `/etc/passwd` into `/etc/ftpgroups`.

/etc/ftphosts

If you want to restrict access to particular accounts from a particular host, this is the file you need to modify. By default, OpenLinux has no settings, so anybody can FTP in, as demonstrated in the following example. This file has no parameters set.

```
# Example host access file
#
# Everything after a '#' is treated as comment,
# empty lines are ignored
```

The following code is a possible setting to prevent user jack from domain notwelcome.com from getting FTP access, and allowing in user friend either from domain welcome.com or from 172.121.34.* (which group of numbers means that user friend can FTP in from any host belonging to the 172.121.34 network).

```
# Another ftphosts example
deny                    jack           notwelcome.com
allow                   friend   welcome.com 172.121.34.*
```

/etc/ftpusers

The user accounts listed in this file are denied FTP access due to the potential security risk that these user accounts pose. Here's an example:

```
root
bin
daemon
adm
lp
sync
shutdown
```

```
halt
mail
news
uucp
operator
games
nobody
```

/var/log/xferlog

The `/xferlog` file is like an audit trail. It contains all transfer information carried out by *WU-FTPD*; as you will see, it can be very useful in troubleshooting. Each transfer entry is composed of a single line, containing the following fields, separated by spaces:

```
Mon Apr 3 16:22:01 1999 5 ftp.ol23.com 568881 /file.Z a _ o g tho@friend.com ftp 0 *
```

The following list describes the fields in the preceding example, moving from left to right.

- `Mon Apr 3 16:22:01 1999` is the current time in the form DDD MMM dd hh:mm:ss YYYY
- `5` is transfer time in seconds
- `ftp.ol23.com` is the remote host name
- `568881` is the file size in bytes
- `/file.Z` is the name of the file
- `a` is the transfer type (a for ASCII and b for Binary)
- _ is one of the four values (concatenated if necessary) described in the following table

This table describes what possible values can be used.

Value	Description
C	file was compressed
U	file was uncompressed
T	file was tarred
_	no action taken

- `o` means the file was sent to the user (o for outgoing) or received from the user (i for incoming)
- `g` means accessed as guest (a for anonymous, r for real)
- `tho@friend.com` is the local username

- `ftp` is the service name
- `0` means the authentication method (0 for none and 1 for RFC931 Authentication)
- The asterisk at the end stands in here for the authenticated user id, because there is none in this case

Configuring WU-FTPD

There really is not much one needs to do to configure the FTP server out of the box. After a standard OpenLinux installation, WU-FTPD and its configuration files are installed and configured for you. If you don't intend to connect your FTP server to the Internet, there are no further configurations needed. However, if you want to make your FTP server accessible over the Internet, then you need to fine-tune the default FTP configuration files.

Configuring the FTP server requires modification to these files:

- `/ftpaccess`
- `/ftphosts`
- `/ftpusers`
- `/ftpgroups`
- `/ftpconversions`

These five files are in the `/etc` directory. The main configuration file is `/ftpaccess`; this file is used to configure both basic server information and access to specified directories. The next three files in the list relate to access by other computers. The last one deals with file conversions during file transfer.

Basic FTP Configuration in the /ftpaccess File

Following are the parameters required for basic configuration.

class classname users ip-address

Use this parameter to manage which area of your file system a group (class) of users can access. The default installation created a class called `all` that is composed of real, guest, and anonymous users from any domain, who can access whatever area of your file system you permit them to. Here's an example:

```
class xfiles  sculley,mulder *
```

A class called `xfiles`, consisting of users called `sculley` and `mulder`, can access restricted areas of my file system, with specified permissions that I need to define later on. (See the "Modifying Access Rights" section later in this chapter.) If `sculley` and `mulder` can log in only from certain hosts, then replace the * with the host range of IP addresses, for instance, `172.155.32.*`.

deny ip-address message

Use this command to deny access based on IP address or host name. Here's an example:

```
deny foe.com /usr/local/ftp/not-welcome.txt
```

This prevents any users from `foe.com` from logging in, and displays the content of the `not-welcome.txt` file.

limit class maxuser time message

Use this command to manage the number of users who can access your FTP server simultaneously by class or time. This prevents your FTP server from being overburdened. Here's an example:

```
limit xfiles 2 MoTuWeThFr600-1800 /usr/local/ftp/very_busy.txt
```

This allows a maximum of two users from the class `xfiles` to access the FTP server from 6 am to 6 pm, Monday through Friday. If the maximum is reached, the content of the /`very_busy.txt` file is displayed.

loginfails number

Use this to specify the maximum number of failed attempts to log in before closing the FTP connection. Usually, the default value is 3.

```
loginfails 3
```

banner message-file

This displays the content of the file named `message-file` before the user is prompted for log on. Here is an example:

```
banner /usr/local/ftp/ftp_greeting.txt
```

email address-name

This states the e-mail address to display to the user if the message file contains the %E parameter. By default, the e-mail address displayed is mailto:root@localhost. You should change this to something more appropriate, such as mailto:ftpadmin@myserver.com, and make sure there is an account on your OpenLinux server called ftpadmin. For example:

```
email mailto:ftpadmin@myserver.com
```

```
message messagefile event class
```

The preceding displays the content of the file named /messagefile whenever there is an event caused by a user logging in or changing the directory for a particular class. Following is an example to display the content of xfile_message.txt whenever a user belonging to the class xfiles logs in.

```
message /usr/local/ftp/xfile_message.txt login xfiles
```

And here is an example to display the content of restricted.txt whenever someone changes into the directory /home/xfile/restricted.

```
message /usr/local/ftp/restricted.txt cwd=/home/xfile/restricted
```

Following are some of the commonly used message codes to include in your message files:

Message Code	Description
%C	Current directory
%E	E-mail address specified in the e-mail command
%F	Free space in the current directory
%L	FTP server name
%M	Maximum number of users allowed for this class
%N	Current number of users for this class
%R	Client host name
%T	Local time, in the form Mon Sep 27 22:00:00 1999, for example
%U	User login name

log commands user

This logs all commands issued by one or more users. For example,

```
log commands sculley, mulder
```

log transfers class direction

This logs all file transfers for users belonging to a specified class, and the direction of the transfers (inbound to your FTP server or outbound to a different one). Here is how to log all file transfers, both inbound and outbound, for two classes:

```
log transfers guest,anonymous inbound,outbound
```

alias shortcut long-dir

This command creates a path alias. In this case, the alias called `work` points to a subdirectory several levels down.

```
alias work /home/user1/projects/secret/work
```

Additional Configuration Options

A few other configuration options merit discussion.

Creating Public Directories

Create an incoming directory only if you want people to FTP files onto your site. Remember that any files transferred to this directory might contain illegal software or data. Be sure to check it on a frequent basis. Don't forget to check all files in the incoming directory for viruses, especially if you don't know who uploaded them.

To see what an anonymous user sees when logging in to your FTP server, take a look in the `/home/ftp` directory; this is the directory in which they start. From there, you can structure your file system as required. As a general rule, the `/home/ftp/pub` directory is where the public files are placed. Another standard is the `/home/ftp/incoming` directory. This is where people can upload or download files to or from your server. If you decide to create this directory, make sure the permissions are set properly, so that people can write to it and read from it.

Allowing root to Use FTP

As a security precaution, the default installation does not allow users FTP access to your machine using the `root` account. To allow `root` into your account, edit the `/etc/ftpusers` file to remove `root`, or better yet, insert a hash mark (#) in front of `root`, as shown on the next page.

CAUTION

> We strongly recommend that you leave this default setting in place. Accessing your FTP server with the root account makes it possible to delete system files and crash your system. Even worse, an outsider could upload rogue system files, obtaining backdoor entry!

The following is an example listing of the `/etc/ftpusers` file that allows anyone who knows the password to reach your OpenLinux FTP server using the `root` account. The `bin` account is denied from logging into the FTP server. You must have root privileges to edit this file.

```
#root

bin
```

Modifying Access Rights

By default, all users have the permission to modify or delete any files per their group privileges. There are five permission settings you can control to limit their permission capabilities. (You need to have root privileges to edit the `/etc/ftpaccess` file.) The format of each parameter is `capability permission class`, where `capability` values are as listed in the table following, `permission` is yes or no, and `class` is the name of the class or user.

Capability	FTP User Can...
chmod	Change server file permissions.
delete	Delete files.
overwrite	Replace files.
rename	Rename files.
umask	Change permissions.

In the following example, users of class `real` cannot change the server file permission.

```
chmod no real
```

FTP Administrative Tools

Now that you have finished configuring WU-FTPD, let's review what administrative tools are available to assist us. These tools are `ftpshut`, `ftpcount`, and `ftpwho`. All three commands require that you be using the root account.

ftpshut

The syntax is

```
ftpshut [ -l min] [ -d min] time warning.txt
```

Use this command to shut down the FTP server. After you issue it, a file defined by the shutdown command in `/etc/ftpaccess` is created. To cancel the FTP shutdown, remove that file using the `root` account. The following table describes what the `ftpshut` parameters do.

Parameter	Description
`-l min`	Shuts down and refuses any new FTP requests in minutes
`-d min`	Starts terminating FTP connections min minutes before shutdown
`time`	Shuts down at a specified time, expressed in 24-hour format (eg. HHMM) or in time minutes
`warning.txt`	Displays the content of the `warning.txt` file, which can include message code

Here is an example instructing the FTP server to shut down in 10 minutes with a message from `ftp-shutdown.txt`, and to refuse new FTP requests only at that point.

```
ftpshut 10 /usr/local/ftp/ftp-shutdown.txt
```

ftpwho

This command shows current process information for each FTP user. Additionally, it shows the current number of FTP users for each class. `ftpwho` is useful to gauge how many FTP users your system can take. You must be `root` to issue this command. The following example shows that there is one FTP user belonging to class `all`, and that there is no maximum number of concurrent FTP sessions set for this class.

```
ftpwho

Service class all:

    1 ?        S      0:04 init

   -   1 users (no maximum)
```

ftpcount

This command displays the total number of users for each class (as specified in `/etc/ftpaccess`) that are connected to your FTP server, and the maximum number allowed for that class. You must be `root` to issue this command. For example,

```
ftpcount

Service class all                    -    1 users (no maximum)
```

Advanced FTP Configuration

In most situations, the typical configuration is all you need to have a fully functional FTP server. In spite of this, there are many more parameters you can change in the configuration files for WU-FTPD. In this vein, we'll briefly discuss two advanced topics: virtual hosting and TCP Wrappers configuration.

Configuring Virtual Hosts

Just as you can set up virtual Web hosting, you can set up virtual FTP hosts; you just need to configure the appropriate configuration files. What does this mean? Let's say I want my OpenLinux 2.3 server to act like two or more different FTP servers. Suppose I want a user to see one banner message at one FTP site, and a different banner message at another site: one reading "Welcome to HIS FTP server" and the other reading "Welcome to HER FTP server." Besides having different banner messages, you can set up different directory structures and permissions, as though you had two physical FTP servers; in fact, though, you can use one physical FTP server and the same port to host two or more virtual FTP hosts. You must supply a unique IP address for each virtual FTP host.

A benefit of having virtual FTP servers is lower hardware and maintenance costs because all the virtual FTP servers are running off one computer.

Here's an example configuration to set up the virtual hosts.

```
# Virtual Server at 172.10.100.10

virtual 172.10.100.10 root     /home/ftp/virtual/ftp-serv

virtual 172.10.100.10 banner   /home/ftp/virtual/ftp-serv/banner.msg

virtual 172.10.100.10 logfile /home/ftp/virtual/ftp-serv/xferlog
```

Add lines similar to the preceding example for each virtual server in `/etc/ftpaccess`. The first parameter is the IP address of the virtual server (for example, `172.10.100.10`). The second parameter for that virtual server is `root` or `banner` or logfile. The third parameter is the file system location for the item specified in the second parameter. Note that all the messages, files, permissions, and other settings in the ftpaccess file apply to all virtual servers.

Securing FTP with TCP Wrappers

A special program called a TCP wrapper accomplishes some security purposes by managing WU-FTPD. It is referred to in the /etc/inetd.conf file, which uses the */usr/sbin/tcpd* program. A standard OpenLinux installation has secured WU-FTPD with TCP wrappers. A sample line from the /etc/inetd.conf file is shown here.

```
ftp stream tcp nowait root /usr/sbin/tcpd in.ftpd -l -a
```

This line shows that the TCP daemon program *tcpd* manages the FTP daemon; whenever an FTP request occurs on port # 21 (as named for FTP in the /etc/services file), this program is activated. By encapsulating *in.ftpd* in the TCPD, you control access to the WU-FTPD through the /etc/hosts.allow and the /etc/hosts.deny files. The security rules can be based on

- Which service is requested
- The IP address of the requesting client
- The domain name of the requesting client

Here is an example /etc/hosts.allow file that would allow all FTP (*in.ftpd*) connections from friends.com and *.friends.com machines.

```
ALL: friends.com .friends.com

     in.talkd: ALL

     in.ntalkd: ALL

     in.fingerd: ALL

     in.ftpd: ALL
```

Starting and Stopping the FTP Daemon

The FTP server starts when you boot up your OpenLinux server. To stop the FTP server now, issue the ftpshut now command. To cancel the shutdown, remove /etc/shutmsg, or whatever file is defined by the shutdown parameter in /etc/ftpaccess. To restart the FTP daemon, do the following in the root account.

1. Find the process ID for *inetd*, as shown here.

```
[root@ftp_server/]# ps -ae | grep in
   1      ?       00:00:04    init
 517      ?       00:00:00    inetd
1262      ?       00:00:00    in.telnetd
1464      ttyp0   00:00:00    login
```

2. Kill that process, typing for example `kill -HUP 517`, to shut down and restart your FTP server.

Troubleshooting FTP

You should be able to resolve most FTP problems by re-examining `/etc/ftpaccess`, the main configuration file for WU-FTPD. Other related files, such as `/etc/ftphosts`, `/var/log/xferlog`, and `/etc/passwd`, can be used to help pinpoint the source of your WU-FTPD problems. If you need more assistance, try posing a question to the WU-FTPD mailing list, at **www.landfield.com/wu-ftpd/**. As with other troubleshooting techniques, localize the problem using a "divide and conquer" strategy. If you are really stuck, start with the default configurations provided in the `examples` document at that site.

Here are some common problems you might encounter. Suppose you see the following:

```
FTP server shut down - please try again later.
```

To restart the FTP server, remove the file specified by the parameter `shutdown` in `/etc/ftpaccess`. (Usually, the default value is set to `/etc/shutmsg`.) You need to be in the root account to remove this file. Removing this file allows users to reach your FTP server immediately.

The FTP server might return `login incorrect` when you are using a real, guest, or anonymous account. Make sure you can *telnet* into your system using the real or guest account. If you can, the most likely culprit is the class parameter in `/etc/ftpaccess`. Verify that a class is defined for your real, guest, or anonymous account. The simplest setting to ensure that all three types of FTP users can log in from any host is to add the following line in `/etc/ftpaccess`.

```
class          all          real,guest,anonymous *
```

Make sure there is no space between `real,guest,anonymous`; otherwise, WU-FTPD interprets the words after the space as being part of the domain address. The following line allows only `real` and `guest` accounts to log in, but not `anonymous`—WU-FTPD interprets `anonymous` as a domain name.

```
class          all          real,guest,  anonymous  *
```

Suppose the account `mulder` is denied access. Ensure that `mulder` is not listed in `/etc/ftpusers`, because any users listed in this account are prevented from logging in. If not, then make sure that `mulder` has an account on the system. To verify this, *telnet* into the OpenLinux server, using `mulder` as the username.

For More Information

URL	Resource Name
`http://www.landfield.com/wu-ftpd/`	WU-FTPD Resource Center
`http://www.wu-ftpd.org`	WU-FTPD Development Group
`http://www.calderasystems.com`	Caldera Systems, Inc. Home Page
`http://www.dejanews.com`	Deja.com

Chapter 9: Configuring UseNet News with innd

UseNet Overview

Configuring innd

You can use the UseNet server that comes with OpenLinux, *inn* (InterNet News), to provide discussion group services on a worldwide, company-wide, or local basis. This chapter explains how to configure a small UseNet server, suitable for hosting a few newsgroups. *inn* can handle much more, but as the load grows the configuration becomes considerably more complex, going beyond the scope of this book.

Files Referenced in this Chapter

The following files are used by OpenLinux's innd packages:

File	Purpose
`/etc/cron.d/lib/news.daily`	Handles daily news maintenance
`/etc/cron.d/lib/news.hourly`	Handles hourly news maintenance
`/etc/news/inn.conf`	This is the general *inn* configuration file
`/etc/news/nnrp.access`	Defines which machines can read and post to your news server
`/etc/news/overview.fmt`	Defines how much detail to give in each overview file
`/etc/news/expire.ctl`	Defines when articles should be expired (purged) from the system
`/var/log/news.all`	*inn*'s messages are logged in this file
`/var/state/news/active`	Lists all newsgroups that *inn* knows about
`/var/state/news/newsgroups`	Descriptions for newsgroups are kept here

UseNet Overview

UseNet, also called NetNews, is commonly referred to as "the world's largest bulletin board." Short for *User Network*, UseNet started out as a way to distribute messages on computers without needing a single computer to store them all at once; many computers could share the load. Today, UseNet is a global information, chat, and messaging service, the largest of its kind. A full newsfeed comprising all UseNet newsgroups and articles is dozens, if not hundreds, of gigabytes a day, comprising millions of messages. For this reason, many smaller systems place restrictions on the amount of UseNet information they will carry.

UseNet messages, called articles, are placed into discussion groups, called newsgroups. Each group name consists of several abbreviated words, separated by periods (.), with the most general category being the first word in the name, the next most general name the next word, and so on until the last word in the name is the most specific one. An example of this is the newsgroup ***alt.os.linux.caldera***; **alt** means *alternative* newsgroups, **os** means dealing with *Operating Systems*, **linux** means dealing with the *Linux* Operating System, and **caldera** means dealing with *Caldera Systems'* version of the Linux Operating System, or OpenLinux.

Introduction to inn

Because UseNet is distributed, there is no governing authority per se, although the Internet Software Consortium does a lot of work with UseNet. Each site is responsible for the maintenance of messages sent through it. Even with sophisticated programs, setting up and maintaining a UseNet server requires some day-to-day work. *inn* needs a fair amount of customization to work well.

> As with many programs on OpenLinux, *inn* refers to the suite of programs and not to the individual executable names themselves. There are more than twenty actual programs that are executed at some point or other, the most popular of which is *innd*, the InterNet News Daemon.

NOTE

Planning for a UseNet Server

When you decide to run a UseNet server, there are a few planning issues to consider before setting it up. First, how much of the entire UseNet system do you want to carry? If your answer is "all of it," pause a moment to reconsider. Carrying the entire UseNet newsfeed takes gargantuan computing resources; don't do it if you have a T-1 Internet connection and a few gigabytes of hard disk space—that won't be enough. Expect it to take 50 to 100 gigabytes of storage and to max out a T-3 connection. Consider carrying only part of UseNet if you don't have enough—or don't want to use that much—storage.

Next consider why you want to run a UseNet server. If you are a small ISP and just want to provide a news server for your customers, try using one of the news outsourcing companies, such as SuperNews or GigaNews. They let you use their servers for news, and your customers won't know that you don't keep your news systems yourself. Using such services can save you a lot of hassle and headache.

Many software companies, including Microsoft, use UseNet to provide forums for feedback on their products. Having your own news server allows you to keep track of what messages and newsgroups you want to carry (that is, only those that pertain to your business) and to cut maintenance costs. You can configure these systems so that your messages do not propagate to the rest of the Internet, and you can assign moderators to each newsgroup so that messages can be approved before they are posted.

Configuring innd

You need to do some configuration no matter what you use *inn* for. The necessary steps are listed in the following section, "General Configuration." inn places in the `/etc/news` directory lots of configuration files, many of which need changing. The "General Configuration" section details what needs to be changed for a minimally functional UseNet server.

To specify which groups you want to carry, browse the "Specifying Your Available Newsgroups" section. In the "Advanced Configuration" section, configuration files are listed that can be tweaked based on personal preference; changing these files is not absolutely necessary, but doing so can be beneficial for performance tuning.

General Configuration

The most important file for *inn* is the `/etc/news/inn.conf` file. This file lists several configuration values that are used by all the programs that make up the inn suite. This file is created as `/etc/news/inn.conf.sample`. Copy it from `inn.conf.sample` to `inn.conf` before editing it. You must change many values, as detailed in the following sections.

Organization

```
organization:    Cheek Consulting, Inc., Seattle, WA
```

The organization line appears on outgoing messages from your server; change it to something descriptive of your organization. It can also be helpful to specify a location (I used my business name and location).

Server

```
server:    saltlake.cheek.com
```

This line is the fully-qualified domain name of your server, saltlake.cheek.com in my case. If you will be propagating messages to the Internet from this machine, and vice versa, machines will connect to the hostname specified on this line. Put only the official name of the server here—do not use any aliased names on this line.

Pathhost

```
pathhost:    saltlake.cheek.com
```

Similar to the server line, this line is the name by which other machines will know your server. It is generally the same as the server line. You may choose to put an alias, such as news.cheek.com, here instead.

moderatormailer

```
moderatormailer:     %s@moderators.isc.org
```

Messages posted to moderated newsgroups need to be approved before they can be posted. Each message is sent to the e-mail address specified by this line; the `%s` is replaced by the name of the newsgroup, which has the dots in the name replaced by dashes.

domain

```
domain:     cheek.com
```

The domain line should be set to your server's domain name; in my case, cheek.com.

fromhost

```
fromhost:     saltlake.cheek.com
```

`fromhost` is the name of your server again; this time it is used for outgoing messages. It is also generally the fully-qualified domain name of your server. If you use an alias, such as news.cheek.com, you can use it here instead.

The next file to edit is the `/etc/news/nnrp.access` file. This file determines who can read messages from and post messages to your news server. At the end of the file, add a line, such as this:

```
*.cheek.com:Read Post:::*
```

In this example, I allowed all machines in the cheek.com domain to access my news server. They can both read and post messages. I could have allowed read-only access by removing the Post from this line.

All other lines in this file are fine as they stand; they do not need to be changed.

Last, the `/etc/news/overview.fmt` file needs to be edited. You can see this line in the following file:

```
Xref:full
```

Delete the *full* from this line:

```
Xref:
```

This saves disk space by reducing the amount of information *inn* stores for each message.

Specifying Your Available Newsgroups

The *inn* package that comes with OpenLinux has a standard list of more than 27,000 active newsgroups. You can get a current list via ftp from ftp.isc.org in the `/pub/usenet/CONFIG/` directory; the file `active` is the latest file. Keep in mind that this file lists all newsgroups that the Internet Software Consortium knows about, not necessarily what you can access.

Most likely, however, you can pare the list down to a manageable level. On my server, for example, I just wanted to have local *cheek.test* and *cheek.linuxkb* newsgroups. In the `/var/state/news` directory, I edited the active file so that it looked like Listing 9-1.

Listing 9-1 An example /var/state/news/active file

```
cheek.linuxkb 0000000000 0000000001 y
cheek.test 0000000000 0000000001 y
control 0000000000 0000000001 y
control.newgroup 0000000000 0000000001 y
control.rmgroup 0000000000 0000000001 y
control.sendsys 0000000000 0000000001 n
control.cancel 0000000000 0000000001 n
control.checkgroups 0000000000 0000000001 n
junk 0000000000 0000000001 y
```

This file lists all newsgroups that your server carries. The numbers after the newsgroup name tell the highest and lowest article numbers for each group; the last letter on each line tells whether each group can be posted to or not, and under what conditions. All new groups should start out with the group name, the zeros, the zero-filled one, and a y or an n, as appropriate. Similarly, I edited the `/var/state/news/newsgroups` file, as in Listing 9-2. Descriptions for each newsgroup should be listed in this file.

Listing 9-2 example /var/state/news/newsgroups file

```
cheek.linuxkb        Discussion about the Linux Knowledge Base
cheek.test           Test newsgroup
control              Pseudo-group where news system directives are filed.
control.cancel       Pseudo-group where news system directives are filed.
control.checkgroups  Pseudo-group where news system directives are filed.
control.newgroup     Pseudo-group where news system directives are filed.
```

control.rmgroup	Pseudo-group where news system directives are filed.
control.sendsys	Pseudo-group where news system directives are filed.
Junk	Pseudo-group where non-standard messages are placed.

Both of these files need to be owned by the user and group `news`:

```
chown news.news active newsgroups
```

The control and junk newsgroups are needed for proper *inn* use—always keep them.

Advanced Configuration

You can edit certain files to provide better control of your server resources. The editing explained in this section is optional; your server can work without these changes. If you want, you can skip to the next section, "Starting and Stopping innd."

These files have many lines and options available and, for brevity's sake, I discuss only those I think need changing. Each file is listed with relevant options.

/etc/news/expire.ctl

The messages expiration is controlled by the file `/etc/news/expire.ctl`. Toward the top of the file, you can find the following line:

```
*:A:1:10:never
```

This says that all groups have a minimum expiration of 1 day, a default expiration of 10 days, and a maximum of no expiration. You can change this line to regulate the amount of time an article stays on your system (and takes up precious disk space). To change these settings to a minimum of 1 day, default of 5 days, and maximum of 14, use the following line:

```
*:A:1:5:14
```

Later in the file, you can specify exceptions to this rule. For example, you could make all articles in the rec category (`rec.*`) stay for up to 90 days, and all test newsgroups (`*.test`) expire messages in 1 day:

```
rec.*:A:1:10:90

*.test:A:1:1:1
```

/etc/news/hosts.nntp

If you plan to propagate newsgroups from other machines, such as upstream or downstream UseNet connections, you need to list their hostnames and/or IP addresses in this file. List them one per line, with a colon (:) at the end of each line.

/etc/news/newsfeeds

The `/etc/news/newsfeeds` file establishes which newsgroups are allowed to propagate where; this file ships with an utterly confusing default:

```
ME\
        :*,@alt.binaries.warez.*,!junk,!control*,!local*,!foo.*\

/world,usa,na,gnu,bionet,pubnet,u3b,eunet,vmsnet,inet,ddn,k12\
     ::
```

I suggest changing this to

```
ME:*/!local::

 TEST:!*::
```

This tells *innd* to send all newsgroups to the outside world, except for those specified with a local distribution. If you want to force certain messages to stay local, you can do this:

```
ME:*/!local,!cheek.*::

TEST:!*::
```

Now messages to any cheek groups on my server (such as cheek.test) will not get propagated to the outside world.

Starting and Stopping innd

Before you start *innd,* you need to create a few files. Executing the following commands will create history files for your new *inn* server; the commands will also give these files proper permissions and ownership by the *news* account.

```
touch /var/state/news/active.times
cd /var/state/news
/usr/libexec/inn/bin/makehistory -or
chown -R news.news /var/state/news
chmod 644 history
```

Starting *inn* is just like starting most other services in this book. Use `/etc/rc.d/init.d/news start` to start the daemon, and use `/etc/rc.d/init.d/news stop` to stop it. To make the daemon start automatically at system boot, enable the InterNetNews news transport system (innd) system daemon from within *COAS* (see Chapter 2, "Configuring OpenLinux's Basic Network").

The first time you start the service, you'll receive an e-mail message mailed to the root account:

```
Boot-time Usenet warning on saltlake.cheek.com

No .news.daily file; need to run news.daily?
```

You can safely ignore this message—it serves as a reminder that a few cron jobs need to be added. The first one calls a script that does daily cleanup; the second serves as a backup in case all the news doesn't get sent. In the `/etc/cron.d/lib` directory, create the files shown in Listing 9-3 and Listing 9-4.

Listing 9-3 The /etc/cron.d/lib/news.daily file

```
#!/bin/sh
#news.daily - run innd's news.daily script

su news -c /usr/libexec/inn/bin/news.daily
```

Listing 9-4 The /etc/cron.d/lib/news.hourly file

```
#!/bin/sh
#news.hourly - clean up news on an hourly basis

su news -c "/usr/libexec/inn/bin/rnews -U"
```

Make these files executable with the following command:

```
chmod a+x /etc/cron.d/lib/news.daily /etc/cron.d/lib/news.hourly
```

Then, create links from the appropriate Hourly and Daily directories:

```
ln -s ../lib/news.hourly /etc/cron.d/Hourly

ln -s ../lib/news.daily /etc/cron.d/Daily
```

Troubleshooting innd

If you start the server and do not receive errors, congratulations! *inn* is pretty picky; you have to follow the instructions in this chapter very meticulously. If you receive errors, the best place to check is the file `/var/log/news.all`. This file has messages from the *inn* system. You should see something like this:

```
Nov 29 17:03:49 saltlake ctlinnd[2822]: Reading config from /etc/news/inn.conf
```

If you see any errors after this message, stop the *inn* daemon and fix the error, and then start *inn* again.

If you cannot connect to your server, check the `/var/log/news.all log` file. A normal connection shows the following:

```
Nov 29 17:29:06 saltlake innd: localhost connected 16 streaming allowed

Nov 29 17:29:14 saltlake innd: localhost:16 closed seconds 8 accepted 0 refused 0
rejected 0
```

You can force a connection via telnet. To telnet from your own machine to your news server, try this:

```
telnet saltlake.cheek.com nntp
```

After you connect, you can use the commands `help`, `list`, and `quit` to check whether the server is running correctly.

For More Information

You can find much more information about UseNet and *inn* at these URLs:

URL	Resource Name
http://www.isc.org/products/INN/	Internet Software Consortium's *INN* home page
http://linuxkb.cheek.com/page.php?usenet	Linux Knowledge Base UseNet page
http://www.supernews.com/	SuperNews, an outsourced News Server company
http://www.giganews.com/	GigaNews, another outsourced News Server company

Chapter 10: Configuring RADIUS with Lucent's radiusd

RADIUS and radiusd Overview

Installing and Compiling the radiusd Source

Installing the radiusd Binary

Administering radiusd

radiusd Configuration Files

RADIUS Accounting

Security Considerations

RADIUS (*Remote Authentication Dial-In User Service*) is a protocol designed to authenticate users who access networks remotely, such as via modem. The RADIUS protocol uses a client/server model to authenticate users. RADIUS is designed to centralize user management to a single machine, so all remote users can be managed from one central location. It uses MD5 encryption when transmitting passwords over the network. By doing so, any information sniffed from the network will be unusable, as the data is encrypted.

Files Referenced in this Chapter

File	Purpose
`/etc/raddb`	radiusd configuration files are stored in this directory
`/etc/raddb/clients`	contains all the names of RADIUS clients and their shared secrets
`/etc/raddb/users`	contains the list of RADIUS users and all their attributes
`/var/log/secure`	normal radiusd log messages will go here
`/var/log/radacct`	RADIUS accounting information will be stored in files in this directory

RADIUS and radiusd Overview

While RADIUS is a protocol, the term can be used to refer to the entire system as well. A piece of the RADIUS system is the RADIUS server, *radiusd*, which stores all of the RADIUS passwords. The RADIUS server handles all requests from RADIUS clients, such as Lucent (formerly Livingston) Portmasters, Lucent (formerly Ascend) MAX switches, or other computers. *radiusd* can check a user's password in its own database, or via the system's own authentication method, such as `/etc/passwd` and `/etc/shadow`, NIS (*Network Information Service*),and so on.

Additionally, in order for RADIUS to be of any use to you, you will need a RADIUS client that has been properly configured to accept remote users and talk to your OpenLinux RADIUS server. RADIUS clients are machines whose job it is to connect a remote user (over a modem, for example), and then ask a RADIUS server if this user can use the network's resources. If yes, the client negotiates a suitable connection with the remote user's machine, and allows access to the network. Configuration of a RADIUS client is also beyond the scope of this book.

NOTE

> To learn all the gory details of the RADIUS protocol, see RFCs 2138 and 2139. These can be found at any RFC repository, such as http://www.faqs.org/rfcs/.

What is RADIUS?

Back when networks contained only one computer, managing user accounts was simple. As networks evolved to include many different computers and proprietary systems, managing login accounts became much more complex, because all the systems were scattered across the enterprise.

Most enterprises contain many different computers and networks, each with its own login database. Other systems—like modem pools, databases, and Web servers—have their own password databases. Ideally, all of this information is centrally managed so that administrators can manage all users.

Various schemes to centralize user login information have been tried, with varying degrees of success. (Examples of these schemes include NIS, Kerberos and LDAP.) Traditional networks can be secured using some form of physical security. Dial-in access (through modems), though, has always represented a potential hole through which unauthorized users can access a network. RADIUS helps to close this hole by creating a central repository where dial-in access can be managed.

All user information is stored on a central RADIUS server. RADIUS clients, such as Lucent Portmasters or Ascend MAX switches, are usually terminal servers that support the RADIUS protocol. When a user attempts to log in, they connect to the RADIUS client, then are prompted for their username and password. The Portmaster then checks this username and password against the master username/password database stored on the RADIUS server.

To allow communication only between trusted RADIUS clients and servers, both computers must agree on a common password of their own, called the *shared secret*. If the client does not know the shared secret, then the RADIUS server will not allow it to authenticate users. The RADIUS server maintains a list of hosts that are allowed to communicate with it and each of the hosts' shared secrets.

After authentication the RADIUS server responds by telling the client what kind of framed service and protocol (such as PPP or SLIP) the user is allowed and the IP address they are assigned (static or dynamic). What information the RADIUS server responds with is determined by how the user's information is configured, and what information the client supports or requires. It is also important to note that when the client and server exchange passwords over the network, the passwords are encrypted to make it difficult for password sniffer programs to capture.

What is radiusd?

radiusd is a UNIX daemon which provides all of the RADIUS server functions. As of this writing, the current version of *radiusd* is version 2.1. (The source code is available via anonymous FTP at `ftp://ftp.livingston.com/pub/le/radius/radius21.tar.gz`,

Lucent's Livingston FTP site.) *radiusd* can be compiled for a variety of UNIX platforms, including Caldera's OpenLinux.

Associated with *radiusd* is a utility called *radtest*, which can be used to check the *radiusd* configuration and verify that it is working correctly. *radiusd* listens to ports 1645, 1646, 1650, and 1651; it is important to make sure that no other services are running on these ports.

radiusd uses its own password database by default, but it also has the ability to use Linux's password file instead; by doing so the system administrator does not have to maintain two different sets of passwords. All of the configuration files for *radiusd* are stored in `/etc/raddb`.

Installing and Compiling the radiusd Source

To install the *radiusd* source, copy the file `radius21.tar.Z` to `/usr/src`. Uncompress the file using the command `tar xvzf radius21.tar.Z`.

Before you compile *radiusd*, you need to make a few file changes. First, edit the *radiusd* `Makefile`, which is in `/usr/src/radius/src`. (The `Makefile` can be changed with any text editor.) Comment out line 23, changing it from

```
CPPFLAGS            = -DNOSHADOW
```

to

```
#CPPFLAGS           = -DNOSHADOW
```

This will allow *radiusd* to work with OpenLinux's shadow password functionality. In addition, you must create a configuration file for OpenLinux; create the following file as `/usr/src/radius/src/conf/OpenLinux_2.3` (see Listing 10-1):

Listing 10-1 The radiusd compilation configuration file /usr/src/radius/src/OpenLinux_2.3

```
# System: Linux 2.2.10 #1 SMP Fri Aug 6 00:46:43 CEST 1999 i686
# Caldera OpenLinux 2.3
#
RADLIBS = -ldb -lcrypt
```

Additionally, edit the /usr/src/radius/src/radius.h file, changing the location of the radius accounting directory:

```
#define RADACCT_DIR            "/usr/adm/radacct"
```

to

```
#define RADACCT_DIR            "/var/log/radacct"
```

Finally, to compile *radiusd*, use the command: `make EXT=OpenLinux_2.3 build`

Installing the radiusd Binary

radiusd should be installed by the root user. In order to install *radiusd*:

1. Change to the directory where the *radiusd* binary was generated.

   `cd OpenLinux_2.3`

2. Copy the *radiusd* binary to /usr/local/sbin.

   `cp radiusd /usr/local/sbin`

3. Create the directories /etc/raddb and /var/log/radacct.

   `mkdir /etc/raddb /var/log/radacct`

4. Copy the *radiusd* configuration files to the directory.

   `cp -R /usr/src/radius/raddb/* /etc/raddb`

5. Change the ownership on the configuration files so they are owned by root.

   `chown -R root.root /etc/raddb`

6. Change the permissions on the configuration file so it can be read only by root.

   `chmod 600 /etc/raddb/*`

7. Append the following four lines to /etc/services.

```
radius          1645/udp        radiusd
radacct         1646/udp
radius-proxy    1650/udp
radacct-proxy   1651/udp
```

Administering radiusd

In this section, you'll learn how to administer *radiusd*. Basic day-to-day operation, starting and stopping, troubleshooting, and other matters will be covered.

radiusd Configuration Files

radiusd uses several configuration files, which are detailed below.

- **Clients.** This file contains the clients that can communicate with the server, and their shared secret keys.
- **Users.** This is the RADIUS users database. It contains a list of who is authorized to authenticate, what service they connect to, and other related parameters.
- **Dictionary.** This is the dictionary of RADIUS attributes. It defines the attributes that are passed between the RADIUS client and the server. In general, you will likely never need to modify this file unless you are adding vendor specific RADIUS attributes that are not in the standard RADIUS attributes.

The Users File

The `users` file is a text file that contains the users who can authenticate via the RADIUS server. Each entry in the file contains three items: the username, the check items, and the reply items. The username and check items (see table 10-1) are on the first line of the entry. Reply items are on subsequent lines. For a RADIUS authentication request to be granted, all check items must match. Reply items (see table 10-2) specify to the RADIUS client which type of service is to be granted, as well as any parameters about that service.

Table 10-1 Common RADIUS Check Items

Check Item	Definition	Valid Values
Password	The user's password	The password in double quotes
Auth-Type	Authentication type	Local, System
Expiration	Password Expiration Date	A date in MMM DD YYYY format
Prefix	Username prefix	
Suffix	Username suffix	
Group	User group	
NAS-IP-Address	RADIUS client IP Address	An IP address
NAS-Port	RADIUS client user's port	
NAS-Port-Type	RADIUS client user's port type	ISDN, Async, Sync

Table 10-2 Common RADIUS Reply Items

Reply Item	Definition	Valid Values
Service-Type	Type of service	Login-User, Framed-User
Login-Service	Type of login service	Telnet, Rlogin, TCP-Clear
Login-IP-Host	Remote host address	An IP address
Login-TCP-Port	Login Service TCP Port	A port number
Framed-Protocol	Framed Protocol	PPP, SLIP
Framed-IP-Address	IP address for user	An IP address
Framed-IP-Netmask	IP netmask for user	A netmask
Framed-Route	Pass routing info	<Dest Net>/<Net Size> <Gateway IP> <Hops>
Framed-Routing	Route broadcasts	None, Broadcast, Listen, Broadcast-Listen
Filter-Id	Filter identifier	
Framed-MTU	Maximum Transmit Unit	
Framed-Compression	Compression type	None, Van-Jacobson-TCP-IP
Session-Timeout	Session time limit	Number of seconds
Idle-Timeout	Session idle time limit	Number of seconds

The Username

The username can be up to 63 printable characters long with no whitespace (spaces, tabs, etc). However, vendor's hardware could impose further limits. A username called "DEFAULT" will match any user given. If used, DEFAULT should always be the last entry in the `users` file.

Check Items Definitions

- `Password`. The user's password in double quotes. Maximum supported password length is dependent on the equipment vendor.
- `Auth-Type`. The authentication type. When set to Local, the Password specified in the check items is used; when set to System, RADIUS authenticates the password against OpenLinux's (i.e. `/etc/passwd`, NIS, etc) authentication system. When local authentication is desired, `AuthType=Local` can be omitted and just a `Password=value` can be used.
- `Expiration`. Defines the expiration date of user's access. The format used is MMM DD YYYY. For example, `Expiration="Dec 31 2000"`.

- `Prefix`. Defines a username prefix so attributes can be set differently based on a username prefix. For instance, you can define Joe with a `Prefix="PPP%"` as a PPP user, and `Prefix="SHELL%"` as a telnet login user. When Joe logs in as PPP%joe, he starts a PPP network session. When he logs in as SHELL%joe, he gets connected via telnet to an OpenLinux server.
- `Suffix`. Same idea as Prefix, but defines a suffix instead.
- `Group`. The user must be a member of the specified group in order to authenticate. You could use this to separate users into groups, and give different service attributes depending on the user's group. For example, you could have a group staff and a group users, and create two `users` file entries for user Bob. One has `group=staff` and the other `group=users`. If Bob is then to have his staff attributes disabled, simply moving Bob from group staff to group users removes his ability to authenticate with staff attributes. If users are in multiple groups, you could define one entry with `Group="users", "staff"`. In this case, to authenticate the user needs to be in both groups.
- `NAS-IP-Address`. The IP address of the RADIUS client (i.e. Lucent Portmaster). This can be used to restrict where particular users can authenticate. For instance if you have an NAS for employee use and one for general use, you can restrict users to one or the other by using this attribute.
- `NAS-Port`. The port on the RADIUS client used for authentication. If there is a dedicated line for a particular account tied to a specific port on, for example, a Lucent Portmaster, you could use this attribute to restrict the account to only that port.
- `NAS-Port-Type`. Restricts a user to a particular port type. You could use this to keep normal async (modem) users from using ISDN ports, and ISDN users from using async ports.

Reply Item Definitions

- `Service-Type`. The type of service. Can be `Login-User` or `Framed-User`. `Login-User` is a character-based service, which allows users to connect to an OpenLinux login prompt (using either telnet or rlogin). `Framed-User` is a network type connection, which could be an SLIP or PPP connection.
- `Login-Service`. When the `Service-Type=Login-User`, set `Login-Service` to the connection type desired. Supported `Login-Service` types are `Telnet`, `Rlogin`, or `TCP-Clear`.
- `Login-IP-Host`. The host IP address to connect Login-Usersto. For instance, this would be the IP address of the OpenLinux machine you have set up for people to log into.
- `Login-TCP-Port`. This is the TCP port number to connect Login-Users to. For standard telnet this would be port 23. For connecting a dial-up user to *uucpd* (providing you are running *uucpd*) you would set this to 540.

- `Framed-Protocol`. Specifies the protocol for a Framed-User. Valid values are `PPP` and `SLIP`.
- `Framed-IP-Address`. Specifies the IP address for the user. In most NAS vendor's implementations, leaving this blank allows the NAS to hand out a dynamic IP address based on a pool defined by that NAS. If it is set to 255.255.255.255, it allows the user to request an IP address. If it is set to 255.255.255.254, the NAS equipment gives the user an address from its dynamic IP address pool.
- `Framed-IP-Netmask`. Specifies the netmask for the user. If omitted, most NAS equipment will use 255.255.255.255.
- `Framed-Route`. Specifies a route for the NAS equipment to insert into its routing tables. The form is `<Destination Network IP>/<Network Mask Length> <Gateway IP Address> <Hop count>`. The uses of `Framed-Route` are discussed later in the chapter.
- `Framed-Routing`. `Framed-Routing` defines how broadcast routing protocols are handled. Valid values are `None`, `Broadcast`, `Listen`, and `Broadcast-Listen`. If you wanted to send broadcast routing information to a connected user, but not listen to any the user may send to you (a good idea for security reasons), you would set `Framed-Routing=Broadcast`.
- `Filter-Id`. Specifies a filter identifier to be associated with the user's connection. These can be handled slightly different due to various NAS equipment. For example, on Lucent Portmaster equipment, if you specify `Filter-Id="safe"`, the NAS will look for filters defined in its configuration (called `safe.in` and `safe.out`) and apply whatever filters it finds in the appropriate direction (in or out). Cisco equipment, on the other hand, requires that `Filter-Id` be set to the `access-list` number followed by `.in` or `.out`, depending on which direction the filter should be applied. For example, `Filter-Id="110.in"` would cause Cisco equipment to apply access-list 110 inbound to form the user's connection. Check with your NAS equipment documentation to determine how to use `Filter-Id` with your equipment.
- `Framed-MTU`. Specifies the Maximum Transmission Unit size for the Framed-User connection.
- `Framed-Compression`. Specifies the compression type. Valid values are `None` and `Van-Jacobson-TCP-IP` (which would enable Van Jacobson TCP/IP header compression).
- `Session-Timeout`. Specifies the maximum session length in seconds. Setting this value to 600 would limit connections to 10 minutes in duration.
- `Idle-Timeout`. Specifies the maximum idle time for a connection. Setting this value to 600 would result in connections being dropped after 10 minutes of idle time.

Creating a New User

To add users you will need to modify the `users` file, located in `/etc/raddb`. The `users` file that comes with the *radiusd* source contains some example users. Before you use this file, remove the example entries, either by deleting them or by adding a # character to the start of each line. If you don't remove the example entries, you will be opening up your RADIUS clients to all your OpenLinux users, which is something you don't want to do.

Simply add the user and appropriate check and reply items to the `users` file. Here are some examples:

Joe is a dial-up user, dialing in to establish a PPP session, and will receive a dynamic IP address by the NAS equipment answering his call:

```
joe     Auth-Type=Local, Password="password"

        Service-Type=Framed-User,

        Framed-protocol=PPP,

        Framed-IP-Address=255.255.255.254,

        Framed-IP-Netmask=255.255.255.255,

        Framed-Routing=None,

        Framed-Compression=Van-Jacobson-TCP-IP
```

This entry is long for a single dial-in PPP user; however, it can be greatly simplified by exploiting defaults of RADIUS and of many NASes. When you have thousands of users, keeping each entry to the minimum required will save you space and time. The simplest form of the above is:

```
joe     Password="password"

        Service-Type=Framed-User
```

Mark is a *uucp* mail customer of an ISP. The ISP runs *uucpd* on a mail server located at 192.168.14.22. The RADIUS entry that ISP is probably using is:

```
mark    Password="getmymail"

        Service-Type=Login-User,

        Login-Server=Telnet,

        Login-IP-Host=192.168.14.22,

        Login-TCP-Port=540
```

This simplifies dial-in scripting and NAS configurations on the part of the customer and ISP.

User Tom dials in with several different computers, using a variety of servers. He wants to connect to his PC via PPP, an older home computer that uses SLIP, and from a terminal and modem, to access his collocated OpenLinux server at his ISP. The following entries in the ISP's `users` file provide Tom with the multiple types of accesses he needs:

```
tom     Auth-Type=system, Suffix=".ppp"

        Service-Type=Framed-User,

        Framed-Protocol=PPP

tom     Auth-Type=system, Suffix=".slip"

        Service-Type=Framed-User,

        Framed-Protocol=SLIP

tom     Auth-Type=system, Sufix=".shell"

        Service-Type=Login-User,

        Login-Service=rlogin,

        Login-IP-Host=192.168.10.2,

        Login-TCP-Port=513
```

Here the ISP also uses the Unix system's authentication mechanism.

User Jane has a dialup account with her ISP. Her ISP also offers a Web filtering service (by using http proxy). Jane has to have two `users` file entries. One is a normal dial-up and the other enables filters that will not allow Web access to the outside world by invoking a filter called kidsafe on the NAS device. This prevents Jane's children from accessing the Web without going through the content filtering service her ISP offers. Here are Jane's two entries:

```
jane    Auth-Type=system

        Service-Type=Framed-User

jane    Password="mykids", Suffix=".filtered"

        Service-Type=Framed-User,

        Filter-Id="kidsafe"
```

XYZ corporation has a dialup ISDN connection. They have a 16 IP address range of 192.168.2.16 through 192.168.2.31. They also have a static IP address of 192.168.42.18. The ISP configures RADIUS so that the NAS the user dials into is told about how to insert the customer's LAN information into its routing tables. When the customer logs in, the NAS knows how to reach the customer's IP addresses, which it could then share via another routing protocol within the ISP's network. Here is the RADIUS entry used:

```
xyzlan   Password="xyzpass"

         User-Service-Type=Framed-User,

         Framed-Protocol=PPP,

         Framed-Address=192.168.42.18,

         Framed-Netmask=255.255.255.255,

         Framed-Route="192.168.2.16/28 192.168.42.18"
```

Another useful RADIUS feature is the DEFAULT feature of the `users` file. A `users` file can be trivially simplified if everyone in the OpenLinux's password file has PPP based network access. This is all that is required:

```
DEFAULT     Auth-Type=system

            Service-Type=Framed-User,

            Framed-Protocol=PPP
```

This is a nice feature, but keep in mind that accounts like root, and other system accounts on the server (as well as accounts you may have added for *httpd*) that have valid passwords, can also authenticate for PPP network access.

RADIUS has many features that make these highly configurable, flexible user entries to be created. NAS vendors also have several of their own features, which can usually be added to RADIUS by incorporating the vendor specific attributes into the dictionary file.

Deleting a RADIUS User

To delete a RADIUS user, either delete the username and attributes from the `users` file in `/etc/raddb`, or place a # character at the start of each line for the user. Keep in mind that if you are using a `DEFAULT` user with system passwords, you must instead delete the user account from your OpenLinux system.

Changing a User's Password

Change a RADIUS password by changing the Password attribute for the user account in the `users` file. Because the file can be accessed only by the root user, only the root user can change a RADIUS password.

Of course, users that have their `Auth-Type` set to `system`, can change their passwords through the normal OpenLinux means. This includes any users covered by a DEFAULT users entry.

Connecting to a RADIUS Client

Before you try to connect to a RADIUS client machine, such as a Lucent Portmaster, both the hostname and the shared secret of the client need to be added to the `/etc/raddb/clients` file on your server. Listing 10-4 shows an example of this file.

Listing 10-4 The /etc/raddb/clients file, containing a list of hostnames of RADIUS clients, and their shared secret password

```
#RADIUS Client          Shared Secret
#=============          ================
portmaster              trust@me
localhost               testing!123
```

Each RADIUS client will need to be listed in this file, or else *radiusd* will not let it authenticate users. For this to work, the shared secret in this file must be configured separately on the client side. Shared secrets consist of up to 14 ascii characters. No whitespace characters are allowed in a shared secret. There are no limits to the number of clients in the `clients` file.

RADIUS Accounting

RADIUS accounting daemon is a child process of the RADIUS authentication daemon. It starts when you start RADIUS, and it listens on port 1646. RADIUS clients send accounting information when users connect and disconnect from provided services. Logs go to `/var/adm/radacct/detail`. Each record in the logs has a timestamp and the attributes about the connection, along with the action (`START` or `STOP`).

Accounting Attribute Definitions

- `Acct-Status-Type`. Account status type. This is either `START` or `STOP`.
- `Acct-Delay-Time`. The delay time between when the event occurs and when the NAS sent the record.
- `Acct-Session-Id`. A unique identifier for the session assigned by the NAS equipment.
- `Acct-Authentic`. Indicates whether the user was authenticated by RADIUS or a local NAS user.
- `Acct-Session-Time`. The connection time of the session in seconds.
- `NAS-IP-Address`. The IP address of the NAS to which the user is connecting.
- `NAS-Port-Type`. The port type on the NAS to which the user is connecting (Async, Sync, ISDN).
- `Framed-IP-Address`. The IP address assigned to the user for a Framed-User connection.
- `Framed-IP-Netmask`. The IP netmask assigned to the user for a Framed-User connection.
- `Acct-Input-Octets`. The number of octets (bytes) received from the user.
- `Acct-Output-Octets`. The number of octets (bytes) sent to the user.
- `Called-Station-Id`. The phone number called.
- `Calling-Station-Id`. The phone number of the calling station.
- `Timestamp`. The time the record arrived on the server in seconds from the epoch (1/1/1970 00:00:00).
- `Request-Authenticator`. Appears when the accounting record has a problem with its digital signature. A value of `None` indicates it was not signed. A value of `Unverified` indicates the signature did not match the expected signature.
- `Acct-Terminate-Cause`. The reason the session was terminated. If the terminate cause is `Admin-Request`, the session was terminated by an administrator. If it's `Host-Request`, the Login-User session was terminated by the Login-IP-Host. Idle-Timeout termination is due to excessive idle time. Session-Timeout is seen when the user exceeds the maximum session time. A problem with the phone line can manifest itself as a Lost-Carrier reason. A normal Framed-User session is ended with a terminate cause of `User-Request`.

Many ISPs offer limited accounts which include a certain amount of base time per month and a charge for additional hours used in addition to the base hours. RADIUS accounting is the method used by most ISPs to determine how many hours each of their users have used each month. That way, they can determine how much to bill each one based on the individual plan and how much time each used.

Here is an example start and stop for a Framed-User session:

```
Sun Feb 13 09:03:29 2000
User-Name = "sample"
NAS-IP-Address = 10.244.43.212
NAS-Port = 5
Framed-Protocol = PPP
Framed-IP-Address = 10.180.42.133
Called-Station-Id = "5552428"
Calling-Station-Id = "5558302"
Acct-Status-Type = Start
Acct-Delay-Time = 0
Acct-Session-Id = "306488966"
Acct-Authentic = RADIUS
NAS-Port-Type = Async
Timestamp = 950450609

Sun Feb 13 09:38:42 2000
User-Name = "sample"
NAS-IP-Address = 10.244.43.212
NAS-Port = 5
Framed-Protocol = PPP
Framed-IP-Address = 10.180.42.133
Called-Station-Id = "5552428"
Calling-Station-Id = "5558302"
Acct-Status-Type = Stop
Acct-Delay-Time = 0
Acct-Input-Octets = 433167
Acct-Output-Octets = 254970
Acct-Session-Id = "306488966"
Acct-Authentic = RADIUS
Acct-Session-Time = 2113
NAS-Port-Type = Async
Timestamp = 950452722
```

A RADIUS accounting start and stop record for a Login-User session:

```
Tue Jul 30 14:48:18 1996
Acct-Session-Id = "35000004"
User-Name = "bob"
NAS-IP-Address = 172.16.64.91
```

```
NAS-Port = 1
NAS-Port-Type = Async
Acct-Status-Type = Start
Acct-Authentic = RADIUS
Service-Type = Login-User
Login-Service = Telnet
Login-IP-Host = 172.16.64.25
Acct-Delay-Time = 0
Timestamp = 838763298

Tue Jul 30 14:48:39 1996
Acct-Session-Id = "35000004"
User-Name = "bob"
NAS-IP-Address = 172.16.64.91
NAS-Port = 1
NAS-Port-Type = Async
Acct-Status-Type = Stop
Acct-Session-Time = 21
Acct-Authentic = RADIUS
Acct-Input-Octets = 22
Acct-Output-Octets = 187
Acct-Terminate-Cause = Host-Request
Service-Type = Login-User
Login-Service = Telnet
Login-IP-Host = 172.16.64.25
Acct-Delay-Time = 0
Timestamp = 838763319
```

Starting and Stopping radiusd

You can start *radiusd* manually by using the command `radiusd`. *radiusd* also supports several command line options to enable/disable features or override defaults.

- `-a`. Specifies an alternate directory for RADIUS accounting. The default directory is `/var/log/radacct`.
- `-b`. Uses a DB version of the `users` file. The db version is created from the plaintext `users` file, using the *builddbm* utility. This speeds `users` file lookups significantly, and is recommended if you have 500 users or more in your `users` file.

- `-d`. Specifies an alternate directory for RADIUS configuration files. The default directory is `/etc/raddb`.
- `-l`. Specifies a RADIUS logfile to use instead of using the *syslog* facility.
- `-s`. Runs RADIUS in single-threaded mode without spawning a child process to handle each authentication request.
- `-v`. Displays the version of RADIUS without starting the *radiusd* daemon.
- `-x`. Debug mode. To send debug output to syslog, use `-x -l syslog`.

To start the RADIUS server each time your OpenLinux machine is rebooted, add the line `/usr/local/sbin/radiusd` to the `/etc/rc.d/rc.local` file. To stop the radiusd server, use this command:

```
killall radiusd
```

Troubleshooting radiusd

When RADIUS does not work, typically you will find that users cannot connect remotely to your servers. This is a pretty ambiguous symptom, but it is useful to see if *radiusd* is the culprit. One way to troubleshoot *radiusd* is to run the program with the `-x` flag. This causes *radiusd* to write log messages to standard output. This allows the system administrator to see all of the requests being made from RADIUS clients and whether the requests succeeded or not. If *radiusd* is failing:

- Make sure each RADIUS client is listed in the /etc/raddb/clients file on your server.
- Verify that the shared secret in the /etc/raddb/clients file matches the shared secret configured on each RADIUS client.
- Check to make sure the RADIUS client is using the proper RADIUS server. This should be explained in your client's (i.e., the Portmaster's) manual.
- Check the RADIUS client's documentation to make sure the users file defines all the attributes it requires.

You can perform additional troubleshooting by checking your server's logs. *radiusd* logs a little bit of information to the file /var/log/secure, and also logs client information in the directory `/var/log/radacct`. In that directory there is a directory for each RADIUS client's accounting information. Checking the logs can be a good way not only to see what *radiusd* is using, but also to identify who is logging in using a RADIUS client and when.

New to radiusd 2.1 is a feature that lets you turn debugging on and off without having to stop and restart the daemon. Sending *radiusd* a `USR1` signal will turn debugging on, and sending it a `USR2` signal will turn debugging off. Debugging messages are logged via *syslog*.

In addition, the *radtest* program provided with radiusd 2.1 aids in debugging by giving you a simple testing tool to determine what your RADIUS server is doing. *radtest* uses localhost (127.0.0.1) as the originating client IP, so you need to define a secret key for localhost in your RADIUS `clients` file. If you do not do this, you will not be able to used *radtest* to test your configuration.

Security Considerations

RADIUS itself is reasonably secure, since all the passwords are encoded in MD5 encrypted packets between authorized RADIUS clients and the RADIUS server, using a private shared secret key known only to the client and the server. Therefore, security of your RADIUS server is very important to the security of your network. A compromise of your RADIUS server is likely to result in a compromise of your entire network.

Most RADIUS servers are dedicated boxes so that a limited number of people (administrators) have login access to the RADIUS server. When this is not possible, adhering to secure file permissions is a must. If your `users` file is world readable and has plain text passwords, then the access of those users is compromised. If your `clients` file is world readable, then they will have the shared secret (which wouldn't be much of a secret anymore), and could run decryption routines on any sniffed data between a client and server. If that occurs, any RADIUS user's password can be compromised.

For PPP based network access authentication, the protocols used are PAP (Password Authentication Protocol) and CHAP (Challenge Handshake Authentication Protocol). Most people use PAP, but CHAP is increasing in popularity. CHAP is more secure because of a challenge response handshake, encrypting the password yet one more time (in addition to the MD5 the RADIUS packets are encrypted by). However, in order to use PAP, your RADIUS users must use `Auth-Type=local`, and have plain text passwords in the RADIUS `users` file (versus using `Auth-Type=system`).

Be sure all RADIUS configuration files are owned as root and have permissions set (600 for file, 700 for directories). Your logging directory (`/var/log/radacct`) should be protected as well, so RADIUS accounting and logfiles are not accessible other than to the system administrators.

If you really want the ultimate in security, you want your RADIUS server behind a firewall. A firewall will allow you to control network transmission between your RADIUS server and the world. Allowing udp ports 1645 and 1646 from only those sources that are clients, and generally tightening login and other accesses will result in the best security you could have for your RADIUS server. See Chapter 11 "Building a Firewall with ipchains" for more information on firewalls, and how to build one with an OpenLinux box.

For More Information

For more information on RADIUS, check the following URLs:

URL	Resource Name
http://www.livingston.com/marketing/products/radius.html	Lucent's (formerly Livingston) RADIUS page
http://www.faqs.org/rfcs/	Internet RFC's (2138 and 2139 are helpful)
ftp://ftp.livingston.com/pub/le/doc/manuals/pc/radius.pdf	RADIUS Administrators Guide

Chapter 11: Building a Firewall with ipchains

Firewall Overview

Linux's Firewall Features

Configuring ipchains

Applications and IP Masquerading

Many people think that if you have a firewall your computer network is completely secure. This is a myth! Firewalls are simply one tool to make a network more secure than it was before. A network will always be vulnerable to internal corruption.

Files Referenced in this Chapter

File	Purpose
/etc/rc.d/init.d	File where firewall start script is located
/etc/ipchains.rules	File defining your ipchain ruleset
/etc/modules/default	Configuration file for IP forwarding modules

Firewall Overview

Security can be compromised from within. For example, a disgruntled employee can do significant damage by corrupting the files on the server. This same user might change other users' passwords to stop them from using their accounts while the data is being systematically destroyed.

So what does a firewall do? A firewall simply provides an additional line of protection to your computer network and data. Whether it's additional computing power, more bandwidth, or simply the numbers, your network might contain exactly what every attacker wants. Consequently, you need a firewall to protect yourself, even if it can't provide perfect protection.

You can make a firewall as complex and time-consuming as you want. You can save every packet that goes in and out of the firewall, and you can make sure that a human looks at every packet to verify the content, although this would be overkill in most networked environments.

For a firewall to provide any type of security, it needs to do some type of *packet filtering*. In packet filtering, the firewall looks for specific information in a packet to determine its type, source, destination, port, and protocol. Based on this information, the firewall either permits the packet to pass through or rejects it.

A firewall is a computer (or computers) that is connected to both the internal network and the external network directly. This means that these computers have a direct interface with both worlds. In many cases, this is done by having multiple network interface cards, or a network interface card along with a card that is specific to your Internet connection. Because the internal and external networks are connected through a computer that requires the packets go from one network interface to another, this cannot occur without going through the firewall.

The requirement that the packet must pass through the firewall is useless unless there is a rule regarding that packet. The rules in the firewall can be as complex or as simple as the administrator desires. For example, a simple ruleset could instruct the firewall to permit every packet to leave the firewall and deny all the packets that want to enter. A more complex ruleset might allow common Internet services in and out, such as http, ftp, smtp, pop3, and dns, yet deny other protocols used inside the local network (nfs, nis, dhcp, lpr, netbios, etc).

Using Firewalls vs. Proxy Servers vs. IP Masquerading for Security

There are several procedures to follow in order to create a firewall. You can use a standard firewall, which provides transparent security to your network. You also can use a proxy firewall, which is plainly visible to your clients and transparent to those outside your network. Last, you can use IP masquerading by having a gateway that provides your way to the Internet, which allows your network to use only one IP address or a block securely. In addition, this method is transparent to most of your client's applications. Combining masquerading and packet filtering adds extra security to your network.

Using Firewalls

Using a transparent firewall benefits both the end user and the administrator. With a transparent firewall, users don't have to make obtrusive changes to their systems to be able to access the outside world. A transparent firewall also acts as a packet filter, which allows you to use a single system and possibly fewer resources than with other methods. You can purchase a packet filter out of a box—you don't need an in-depth understanding of how the firewall acts. This method can potentially decrease the number of logs the System Administrator needs to go through.

Naturally, there must also be disadvantages to using transparent firewalls, or else everybody would use this solution. One negative is that you must have a range of IP addresses, unlike with a masqueraded solution. Additionally, you cannot cache any of your data (as is possible with a proxied firewall). Finally, unless you go through the process of making a large set of rules, you cannot log your users or potential intruders.

Imagine that you have acquired a block of IP addresses, say 12.34.56.1–70. Using these IP addresses, the local network computers communicate directly with the computers on the Internet. All packets will pass through your router and out onto the Internet without needing to use a proxy server, or be masqueraded. Since there is still a single point where all connections go through, you can still filter the packets with your firewall.

The following steps illustrate the process of a browser requesting a Web page in a public network.

1. The computer (12.34.56.18) uses its browser to connect to its default gateway/router and requests a Web page. No special browser configurations are required.
2. The firewall allows all http (port 80) traffic, has DNS properly configured, and then passes the request to the next router.
3. The computer gives the request to the Web server on port 80; the Web server tells the computer to use port 3248 for further communication and sends the Web page to the computer on port 3248.
4. The request passes through all the routers on the way back, just as it did on the way to the site, and begins to receive the packets on port 3248.
5. The browser reads the packets and delivers the Web page.

Here, the only connection is between the computer and the Web server. These are the only computers (at this time) to send the request on port 80 and to have the request negotiated and sent back to the computer on port 3248. To deny all access to Web sites, you only have to deny all outgoing packets from the internal network on port 80. This way, the request never reaches the Web server and the negotiation (and sending) of the Web page never occurs.

Proxy Server

A proxy server is an intrusive but effective method of logging clients and potential intruders. By having a proxy server, the Administrator has complete control over your network; this complete control can also benefit the client. For example, you could spare clients from having to see annoying pop-up windows on certain Web sites. As a proxy, any or all of the data that goes through your network can be cached, which can be beneficial. For example, an ISP might find that most users visit specific sites such as news, sports, and search engines. When the first client accesses the site, that day's news can be cached and then frequently updated. This use of cached data can save ISP's money by reducing the amount of bandwidth they need from their upstream providers.

Clients need to make certain adjustments to their systems to use the proxy. Because there is a very limited amount of proxying software, the services the client can access are sometimes very limited.

IP Masquerading

IP masquerading benefits both the client and the Administrator. The client has a transparent connection where everything acts as if it is connected directly, even though it is not. The Administrator can use a single IP address for the server and then allocate IP addresses to the clients from the allocated private network blocks (RFC 1597 blocks of addresses). By doing this, all clients are protected because those outside the internal network cannot access the private network over the Internet.

The disadvantages of IP masquerading relate to the services that can be provided by other systems on your network. If you are masquerading your entire network (using a single real-world IP address), the system doing the masquerading is the only one that can be your external Web, ftp, mail, or dns server unless you forward the connection to an inside machine. This can dramatically increase the load on your server, and because this server is exposed to the Internet in more ways, there are more potential vulnerabilities.

A proxy is a program that does the packet filtering automatically, and it might cache data as well. Packets using traditional proxies will never directly access the Internet from your internal network because they all are required to pass through your packet-filter. You can find several programs that act as proxies, but this is much more limited than other methods of masquerading. One program that acts as a caching proxy is *squid* (Web proxy). Several other proxy programs also exist for your use.

> **NOTE:** When using traditional proxies, your internal network should assign IP addresses from the RFC 1597, Private Network Allocations (that is, 10.*.*.*, 172.16.*.* or 192.168.*.*).

If you want to use *squid* on your firewall, follow these steps to enable your browser to access a Web page:

1. Configure the computer's browser to use the proxy at port 8080.
2. The computer (192.168.1.52) connects to the firewall's internal network interface (192.168.1.1) on port 8080 (the port where squid runs).
3. *squid* indicates its acknowledgment of the request and tells your computer to go to port 3248 (or any arbitrary port number) for further communication.
4. The firewall connects to the Web site using its external network interface (134.56.7.89) on port 80.
5. The Web server acknowledges the firewall's request and tells it to switch to port 3587 (or any arbitrary port number).
6. The Web server sends the data to the firewall.
7. The proxy processes the data and remembers that the request for this data was from 192.168.1.52, which is on the internal network, and sends the data to the computer on port 3248.
8. The browser on the computer processes the page, and the user sees the Web page.

It might seem like there is a great deal going on just to retrieve the Web page, but in reality, this isn't very much for the firewall or any other computer to process. Because this was a proxy, the Web server thinks the request was made by the firewall and there aren't any additional computers on the network. From your computer, the request was sent only to the firewall. This benefits the System Administrator because the request passes through the firewall (a very easy way to log traffic). As I mentioned previously, the only problem is that there is a limited number of services that can be provided this way. Even though additional ports are used, there's no problem because there are 65,536 ports available for use, and only 1,024 of these ports have defined functions associated with them.

Standard masquerading does not have a proxy—all the masquerading is performed by the kernel instead of by special proxies, which is simpler. If this is a simpler solution, however, why isn't it used for all masquerading? Proxies have benefits other than just simple masquerading. For example, *squid* can cache requests to the Web, which allows frequently–accessed Web pages to appear without traversing the Internet. Proxies also typically provide logging features, which can help the System Administrator.

In the kernel-level process, each packet is rewritten as it passes through the firewall. The outbound requests appear as if they come directly from the firewall (like a proxy without the proxy), and the inbound packets appear as if they come directly from the requested location.

The rewriting process can be CPU-intensive and, with some protocols, fairly inefficient. To combat this problem there are specific kernel modules for individual cases. There are modules for quake, real audio, ftp, irc, and so on. Precompiled masquerading firewall modules in OpenLinux are located in the `/lib/modules/(kernel version)/ipv4/` directory.

As with traditional proxies, the packets from your local network cannot go to the Internet without passing through the packet filter, and vice versa. In some cases, there are no kernel modules, and the process of rewriting each packet through the CPU is too intensive. In such situations, the kernel changes only the header information of the packet, and then uses the auto forwarding feature in the kernel.

The section on standard proxies describes the process of a request to obtain a Web page from a browser. The following steps demonstrate how this process works in a standard masqueraded network.

1. The computer (192.168.1.52) connects to the firewall's internal network interface (192.168.1.1) on port 80 (no special configuration of the browser is required). The firewall is the default route (gateway) for the computer's requests.
2. The firewall acknowledges the request and tells your computer to go to port 3587 for further communication.

3. The firewall looks up the DNS entry for the request.
4. The firewall connects to the Web server on port 80. It acknowledges the request and tells you to go to port 3248.
5. The Web server sends the data to the firewall using port 3248.
6. The firewall rewrites the packets and sends them on port 3587 as it receives them (the firewall does not need to receive the entire Web page, picture, or song before retransmission).
7. The computer's browser processes the page as it comes from the requested site (with little delay, because the firewall sends the packets as they are received).

In this case, the computer thinks the Web page came directly from the requested site. With a proxy, however, your computer thinks the Web page came from the firewall and the Web server thinks the request came directly from the firewall.

Linux's Firewall Features

The firewall features in the Linux kernel are made up of chains of rules. *Rules* consist of a set of matching criteria and a target. When the packet matches the criteria of the rule, the kernel looks to the target to decide what to do with it. That target can be another user-defined rule to match the packet against, or an internal action telling the kernel what to do with the packet.

The *ipchains* program controls the chains stored in the running kernel. By having a separate program, you can add or remove rules without having to recompile your kernel. It also allows you to view statistics about the matching of each particular rule in a chain.

Configuring ipchains

The *ipchains* program allows you to control, modify, and inspect the chains in the kernel. Each rule in the chain will have its matching criteria and the associated target. Targets are either user-defined chains, or the kernel built-in actions. These actions are `ACCEPT`, `DENY`, `REJECT`, `MASQ`, `REDIRECT`, and `RETURN`. See table 11-1 for a description of the kernel built-in actions.

The three built in chains, are input, output, and forward. They are applied to packets as their names imply. Packets arriving on an interface are evaluated against all input rules that apply to that interface. Packets leaving the firewall are evaluated against the output rules that apply to the outbound interface. Finally, packets that are being forwarded through the box are evaluated against the rules in the forward chain. User-defined chains can be written, and may be used as targets in other chains (user-defined, or system built-in chains).

Table 11-1 Kernel built in actions

ACCEPT	Let the packet through.
DENY	Drop the packet.
REJECT	Drop the packet and send an ICMP message back to the sender indicating that it was dropped.
MASQ	Masquerade the packets as if they came from the firewall host. Return packets will be demasqueraded automatically (this can only be used on the forward chain).
REDIRECT	Redirects traffic to a port local on the firewall. Used for instance for transparent proxying (see the chapter "Configuring the Apache Web Server"). (This target can only be used on the input chain and user-defined chains).
RETURN	With this target, the next rule to be examined will be next rule in the chain that called the current chain. If there is no calling chain to return to, the chain policy target is used.

The `ipchains` command has many options to allow you to control and inspect the chains. Each rule you define will be added to the chains with individual `ipchains` commands; one per rule. The command line options for *ipchains* are documented in Table 11-2.

To create a firewall rule, you need to use a `chain`, `target`, and at least one `rule` (typically several). All firewall rules are executed in the order of creation. You can change this by changing the index of the rule. Table 11-2 lists commands (ipchain command line options), along with a short description of each.

Table 11-2 ipchains Command Line Options

Code	Name	Description
-A	Append	Adds one or more rules to the chain.
-D	Delete	Deletes one or more rules from the chain. Do this by numbering 1 - ... (top to bottom) or by matching the rule.
-R	Replace	Replaces a specific rule. You must be specific—if there is ambiguity due to matching addresses, the replace function will fail. As with deletion, you can specify the rule by number 1 - ... (top to bottom).

Table 11-2 ipchains Command Line Options *(continued...)*

Code	Name	Description
-I	Insert	Inserts or places the rule in a specific location based on order. For example, 2 makes it the second rule under the specified chain.
-L	List	Lists all the rules of a specified chain. When you do not specify a chain, all the chains will be listed (input, forward, and output) in this order.
-F	Flush	Removes all the rules under a chain, therefore flushing or clearing the chain. If you want to delete all or most of the rules, this typically is faster than deleting them one by one.
-Z	zero	Clears all the incrementation of the counters at start-up of the rule. This allows your accounting to start fresh.
-P	Default policy	Sets the default action for a chain. We can set it to any of the normal targets: ACCEPT, REJECT, DENY, etc.
-M	Masquerading	Allows you to view the masqueraded connections specified by rules when you use -L in conjunction with it. You also can use this with -S to set/specify the kernel's masquerading parameters, that is start masquerading and set the various time-out values.
-S	Set	Allows you to set the time-out values for tcp, tcpfin, and udp connections. If you want to set one of these, you are required to must set all of them all (-S tcp 3 tcpfin 6 udp 5). If you do not want to change a value, you can type 0. This indicates that you use the current value. Because this is setting the time-out values of masquerading in the kernel, this option must be used in conjunction with -M.
-C	Check	Checks a rule. You send real packets faking all the parameters -s (source), -d (destination), -p (protocol), and -i (interface). Your system requires you to fill in all the parameters.
-h	Help	Gives you help.
-P	Protocol	Identifies the protocol type that your rule involves. Because the same port can be used by multiple protocols, you can specify tcp, udp, icmp, or all.

Table 11-2 ipchains Command Line Options *(continued...)*

Code	Name	Description
-s	Source	Specifies the source in regard to the specified chain. You must specify the address and mask. In the specification of the address, you can use a hostname (jack.foo.com), network name (foo.com), or an IP address (192.168.1.1). You can also specify the port or port range (1024:5000). If you specify a port or port range, you must specify the protocol as well.
-d	Destination	Just the opposite of source, but you use the same rule structure.
-j	target	What to do with the packet that matches the rule. You can specify ACCEPT, REJECT, DENY, MASQ, REDIRECT, RETURN and (null).
-f	Fragment	Allows you to decide what to do with fragmented packets. A rule here is good because using packet fragments is a common method of attacking a system.
-b	Bi-directional	Makes the rule applicable in both directions.
-v	Verbose	Gives you more data and information about what is going on.
-n	Numeric	Says that you only want IP addresses and port numbers, and no hostnames (fred.foo.com) or port names (ftp).
-l	Log	Turns on kernel logging of packets. You can get specific information about certain rules (such as who tried to telnet into or out of your firewall).
-y	syn	Match TCP packets with the SYN bit set and the ACK and FIN bits cleared. Packets that match this criteria are used to request TCP connections. When preceded by a "!" (i.e. ! -y) inverts the option.

Now that you know all about masquerading and firewalling, it is time to configure ipchains. This process involves:

- Testing the firewall to see if it accomplishes all tasks correctly.
- Enabling IP forwarding (or all the packets will be denied at the firewall).
- Determining a ruleset (firewall rules/laws).
- Implementing the firewall rules.
- Making the firewall last forever (or until you decide to change it).

Determining Rulesets

Now that you are aware of all the options you can use in your rules, it is time to decide what your rules should be. To determine the specific needs for your firewall, you should consider the following:

- What services do your clients want? This will determine which ports and services you need to leave open.
- Are any of these services security risks for your network or your company? Why? The service may be too risky to allow.
- What would be the damage to the company or the network if your network were compromised for the specific services? This will also determine if the risk outweighs the benefit.
- Is the likelihood of these services being compromised so minimal that it is very unlikely that any problems caused by the specific service exist?
- Is the risk of a given service worth the benefit to you or the end user?
- Do you want any specific backdoors that would be unlikely to be exploited by those outside the company (REDIRECT)?
- Do you want lengthy, verbose logs?
- Do you want numeric-only logs?
- Do you want logs at all?
- Do you want to use real IP addresses, or do you want to use IP masquerading? Will your applications support IP masquerading (most all do)?
- What services can be provided another way and still be useful?
- What is the most efficient method of creating a rule set?

Let's look at an example. Here, masquerading has been chosen. The private network space 192.168.1.0/24 was chosen for the protected LAN. The `eth0` interface is the interface facing the outside world, and the `eth1` interface will connect to the protected LAN. A Web server is running on the firewall and needs to be reached by the outside world. The clients on the protected LAN are configured to use the upstream ISP's DNS servers. In addition, a mail server is running on the firewall.

Here is the `ipchains config` that meets the above requirements with explanations of what we are doing:

```
ipchains -P forward DENY
```

This sets the default action for the forward chain. If a packet to be forwarded fails to match any of the matching criteria in the rules of the forward chain, the packet will be dropped.

```
ipchains -P input DENY
```

This sets the default action for the input chain. If a packet coming into an interface on the firewall fails to match any of the matching criteria of the rules in the input chain, it will be dropped.

```
ipchains -A forward -i eth0 -s 192.168.1.0/24 -d 0/0 -j MASQ
```

All internal ips (192.168.1.0/24) to be forwarded to the outside world will be masqueraded. The resulting packets forwarded out of the network will have their from IP address changed to that of the exterior IP address of the firewall. Returning packets will be demasqueraded automatically, and will bypass the forward chain.

```
ipchains -A input -i eth1 -p tcp -s 192.168.1.0/24 -d 0/0 80 -j REDIRECT 3128
```

Outbound Web connections (port 80) from the protected LAN (192.168.1.0/24) to the outside world will be transparently redirected to port 3128, where the firewall is running the squid proxy server.

```
ipchains -A input -i eth1 -s 192.168.1.0/24 -d 0/0 -j ACCEPT
```

Allow the protected LAN to send packets to the outside world. Our specifications placed no limits on outbound traffic, so allow it all. This doesn't mean the resulting response packets will get back in, it just allows them to be sent out.

```
ipchains -A input -i eth0 -s 192.168.1.0/24 -d 0/0 -l -j DENY
```

If you receive a packet from the outside world that claims to be from an address used on the protected LAN, drop it, as this only happens when someone is spoofing (faking) their return IP address in their TCP packets. Since this is usually someone trying to break your security we log these packets.

```
ipchains -A input -i eth0 -p tcp ! -y -j ACCEPT
```

Packets entering from the outside world that are responses to tcp requests sent from the protected LAN will be allowed in. This rule looks at the TCP connection bits (SYN, ACK, FIN) to determine whether the packet is a request for a new connection (SYN bit set, ACK and FIN bits cleared), or a response to a request made from the protected LAN (SYN bit cleared, ACK or FIN bits set). Remember to escape the ! character (with a \ character) if the command is being run by a shell that will interpret the ! character (i.e. csh and tcsh).

```
ipchains -A input -i eth0 -p tcp -s 0/0 -d 0/0 80 -j ACCEPT
```

Incoming packets from the outside world destined for port 80 are accepted. Since we are not using anything other than one real world IP (ISP assigned) facing the outside world, it is not necessary to specify the actual destination. If so desired, one could have used `-d 10.5.8.19` instead of `-d 0/0` (where `10.5.8.1.9` would be the real world IP address assigned to your `eth0` interface).

```
Ipchains -A input -i eth0 -p tcp -s 0/0 -d 0/0 25 -j ACCEPT
```

This allows incoming SMTP requests (port 25) to the firewall which is running your mail server. As above, it is not necessary to specify the actual destination (the external IP address used on `eth0`).

```
ipchains -A input -i eth0 -p udp -s 0/0 53 -d 0/0 -j ACCEPT
```

DNS is a UDP protocol, so when we make a DNS request out to the upstream ISP's DNS server, the packets coming back are not TCP, so there is no ACK or FIN bit (since it is not TCP), so we need to specify that DNS (port 53) packets originating from DNS servers can enter.

```
Ipchains -A input -i lo -s 0/0 -d 0/0 -j ACCEPT
```

Allow the firewall to speak from itself to itself via the loopback interface. This is used by some applications to talk between component server processes (such as *squid*).

Any packet not meeting any of these rules will follow the default targets we set for the chains (we set these up front to `DENY`). Make sure you have enabled IP forwarding, or you will find the server is accessing the net as you expect, but the protected LAN can't contact anything on the outside!

An improvement to the above to aid in debugging would be to set the default target for the input and forward chains to accept, then add specific deny rules with the logging flag at the end of each of the chains. This will cause anything you are not permitting to be logged to your `/var/log/messages` file. This way if you're having problems, you should be able to see why, and if someone is attempting to probe your firewall you will have a log of it. The modified rules look like so:

```
ipchains -P forward ACCEPT
ipchains -P input ACCEPT
ipchains -A forward -i eth0 -s 192.168.1.0/24 -d 0/0 -j MASQ
ipchains -A forward  -s 0/0 -d 0/0 -l -j DENY
ipchains -A input -i eth1 -p tcp -s 0/0 -d 0/0 80 -j REDIRECT 3128
ipchains -A input -i eth1 -s 192.168.1.0/24 -d 0/0 -j ACCEPT
ipchains -A input -i eth0 -s 192.168.1.0/24 -d 0/0 -l -j DENY
ipchains -A input -i eth0 -p tcp \! -y -j ACCEPT
ipchains -A input -i eth0 -p tcp -s 0/0 -d 0/0 80 -j ACCEPT
ipchains -A input -i eth0 -p tcp -s 0/0 -d 0/0 25 -j ACCEPT
ipchains -A input -i eth0 -p udp -s 0/0 53 -d 0/0 -j ACCEPT
ipchains -A input -i lo -s 0/0 -d 0/0 -j ACCEPT
ipchains -A input -s 0/0 -d 0/0 -l -j DENY
```

While there is no defined limit for how large your chains can be, it is always best to keep them as small as possible, as each packet has to be evaluated by the chain (or chains) until a match is found, or a default action taken if no match is found. The more rules, the longer it will take to analyze each packet to make a determination as to what to do with it.

Enabling IP Forwarding

In order to use real, routable addresses, or to use IP masquerading, the kernel needs to forward packets. By default, IP forwarding is disabled. In order to enable IP forwarding, you need to execute the following command:

```
echo 1 > /proc/sys/net/ipv4/ip_forward
```

Your next machine reboot will clear this value, it is defaulted to not forward at boot time. We'll cover how to deal with this on a reboot shortly.

Applications and IP Masquerading

Many applications work with IP masquerading just as they do in non-masquerading environments. Some, however, have problems. In order for IP forwarding to work with some of these applications, you need to load some additional, loadable kernel modules. Here is a list of some known applications and the modules required for them to work properly in an IP masquerading environment:

Table 11-3 Applications needing loadable modules with IP masquerading

Application	Required Module	
ftp	ip_masq_ftp	
irc	ip_masq_irc	
CU-SeeMe	ip_masq_cuseeme	
Real Audio	ip_masq_raudio	*will work without, but works best with
VDOLive	ip_masq_vdolive	
Quake	ip_masq_quake	*only need when more than 1 net player

To load any of these modules, use `insmod`. For example:

```
insmod ip_masq_ftp
```

Making Changes Permanent

Now that you've implemented your firewall, turned on IP forwarding and loaded any relevant kernel modules needed for your applications (if you are using masquerading) you have a running firewall.

Unfortunately next time you reboot your firewall will not automatically initialize. The `ipchains` command does not save your rules to disk, it merely installs them into the running kernel (not the kernel on disk). The `ipchains-save` and `ipchains-restore` command will save your work. It is recommended you save your chains to a file in `/etc`, i.e. `/etc/ipchains.rules`. To do so:

```
ipchains-save > /etc/ipchains.rules
```

This will save the rules, which are then capable of being restored with:

```
ipchains-restore < /etc/ipchains.rules
```

Still, a reboot would not do anything with this file, as it is not looked for as part of the system startup scripts. To have your firewall setup the chains and IP forwarding, we need to create a startup script and install it into the proper location. Here is a script you can create as `/etc/rc.d/init.d/firewall` to start your firewall:

```
#! /bin/sh
     # Script to control packet filtering.
     # If you haven't created any rules, do nothing.
     [ -f /etc/ipchains.rules ] || exit 0
       case "$1" in
         start)
              echo -n "Turning on packet filtering:"
              /sbin/ipchains-restore < /etc/ipchains.rules || exit 1
              echo 1 > /proc/sys/net/ipv4/ip_forward
              echo "."
              ;;
         stop)
              echo -n "Turning off packet filtering:"
              echo 0 > /proc/sys/net/ipv4/ip_forward
              /sbin/ipchains -X
              /sbin/ipchains -F
              /sbin/ipchains -P input ACCEPT
              /sbin/ipchains -P output ACCEPT
              /sbin/ipchains -P forward ACCEPT
```

```
            echo "."
            ;;
        *)
            echo "Usage: /etc/rc.d/init.d/firewall {start|stop}"
            exit 1
            ;;
esac
exit 0
```

NOTE

> When you stop the firewall with the script above, it will disable ALL packets from passing through the system. If you wish to only remove all rules and allow all packets, remote the line that turns off IP forwarding:
> `echo 0 > /proc/sys/net/ipv4/ip_forward`

In addition to the startup script, you will want to add any loadable kernel modules to support the protected LAN's client applications to the `/etc/modules/default` file. To support ftp and irc, you would add:

```
ip_masq_ftp
ip_masq_irc
```

Now we have the startup script and masquerading modules, we need to insert a symbolic link into the `/etc/rc.d/rc3.d` directory to point to the script we created so the system will run our script at the appropriate time during boot. To do this:

```
ln -s /etc/rc.d/init.d/firewall /etc/rc.d/rc3.d/S00firewall
ln -s /etc/rc.d/init.d/firewall /etc/rc.d/rc5.d/S00firewall
```

We use `00` so it will be the first thing run at run level 3. It will run before the network interfaces are started. This is done so the rules will be in place before the interfaces come up. Now our firewall is completely automatic. Should the firewall reboot due to power loss or other reasons, when it reboots, the rules you want, and masquerading modules needed will be handled all automatically.

Once created, add execute permission for the owner (root):

```
chmod u+x /etc/rc.d/init.d/firewall
```

The number 15 is an arbitrary number, but the scripts are started in numeric order, so make sure your firewall is started before your network. It is quite common for the network to be started as the first thing, `S1network`. In this case, type:

```
mv S1network S2network
```

Make sure your firewall is started first either by creating your symbolic link at this time or by moving it. Do this by typing something similar to:

```
mv S15firewall S1firewall
```

At this point, your firewall will be started automatically.

Testing for Accepted or Rejected Packets

Once you have gone through all the work of creating a firewall and configuring it to start automatically on boot, you will want to ensure its quality. One way to do so is to get on a machine that is on your internal network and test the firewall rules that apply to your internal network. You can also get on your computer from home and test your firewalls externally. To prevent holes in security, test your firewall without network connectivity by using the `ipchains -C` option. Test the configuration with some of the rules created before to make sure the expected answer is returned:

```
ipchains -C forward -i eth0 -p tcp -s 192.168.1.100 2048 -d 10.1.2.3 80
```

The system replies with:

```
masqueraded
```

Type:

```
ipchains -C input -i eth0 -p tcp -s 192.168.1.200 2048 -d 192.168.1.100
80
```

The system replies with:

```
denied
```

Type:

```
ipchains -C input -i eth0 -p tcp -s 100.200.0.4 3096 -d 0 80
```

The system replies with:

```
accepted
```

Type:

```
ipchains -C input -i eth0 -p udp -s 10.2.3.4 2112 -d 0 137
```

The system replies with:

```
denied
```

Type:

```
ipchains -C input -i eth1 -p tcp -s 192.168.1.100 3456 -d 10.1.1.1 80
```

The system replies with:

```
redirected
```

You can test each rule this way to see how it will respond to various packets exactly as the kernel will do. Once you have tested the firewall and are satisfied it is set up securely, you can now connect your LAN to the outside world and have some assurance that you have protected your LAN as best as possible while allowing the clients the access to the outside world they desire.

The last piece of security you want to deal with regarding a firewall is making sure it is secure. After all, if the firewall is broken into, your protection is gone. Don't leave your firewall wide open to the world. Only allow what you need to. In addition, don't run unnecessary services. For instance, do you really need to run *fingerd* on a firewall? Comment out those unnecessary services in `inetd.conf`. If you only run what you need to, and you only allow the packets you need to you will have the best security you can have without disconnecting the LAN from the outside world.

For More Information

URL	Resource Name
http://www.rustcorp.com/linux/ipchains	IP chains homepage
http://metalab.unc.edu/LDP/HOWTO/IPCHAINS-HOWTO.html	IP chains HOWTO
http://metalab.unc.edu/LDP/HOWTO/Firewall-HOWTO.html	Firewalling and Proxy Server HOWTO
http://scnc.holt.k12.mi.us/~lachniet/proxy/	Masquerading Proxy Server HOWTO
http://metalab.unc.edu/LDP/HOWTO/mini/IP-Masquerade.html	IP masquerade mini-HOWTO
http://tmservices.com/masq	masq apps site

Chapter 12: Configuring the squid Proxy Server

An Overview of the squid Proxy Server

Configuring squid

Transparent Proxying

Proxy Log Analyzers for Use with squid

A proxy server, such as *squid*, makes it unnecessary to establish a direct connection between a client requesting a resource and a server providing that resource. In an environment where there are no proxy servers, the client requests a resource, the request goes directly to the server providing the resource, and the server's response travels directly back to the client (see Figure 12-1). The client and the server must be interconnected.

When a proxy server is added, all traffic from the client goes to the proxy server instead of directly to the server. The proxy receives the request, processes it, and then transmits the original request on behalf of the original client. When the response from the server is received, the proxy server sends it back to the client (see Figure 12-2). The proxy server and the client must be interconnected, as must the proxy server and the server; the client and the server do not need to be interconnected.

Files Referenced in this Chapter

OpenLinux's *squid* package uses the following files:

File	Purpose
`/etc/squid.d/squid.conf`	*squid's* configuration file.
`/usr/doc/squid-2.2.STABLE2`	*squid's* documentation is stored in this directory.
`/var/log/squid/access.log`	*squid's* access log is stored in this file.
`/var/run/squid.pid`	Contains *squid's* process ID.
`/var/spool/squid`	*squid* caches its data in this directory.

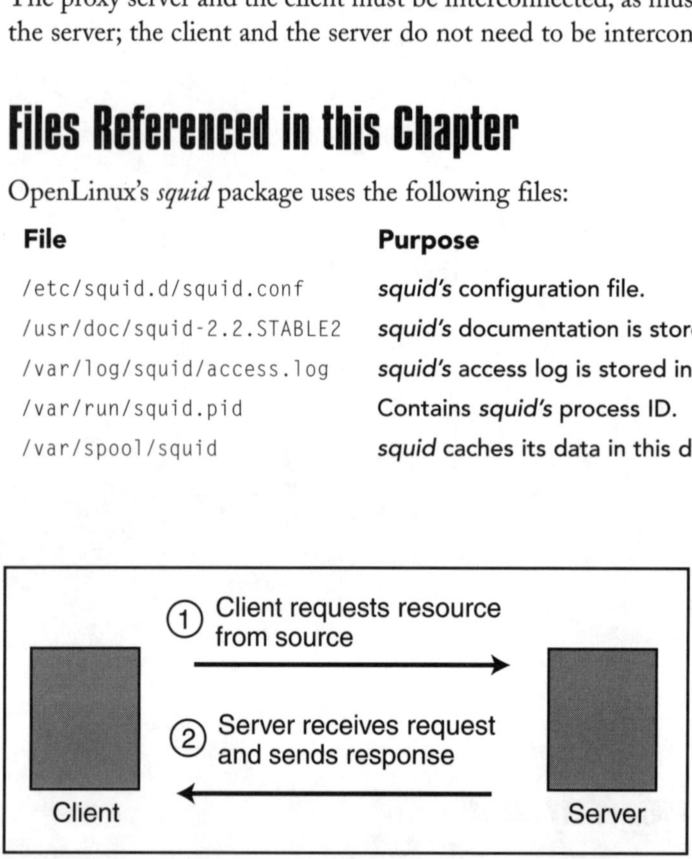

Figure 12-1 *A client and a server typically communicate directly. The client requests a resource; the server receives the request, processes it, and sends the response back to the client.*

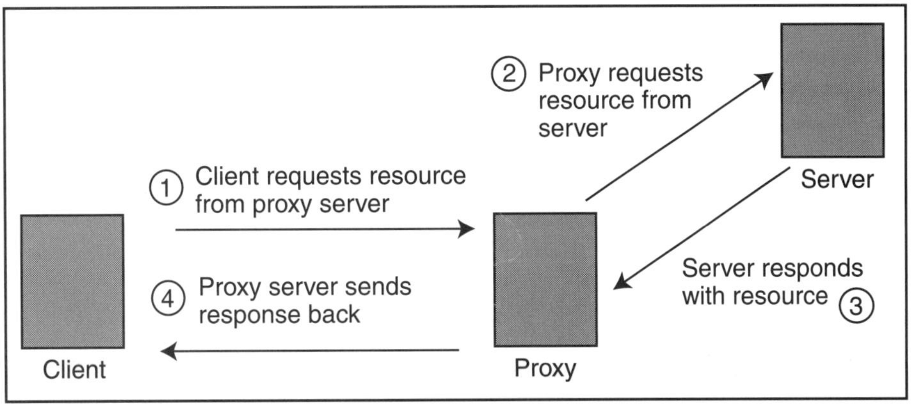

Figure 12-2 *A proxy server acts as an intermediary between the client and the server. The client requests a resource from the proxy; the proxy retrieves the response from the server and relays it back to the client.*

An Overview of the squid Proxy Server

A proxy server's most useful feature is its capability to bring security to an Internet-connected network. When properly configured, a proxy server can halt outside access to a network while allowing outside Internet access from a network; caching proxies, such as *squid*, can even speed up Internet access by keeping local copies of frequently-used Web pages on a hard drive. By forcing all Internet access through a proxy, an administrator can negate the need for a firewall and can keep tabs on all Web and FTP traffic coming from a network. This can then reduce time spent on administrative tasks.

Strengths and Weaknesses of squid

Although one caching Web and FTP proxy server, *squid,* is both fast and secure, it is limited to proxying Web and FTP traffic only. This is probably *squid's* biggest limitation. Other proxy servers, such as Microsoft's Proxy Server for Windows NT, can proxy all sorts of IP traffic, including *telnet*, when *telnet's* proxy client is loaded. Telnetting through a *squid* proxy requires first telnetting to the proxy server gateway machine, and then telnetting out from there, a rather time-consuming process.

On the plus side, *squid* is highly customizable and supports many types of access control lists, which detail who can access what resources at what time on what day of the week, and so forth. It can be used in conjunction with other proxy servers to take information from their caches, so that the actual Internet resource needs to be accessed only on rare occasions. This can greatly speed up Internet access, particularly on heavily loaded Internet connections.

Configuring squid

To get *squid* working, you need to complete four tasks (none of which are particularly difficult):

1. Install *squid* on your OpenLinux server.
2. Perform some *squid* configuration tuning.
3. Start *squid* as a daemon.
4. Reconfigure the Web browser of each user who will use *squid*.

Installing squid

Look for *squid* on the OpenLinux CD within the `/col/contrib/RPMS` directory. It is not installed with a complete OpenLinux installation. Because *squid* is an RPM package and does not need to be compiled, you can simply install it. First, create *squid* user and group IDs. Next, install the `squid-2.2.STABLE2-3.i386.rpm` file.

Creating the squid User and Group

The *squid* proxy server runs under its own user and group IDs. Create these with *COAS* or *lisa*, whichever you feel more comfortable using. The user and group IDs should be *squid*, the home directory doesn't matter, and the account should be disabled. (For more information on using *COAS*, refer to Chapter 2, "Configuring OpenLinux's Basic Network.")

When you install the *squid* binaries, they install with the user and group IDs *squid*. If the *squid* user and group IDs do not exist, root ID is used, and *squid* fails to function correctly.

Installing the squid Binaries

Mount the OpenLinux 2.3 CD with the command `mount /mnt/cdrom`, if it is not mounted already. Then type this command:

```
rpm -ivh /mnt/cdrom/col/contrib/RPMS/squid-2.2.STABLE2-3.i386.rpm
```

You see the following output:

```
squid                   ##################################################
```

rpm, the *Red Hat Package Manager*, loads packages in .rpm format, the format Caldera and many other Linux distributors use. The *i* option means install, the *v* options tells *rpm* to be verbose, and the *h* command tells *rpm* to use hash marks (#) to show progress. If you mounted the Caldera OpenLinux CD, you can now unmount it with the command `umount /mnt/cdrom`.

Configuring the Proxy Server

squid's configuration file, `/etc/squid.d/squid.conf`, is huge but well-documented. Additionally, the defaults work well, for the most part; access control needs to be configured, however, before *squid* can work for any machine besides the machine it is set up on. You should probably configure the following options as well:

- Access control
- IP ports
- Log files and types
- IP forwarding

Configuring Access Control

The *squid* proxy server comes with extensive access control lists, which by default allow only the local server to access the Internet through the proxy server. In a workgroup, you probably want to allow other machines to use the proxy server, and so need to give them access. The configuration file,`/etc/squid.d/squid.conf` contains the access lists under the *ACCESS CONTROLS* section.

The *acl* keyword defines an access control list; the *http_access* keyword implements it. The configuration file (commented out) lists many examples, after which a few rules are actually in force (not commented out). Look for the following line:

```
acl localhost src 127.0.0.1/255.255.255.255
```

This defines an ACL named *localhost* as all access coming from the IP address 127.0.0.1, the local IP address. Define an ACL for your workgroup by using a descriptive name (such as your domain name), an IP address, and a subnet mask. If you are using 192.168.0.1 through 192.168.0.255 for your **domain.com** internal network, with a subnet mask of 255.255.255.0, you use this:

```
acl domain-com src 192.168.0.1/255.255.255.0
```

You just created an ACL called *domain-com,* which encompasses all IP traffic from 192.168.0.1 through 192.168.0.255. (I use the *domain-com* name to remind me that it is for the **domain.com** network, although I could call it anything.) Look further in this configuration file for this line:

```
http_access allow localhost
```

This line tells *squid* to allow http (Web) access for the ACL *localhost*, which is previously defined as all access coming from the IP address 127.0.0.1. Because you defined a new ACL called *domain-com*, insert a line to allow access for this also:

```
http_access allow domain-com
```

Now your entire workgroup on the 192.168.0 network can use the *squid* proxy server for Internet access. There are many other types of access control lists, in which you can disable or enable access on specific ports, or to specific sets of IP addresses or domain names. These all follow the same format: define the ACL with the `acl` command, and then enable or disable it with the `http_access` command.

NOTE

There are no `https_access` or `ftp_access` commands. Define all access rules with the `http_access` command instead. Rules you define with `http_access` will be in force for FTP and secure Web access also.

Each time you modify the `squid.conf` file, you must restart *squid*. How to do so is explained in the "Starting and Stopping squid" section later in this chapter.

Configuring Ports

The *squid* server listens on port 3128 for its commands. You can configure *squid* to use a different port, using the *http_port* command in the `squid.conf` file. Look for this line:

```
#http_port 3128
```

Because this line is commented out, *squid* listens to its internal default, port 3128. If you want this to be a different port, uncomment this line and change the port number. If you want to use port 1500, for example, you can change this line to be as follows:

```
http_port 1500
```

Remember to remove the hash mark to allow *squid* to see the command! Note that because *squid* runs under normal user privileges, you cannot use a port number lower than 1024.

Configuring Logging

The access log is controlled by the `cache_access_log` command in the configuration file.

```
#cache_access_log /var/log/squid/access.log
```

The log's default name is `/var/log/squid/access.log`. You don't need to change this name unless you want to move the log somewhere else. You might want to change the format of the log, however; this is controlled by the `emulate_httpd_log` command.

```
#emulate_httpd_log off
```

squid uses its own log format, which is good for *squid*-specific log analyzers, such as *calamaris*, but not so good if you want to peruse the log files by hand. It can also log in the normal *httpd* Web server log format, so its logs can be analyzed by more common programs, such as *analog*. If you want to use *analog* to analyze the Web logs, change this line to:

```
emulate_httpd_log on
```

This also makes the log file a little more readable, at the expense of detailed information. You can choose whichever format suits your taste. Keep in mind that you must restart *squid* after any changes to the `squid.conf` file.

Configuring the Cache

squid caches copies of each document is receives so that the next time the document is requested, it does not need to go back to the Web to get it. The standard Web cache size is 100 Megabytes; unless your network needs are very involved, this cache size is adequate. You can control the size of the cache, however, as well as how long items stay in cache. Search for the following line:

```
#cache_dir /var/spool/squid 100 16 256
```

This line gives the default cache directory `/var/spool/squid`, as well as the size, 100 Megabytes. You can change the directory and the cache size by altering this line. If you do alter it, remove the hash mark (#) in front of it, so it will not be commented out. To create, instead, a 250 Megabyte cache directory in the `/opt/squid/cache` directory, use the following line:

```
cache_dir /opt/squid/cache 250 16 256
```

The last two numbers, 16 and 256, control how the cache directories are created; normally, you do not need to alter them.

If a document has not been accessed for more than a set amount of time, *squid* deletes it automatically. The default time is one month; this is set by the `reference_age` parameter:

```
#reference_age 1 month
```

One month should be plenty of time, but you might want to shorten the time to a week or two:

```
reference_age 2 weeks
```

Again, if you change this line, remember to remove the beginning hash mark.

Disabling IP Forwarding

A proxy often is used in lieu of a direct Internet connection. In such cases, you might want to prevent users from being able to access the Internet directly, bypassing the proxy and whatever security you placed there. To do restrict access, you need to disable IP forwarding on the machine that is the Internet gateway. If the gateway is the same server that contains the proxy (it normally is), disable IP forwarding by using *COAS*. (This is explained in Chapter 2, "Configuring OpenLinux's Basic Network," under the "Managing IP Routing" section.)

A side effect of disabling IP forwarding is that no machines can get out to the Internet without use of the proxy (except for the gateway machine itself, which doesn't rely on IP forwarding, because it is directly connected to the Internet). If you have machines that require services that the proxy does not handle, such as *telnet*, they cannot access those services. In this case, if you still want to disable direct Internet access, use the *ipchains* firewall tool. (You can find more information on *ipchains* in Chapter 10, "Building a Firewall with *ipchains*.")

Starting and Stopping squid

The *squid* server comes with scripts in the `/etc/rc.d/init.d` directory that start and stop it. Before you use the server for the first time, you must initialize the cache directories by running *squid* with the -*z* option.

```
squid -z
```

If successful, you see the message:

```
Creating Swap Directories
```

After you do this, you can start and stop *squid* with the normal *rc* scripts. Use `/etc/rc.d/init.d/squid start` to start *squid*, and `/etc/rc.d/init.d/squid stop` to stop *squid*. To configure *squid* to start when OpenLinux starts (after a system boot), use *COAS*. (For more information on *COAS*, see Chapter 2, "Configuring Open-Linux's Basic Network.")

The *rc* script also comes with a command to restart *squid* when it is already running. (You need to tell *squid* to restart after any change to the `squid.conf` file.) To do this, give the script the *restart* parameter:

```
/etc/rc.d/init.d/squid restart
```

Configuring the Client Machine's Web Browser

Up to this point, each user's machine probably is configured for direct Internet access, without a proxy. Each machine needs to be told to use the proxy, and needs to be told how to reach it. The specifics of how to do so depend on the Web browser, but the basics are the same: Configure each browser to use the hostname of your OpenLinux server as the proxy server with a port of 3128, or whatever port you chose to use. Here's an example for the Netscape Navigator browser, which comes with Open-Linux 2.3.

1. Choose Preferences from the Edit menu.
2. Expand the Advanced tab in the resulting dialog box.
3. Choose Proxies from the expanded menu.
4. Click the radio button for Manual proxy configuration, and then click the View button.
5. Enter the hostname of the OpenLinux server and the port that *squid* uses, as the values for FTP Proxy, HTTP Proxy, and Security Proxy.
6. Click OK in each of the dialog boxes to return to the browser window.

With Netscape Navigator 2.0 and higher you can automatically configure proxy servers. You do this by creating a javascript file on your webserver that will instruct Netscape where your caches are. You then tell your browser where this javascript file is, and it will automatically configure your proxy servers.

In order to do this, you will have to edit your webserver's `mime.types` file (`/etc/httpd/apache/conf/mime.types`), and add:

```
application/x-ns-proxy-autoconfigpac
```

Then restart your webserver:

```
/etc/rc.d/init.d/httpd stop

/etc/rc.d/init.d/httpd start
```

Create the following file with an extension of `.pac` (I used `cache.pac`):

```
function FindProxyForURL(url, host)
{
    return "PROXY proxy.mydomain.com:3128; DIRECT ";
}
```

Alternately, you could create one with more intelligence, that caches non local websites, and goes direct for local websites:

```
function FindProxyForURL(url, host)
{

    if ( isPlainHostName(host) || dnsDomainIs(host, "mydomain.com"))

                return "DIRECT";

                else

                return "PROXY proxy2.mec.es:80";

}
```

Then in the Netscape client browsers that are to use the proxy, add the URL that points to the `.pac` file (i.e. http://localhost/cache.pac on the server itself) in the Configuration Location box under the proxies setting in the advanced preferences section, then check Automatic Proxy Configuration.

The one problem with autconfiguration is that the javascript is run for each URL to connect to. This will impose a potential performance hit to the browser. This is especially true if you do things like use DNS lookups in your javascript. Manual proxy configuration does not impose this potential performance hit.

It therefore may be faster to replace the `dnsDomainIs`(host, "mydomain.com") call in the last `.pac` file example with `shExpMatch`(host, "*.mydomain.com"). This avoids the `dnsDomainIs` call.

Troubleshooting squid

A proxy server adds another layer of complexity to Internet access, which means, unfortunately, that it is another place where access could break down. When the proxy server doesn't work or is misconfigured or the client's browser is misconfigured, it is your task to troubleshoot.

If the user's Web browser is configured correctly, there are three things you can check on the server to find the problem. First, you can check from the OpenLinux server to see if the site is up, and if the server can access it (if the proxy server can't directly access it, none of the proxy clients can reach it). If you can access the Web site from the server but not from the client, then the problem is most likely one of access rights. If it's not an access rights issue, you need to see what the *squid* logs say about the access request.

Checking Server Connectivity

Use a browser to see if the site in question is up, and can be reached at all. Do this directly, without a proxy configured, so that you can test for physical connectivity. If you can't reach the site, either your server is misconfigured or the site is down. You might want to check connectivity from another machine for comparison. If you can reach the site from the server, but not from a client machine, then it is not a connectivity issue. Check access rights next.

Checking Access Rights

The access control lists can block a site from being viewed on the basis of domain name, IP address, port, and more, on both the remote server and proxy client sides. If access to a site is prevented due to an ACL constraint, you see something like this in the server's log:

```
937256019.522       6 192.168.0.2 TCP_DENIED/403 984 GET http://www.yahoo.com/ -
NONE/- -
```

The message `TCP_DENIED` means that an access control list that denied the request is in place. This log is in the native *squid* format. If you are logging in Web server format, you do not see a `TCP_DENIED` message; you need to check the `/etc/squid.d/squid.conf` file's access lists to verify the rules by hand. If you do see that message, you must check the access control lists by hand anyway to verify which rule is causing the denial; if you alter or remove the rule and restart *squid*, the access should work.

Checking the squid Logs

When all else fails, check the *squid* logs. First see if the request happened at all. You can check based on IP address or hostname of the client, or based on URL request. If you are using Web server logging, you can check the time stamp too. If the request is not logged, the client might be misconfigured. (If the request did happen, and all else checks out, you are on your own.)

Managing the squid Logfiles

squid creates lots of log information. If you don't need or care for the data in the logs simply set the logging statements in `squid.conf` to `/dev/null`, and you will not have to contend with managing the logfiles. If you do want the logfiles, then you will want to manage these logfiles or they will grow to the point where they fill all the space they can grab.

squid includes the ability to rotate its logfiles. You will want to rotate your *squid* logfiles on a regular basis. To do this daily, you could add the following entry to your root `crontab` file (`crontab -e root`):

```
0 0 * * * /usr/sbin/squid -k rotate
```

At any one time, this will keep up to 10 old logs present (with the suffixes .0 through .9). If this is too much, you may want to add a `cronjob` that runs shortly after the log rotate, which will keep only 5 old log versions (.0 through .4):

```
1 0 * * * /bin/rm -f /var/log/squid/*.[56789]
```

The removes all files in `/var/log/squid` that end in .5, .6, .7, .8, and .9. The amount of logs you keep will depend on the disk space you have for logs, and the traffic you put through your proxy server. Only keep the amount of logs required for troubleshooting and any statistics you want to run on them.

Starting squid with a Clean Cache

Should you want to start *squid* with a clean cache, the simplest way to do this is to invalidate the `swap.state` files for all swap areas configured. To do this, you would do the following:

First, stop the server:

```
% /etc/rc.d/init.d/squid stop
```

then for each `cache_dir` configured in the `squid.conf` file:

```
% echo " " > cache/swap.state
```

finally, restart the server:

```
% /etc/rc.d/init.d/squid start
```

Purging and Object from the Cache

In order to purge objects from the cache, you have to configure an `acl` to allow the purge operation. The following `squid.conf` lines allow you to purge cache objects from the *squid* server itself:

```
acl PURGE method purge
acl localhost src 127.0.0.1
http_access allow purge localhost
http_access deny purge
```

With these lines, you could then purge http://www.purgeme.com/ from the cache by doing:

```
client -m PURGE http://www.purgeme.com/
```

If the operation is succesfully, you will get a `200 OK` response. If the object was not in the cache, you will get a `404 Not Found` response.

The Cache Manager

The Cache Manager is a cgi utility that allows you display current statistics about *squid*. The Cache Manager allows you to view these statistics without having to log into the *squid* server. By default when you install the package, it places `cachemgr.cgi` in the `/home/httpd/cgi-bin` directory.

Because you would not want the world to have access to this utility, you need to control access to this URL via the web server. You will want to limit where requests can come from, or install a username and password. See the chapter on the Apache Web Server for more information about protecting a URL.

Here is an example:

```
<Location /home/httpd/cgi-bin/cachemgr.cgi>
order deny,allow
deny from all
allow from host.mydomain.com
</Location>
```

To view these stats use the following URL:

```
http://yoursquidserver.yourdomain.com/cgi-bin/cachemgr.cgi
```

squid has many statistics available via the Cache Manager. The most useful are:

```
Memory Utilization
General Runtime Information
5 Minute Average of Counters
60 Minute Average of Counters
Cache Utilization
```

Making Specific URLs Non-Cacheable

There may come a time when you want to set up *squid* to not cache certain URLs. Usually you would want to do this for pages that update frequently; either because they don't pass good cache expiration indicators in their headers, or because they update so frequently, why waste space caching them.

To do this, you use the `no_cache` option in your `squid.conf` file. As an example, let's say you access a company's inventory, which is dynamic and always updating. The URL is http://www.notarealcompany.com/inventory.html. To make it non-cacheable, add the following to `squid.conf`:

```
acl dontcache url_regex ^http://www.notarealcompany.com/inventory.html$
no_cache deny dontcache
```

You may be working with a Web developer who is frequently changing pages and, because it is a testing site, is not very concerned with putting in header info for caching, etc. The developer is using http://www.notarealwebdeveloper.com/prototype and links to many URLs within that space. To keep that from being cached you would add the following to `squid.conf`:

```
acl dontcache url_regex ^http://www.notarealwebdeveloper.com/prototype.*$
no_cache deny dontcache
```

You can even choose when to cache and not to cache based on time. For example:

```
acl dontcache time 09:00-05:00
no_cache deny dontcache
```

You can also choose not to cache based on IP addresses. For instance an ISP could choose not to cache its own local servers (as an example we'll say the ISP has 1 class C 10.1.2.0) by using:

```
acl localservers dst 10.1.2.0/24
no_cache deny localservers
```

Transparent Proxying

More and more locations these days are using transparent proxying. Transparent proxying does not require any special configuration of the browsers, and works by having outbound port 80 requests redirected to a caching server. Transparent proxying can be done with routers, layer 4 switches, gateways (i.e. a OpenLinux box), etc.

In order for you to use this method, you must be using an OpenLinux box as your gateway or firewall (see the chapter "Building a Firewall with ipchains" for more information on building a firewall with OpenLinux). It also requires *squid* to be installed on the same box.

For this example I first set up my OpenLinux box as a gateway, where its `eth0` interface connects it to the world, and its `eth1` interface is for an inside LAN using private IP space (192.168.1.0/24). It uses IP masquerading to allow the private IP space to access the world. Here is the script that sets this up:

```
ipchains -P forward DENY
ipchains -A forward -i eth0 -j MASQ
echo 1 > /proc/sys/net/ipv4/ip_forward
```

The address on the `eth1` interface is 192.168.1.1. I set up an internal machine on 192.168.1.100 and set that internal machine's default gateway to 192.168.1.1. At this point, I can surf the world, ping it, etc. Now that that is working, let's look at setting up for transparent proxying.

For transparent proxying to work, there are a few additional settings we need to add to the `/etc/squid.d/squid.conf` file.

```
httpd_accel_host virtual
httpd_accel_port 80
httpd_accel_with_proxy  on
httpd_accel_uses_host_header on
```

Once these changes have been made, stop and restart *squid*:

```
/etc/rc.d/init.d/squid stop
/etc/rc.d/init.d/squid start
```

All that is left is to tell the kernel to redirect all outbound port 80 requests to the *squid* port (3128 by default). This is done with the following ipchains command:

```
ipchains -A input -p tcp -s 192.168.1.0/24 -d 0/0 80 -j REDIRECT 3128
```

Now all Web requests from any browser on the 192.168.1.0/24 network are getting transparently proxied. Many ISPs use transparent proxying to reduce the amount of bandwidth used on their expensive upstream links to the net. For more information on transparent proxying with your *squid* server and other vendor equipment, see the Squid FAQ online.

Proxy Log Analyzers for Use with squid

Because you can route all Web and FTP traffic from a company or a workgroup through *squid*, the access logs that *squid* provides can detail all Web and FTP traffic from users to the Internet. *squid* keeps a log file of each access, where it went, whether the requested page was found or not, and more. You can view this data in its raw format, but it is easier to interpret using a log analyzer. Two good log analyzers are *calamaris* and *analog*.

squid can produce logs either in its native log format or in a format similar to that of a Web server log. The *calamaris* analyzer takes *squid*'s native log format and produces HTML graphs for viewing by a Web browser; *squid*'s native log format gives more data, but the raw files do not produce human-readable time stamps for each file download. There is no way of determining at what time or on what day a particular URL was accessed. This is a serious drawback for companies that use a proxy server to monitor Web usage.

Because *squid* can mimic a Web server's log, you can use *analog*, a Web server log file analyzer, to give reports from the proxy server's access log. The reports aren't quite as detailed, but they provide human-readable time stamps. If you use *analog* to provide reports for the Apache Web server, you may already have it loaded on your Open-Linux machine, and you won't need to load another program on your server.

For More Information

squid does not have much information on the Internet. These resources are good, however, for learning more about *squid* and other proxy servers.

URL	Resource Name
http://squid.nlanr.net	*squid* Web Site
http://linuxkb.cheek.com/page.php?proxy	Linux Knowledge Base Proxy Server Information
http://calamaris.cord.de	*calamaris* Proxy Server Analyzer
http://www.statslab.cam.ac.uk/~sret1/analog/	*analog* Web Analyzer

Chapter 13: Configuring telnet, ssh, and DHCP Services

telnet, ssh, and DHCP Overview

Configuring telnet

Configuring Secure Terminal and File Access with ssh

Configuring DHCP

Telnet, *ssh* (*Secure Shell*), and DHCP (*Dynamic Host Configuration Protocol*) are all lumped together in this chapter because they are good programs to know how to use, but aren't complicated enough to warrant chapters of their own. *telnet* is of interest here because of its role in remote server management. *ssh* was built to overcome some of the limitations of *telnet* and other applications used for remote login by providing both remote terminal access and file copy, and including security to boot. DHCP is a method of assigning IP addresses and associated network configuration parameters dynamically, rather than requiring each machine on a network to have a specific, static configuration.

Files Referenced in this Chapter

telnet, *ssh*, and DHCP use the following files:

File	Purpose
`/etc/inetd.conf`	*inetd's* configuration file lists which services the *inetd* super-server handles
`/etc/hosts.allow`	A list of services and hosts for which connections should be allowed
`/etc/hosts.deny`	A list of services and hosts for which connections should be denied
`/etc/securetty`	A list of which devices root can be logged in on
`/etc/rc.d/rc.local`	Contains commands to be executed after system boot is done
`/var/run/sshd2_22.pid`	The PID (*process id*) file for *sshd*, the *ssh* daemon

telnet, ssh, and DHCP Overview

telnet is probably the most widely used manner of remote server management; the capability to inspect and change network and other settings via any text terminal that supports *telnet* is a great asset of OpenLinux. *telnet* doesn't have much in the way of security, nor is it very robust as a file transfer system. OpenLinux comes with both a *telnet* client and server installed and enabled by default.

ssh allows terminal sessions, remote execution of commands, and network file copy. All transactions over the network are encrypted, so they cannot be viewed by packet sniffers. Authentication is performed through the comparison of public and private keys, rather than through identification of machine, username, and passwords. Because *ssh* includes cryptography illegal to export outside the United States, it could not be included on the OpenLinux CD-ROM. You can obtain it from an FTP site in Finland (the FTP URL is at the end of this chapter, in the section "For More Information"). Obtaining the latest *ssh* package can give you both a client and a server.

DHCP's main role is assigning IP addresses automatically. Telling a machine to use DHCP gives it a dynamic IP address, whereas normal addressing always gives it a static IP address. You can configure OpenLinux at installation to receive a dynamic IP address via DHCP, but telling it to act as a DHCP server, whereby it gives other machines DHCP IP addresses and keeps track of those addresses, requires specific configuration.

Configuring telnet

telnet is the easiest to configure; by default, it's always on. It's not a service run from an *rc* script; rather, it is run from *inetd*. *inetd* is called a *super-server*, because all it does is listen for connections on specific ports, and when it finds them, it spawns the actual process that handles the service. It's an alternative to having many, many processes waiting for a connection, taking up server memory. Services such as *telnet*, which don't require fast response to an initial connection, use *inetd*. To see what *inetd* does for *telnet*, browse the `/etc/inetd.conf` file, and look for the line that lists *telnet* on it. It should look about like the following.

```
telnet   stream   tcp      nowait   root     /usr/sbin/tcpd   in.telnetd
```

This line tells *inetd* to run the daemon *in.telnetd* whenever a connection on the *telnet* port is requested. If you want to disable the server, you need to edit this line, placing a hash mark to comment out the line. After any change to this file, you need to restart the *inetd* daemon; send it an `HUP` (hangup) signal by issuing the following command.

```
killall -HUP inetd
```

You can't do a lot of configuration with *telnet*. You can turn off a specific user's capability to *telnet* to the server (or get any type of a shell prompt), you can restrict connections based on the machine the connection is from, and you can allow the root user to be able to *telnet* to your server (otherwise, the root user cannot log in via *telnet*).

Restricting telnet Access

Besides turning off all *telnet* access through the `/etc/inetd.conf` file, you can disable it on a user-by-user basis. To disable incoming *telnet* access for a user, change that user's shell to `/bin/false`. For this task, use the `chsh` command. (You can safely ignore the error message that follows.)

```
chsh -s /bin/false joseph
```

```
Warning: "/bin/false" is not listed in /etc/shells
```

CAUTION

> Changing a user's shell to `/bin/false` also can disable that user's console login and FTP access to your server. Never do this for the root user.

To re-enable a user's capability to login, change the shell back to a normal shell, such as `/bin/bash`.

```
chsh -s /bin/bash joseph
```

You can restrict access on the basis of the user's location by using the *tcpd* daemon, which checks that a connection is coming from an allowed source before granting the connection request. To specifically enable a connection from a host or a set of hosts, you need to edit the `/etc/hosts.allow` file. You can allow connections from a specific host, an IP address, a domain name, or a range of IP addresses. Here is an example:

```
in.telnetd:      .cheek.com 127.0.0.1 192.168.1. host2.domain.com
```

The algorithms for allowing connections are based on pattern matching of both IP addresses and hostnames. The `.cheek.com` means any host from the cheek.com domain; these patterns must start with a period to be valid. `127.0.0.1` matches the localhost IP address—I use that so I can *telnet* from my own machine. `192.168.1.` matches all IP addresses in the 192.168.1.x subnet; the IP address must end with a period to match a range of addresses. I also allow the host host2.domain.com *telnet* access to my OpenLinux server. Finally, successful *tcpd* restriction requires the placement of the following line in the `/etc/hosts.deny` file (the line tells *tcpd* to stop all *telnet* traffic that is not specifically allowed by `/etc/hosts.allow`).

```
in.telnetd:      ALL
```

Allowing root telnet Privileges

Because `root` is such a powerful account, OpenLinux allows only the root user to log in on certain terminals, which by default are only local consoles. This means you cannot *telnet* to your OpenLinux machine and log in as `root` unless you change your configuration. A list of trusted, secure terminals are kept in the file `/etc/securetty`. This file normally has all the local terminal devices listed in it, as in Listing 13-1.

Listing 13-1 A normal /etc/securetty file.

```
tty1
tty2
tty3
tty4
tty5
tty6
tty7
tty8
```

These correspond to the eight normal virtual consoles on an OpenLinux system. To check which console you are using, use the `who am i` command. You see output like the following:

```
seattle.cheek.com!joseph   ttyp1    Sep 29 12:54 (:0.0)
```

I have been logged in to my seattle.cheek.com machine as user `joseph` since September 29 at 12:54 pm, on terminal device `ttyp1`, which is not listed as a secure terminal, so I could not have logged in as `root` on this device. If you want to enable `root` logins over *telnet*, I suggest adding at least `ttyp1` through `ttyp8` to the `/etc/securetty` file.

Troubleshooting telnet

If you cannot *telnet* to your machine, there are a few things you can investigate, based on the symptoms. Here are some items to check:

- *telnet* to my server gives an immediate "Connection Refused" message

  Check to see that *telnet* is enabled and running. It might be commented out in the `/etc/inetd.conf` file, or *inetd* might not be running. Verify that your server is listening to port 23, the *telnet* port, by issuing the following command, which can result in the display of a line with `telnet` on it.

  ```
  netstat -ta | grep telnet
  tcp        0      0 *:telnet          *:*             LISTEN
  ```

  If you do not see a line like this, *telnet* is not running. Make sure it is enabled in the `/etc/inetd.conf` file.

- *telnet* to my server produces a connection, but never a login: prompt. (I get nothing for about thirty seconds, and then a "Connection closed by foreign host" message.)

  This could be one of two things. Either this system is denied access due to TCP wrappers (no entry exists in `/etc/hosts.allow` for the system you are trying to *telnet* from, although an `ALL` entry exists in `/etc/hosts.deny`) or DNS is not properly set up on your OpenLinux server and it cannot verify your hostname. You need to verify that `/etc/hosts.allow` and `/etc/hosts.deny` have what you intend them to have, and that DNS can look up hostnames (reverse DNS lookups are described in Chapter 5, "Configuring DNS and bind").

- *telnet* to my server produces a connection immediately, but it takes about thirty seconds to get a login: prompt.

  This is similar to the previous problem, in that DNS is not properly set up on your OpenLinux server and it cannot verify your hostname. You need to verify that DNS can look up hostnames.

- I can *telnet* to my server but cannot log in as root. I am positive I typed in the password correctly, but I still get a "login incorrect" message.

  You might not have added the correct terminal device to `/etc/securetty`. Log in as a normal user and check your terminal with the **who** command; then check that it is in the `/etc/securetty` file. If you cannot log in as a normal user, check to be sure that you have invoked *telnet* to reach the proper machine.

Configuring Secure Terminal and File Access with ssh

ssh is not included with OpenLinux or in this book's CD-ROM; you must obtain it from an FTP site. After it is obtained, compiled, installed, and configured, it can provide you with encrypted data transfer (both file transfer and remote terminal/shell sessions) over a network.

Installing ssh

ssh's home page is **www.ssh.fi** for the OpenLinux version (**www.datafellows.com** provides a Microsoft Windows version), but the easiest way to obtain it is from the Helsinki University of Technology's FTP site, **ftp://ftp.cs.hut.fi/pub/ssh**. Look for the latest version of *ssh*; at the time of this writing, it is *ssh-2.0.13*. Transfer that file to a local directory. Then unpack it with the command `tar xvzf ssh-2.0.13.tar.gz`—you see many files and directories listed, including a directory named `ssh-2.0.13`. Change to that directory.

NOTE

> *ssh* version 2, the latest version, uses different encryption algorithms than *ssh* version 1, and is generally not compatible. Additionally, *ssh2* must be purchased for commercial use, whereas ssh1 is free.

Compiling *ssh* is a three-step process. It involves use of the commands `./configure`, `make`, and `make install`. Execute these commands in that order.

After executing the `./configure` command, you see lots of `checking` messages. Then there should be a line reading `creating sshconf.h`. Then you return to a command prompt.

After executing the `make` command, you see lots of `make` and `gcc` messages; you can safely ignore any warning messages. Enter the last command, `make install`. This copies the *ssh* clients (*ssh*, *scp*, *sftp*) to `/usr/local/bin`, the *ssh* server to `/usr/local/sbin`, and does some last-minute configuration, such as generating authentication keys. (There is also lots of output here.)

To connect to your server with *ssh*, you must first start the *ssh* server by executing the `/usr/local/sbin/sshd` command. Do this now; it automatically goes into the background, as a daemon. The process ID for *sshd* is stored in the file `/var/run/sshd2_22.pid`; killing the process ID contained in this file disables the *ssh* daemon so that no one can use *ssh* to log in any more. If you want *sshd* to be enabled at system boot, add the command to the end of the `/etc/rc.d/rc.local` file; this file contains commands that are executed after system boot is done.

Using the ssh Client

ssh acts just like *telnet*. To access a remote system, you type the command followed by the hostname of the system you want to connect to; if I wanted to connect to my saltlake server with *ssh*, I would type `ssh saltlake`. This would log me in as the same user as I was using on the local system, so if I was logged in as `joseph` on the local system, it would log me in as `joseph` on the remote system. Because all network traffic is encrypted here, *ssh* has no problem letting me log in as `root`; if I logged in as `root` on the local system, I could *ssh* to a remote system and automatically be `root` there as well. If you want to log in as a different user on the remote system, use the `-l` option with the username specified after it, as follows.

```
ssh -l joseph saltlake.cheek.com
```

When accessing a remote system with *ssh*, you are just prompted for the password, because *ssh* knows which user you want to log in as. You are given three chances to type in your password correctly. If you decide that you don't want to log in, press Enter three times instead of pressing Ctrl+C, because pressing Ctrl+C does not exit the *ssh* client correctly.

scp, one of the *ssh* clients just installed, allows you to file copy to remote systems without having to authenticate in a formal program (like FTP requires). This is handy for copying a file or two at a time; copying more might be better done with FTP. *scp* needs to know the filename on the local system, the name of the remote system, and the path on the remote system. If I want to copy the file `/home/joseph/hello.txt` from my local system to my saltlake server, I use the following syntax:

```
scp /home/joseph/hello.txt saltlake:/home/joseph/hello.txt
```

You can also copy files from a remote host to the current directory on the local system (represented by the `.` at the end of the command line).

```
scp saltlake:/etc/passwd .
```

scp can also copy a file as a different user on the remote side; this is necessary because the *ssh* tools enforce file permissions of whatever user you log in as. You need to be able to read from or write to the directories you are attempting to access. (This is not an *ssh* peculiarity; actually, it is enforced at the kernel level across OpenLinux.) To use *ssh* as a different user on the remote machine, place the username and an @ sign before the name of the remote host, as follows:

```
scp /home/joseph/hello.txt liza@saltlake:/home/liza/hello.txt
```

Here the `hello.txt` file in my home directory is copied to liza's home directory on the **saltlake** machine, using her user id.

The *ssh* utilities have many more functions and capabilities, such as a secure FTP client and server, the capability to log in remotely without requiring a password, and so on. Unfortunately, describing them is beyond the scope of this book. If you want to look further into *ssh*, which I recommend, I suggest checking the Web sites listed at the end of this chapter.

Troubleshooting ssh

ssh doesn't have too many problems. In general, if you can *telnet* to the machine in question, you can use *ssh* to connect. A functioning C compiler and development libraries are required to build the *ssh* utilities; if you install the network server, you cannot compile it without loading the development packages.

If you are in X when you use *ssh* to connect to a remote system, you can run applications on the remote system and have their screens show up locally. If you use the `su` command, however, to become a different user, you might see the following message when you try to execute a graphical application:

```
X11 auth data does not match fake data.
```

```
Fatal IO error: client killed
```

This happens because *ssh* proxies the X application's screen output so it can be encrypted back across your connection. X uses authentication to determine who can display what on which machines; changing usernames confuses the authentication, so *ssh* does not allow the application's display. The easiest way to remedy this is by connecting to the remote machine as the user you need to run applications as; because *ssh* allows connections as `root`, this is preferred.

You can instead bypass the *ssh* X proxy and have your application display directed to your local machine. This has the side effect of disabling the encryption inherent in *ssh* for your X applications, however, so the connection is no longer completely secure. If you want to do this, first you need to reset the `DISPLAY` variable on the remote machine by pointing it to your local machine. Type a command like the following:

```
declare -x DISPLAY=seattle:0
```

`seattle` should be the hostname of the local machine, and `:0` is your X server display number (`:0` is the first display, and `:1` is the second; most of the time, you need `:0`). On your local machine, type the following:

```
xhost +saltlake
```

`saltlake` should be the hostname of the remote machine. This line tells your local X server to allow connections from the saltlake machine. If you forget to enter this line, you see the following error messages when you try to run an X application:

```
Xlib: connection to "seattle:0.0" refused by server

Xlib: Client is not authorized to connect to server

cannot connect to X server seattle:0
```

Configuring DHCP

OpenLinux comes with a DHCP server, *dhcpd*, installed by default—it just needs configuration before it can work properly. My experience has been that DHCP can require almost no administration; just configure it, start it, and forget about it. It's no wonder that many networks, regardless of size, are using DHCP.

A DHCP lease is the process of a DHCP client requesting an address from a DHCP server, receiving a response, and then configuring itself to use the network information provided. These are called *leases* because part of the negotiation between the client and the server in this process covers a specific duration of time for which this information is valid; the client leases the IP address only for that time, and a new lease needs to be negotiated after that amount of time. At that point, the server is free to give the client the same IP address, or to give it a different one and use the recently freed IP address for other purposes. DHCP servers therefore need to keep track of which computer is using which lease.

NOTE

> Do not confuse *dhcpd*, the DHCP server daemon, with *dhcpcd*, the DHCP client daemon. This section discusses the server daemon only.

Creating a Basic Configuration File

The `/etc/dhcpd.conf` file is the configuration file for *dhcpd*. This file is a text file that lists options, one per line, to be given to a client requesting DHCP information. The most common settings used by DHCP clients in this file are the following: default and maximum lease times, subnet mask specifications, gateway and broadcast addresses, DNS and WINS server addresses, domain names, static IP address mappings, and dynamic IP address ranges.

One final setting necessary for the server itself is the server identifier hostname. You can make these settings on a global basis, a subnet basis, or a per-host basis. You probably want to set up a few options globally, and then create a definition for each segment to which the server is physically connected. A DHCP client cannot find a server that is not on the same segment it is on, so this precludes setting up more subnet definitions than there are network segments to which the OpenLinux server is connected. Listing 13-2 gives an example `/etc/dhcpd.conf` file.

Listing 13-2 An /etc/dhcpd.conf file for a simple network.

```
# Sample /etc/dhcpd.conf
default-lease-time 86400;
# default lease of 86400 seconds = 1 day
max-lease-time 604800;
# max lease of 604800 seconds = 1 week
option domain-name "cheek.com";
# all clients will belong to the cheek.com domain
option subnet-mask 255.255.255.0;
# all clients get assigned a subnet mask
option broadcast-address 192.168.1.255;
# and broadcast address
```

```
option domain-name-servers 192.168.1.2, 192.168.1.3;
# also all clients get assigned these two dns servers
subnet 192.168.1.0 netmask 255.255.255.0 {
# define a 192.168.1.0/24 subnet scope
   range 192.168.1.20 192.168.1.254;
# dynamic IP's can be assigned from .20 to .254
   option routers 192.168.1.1;
# and a default gateway
}
```

Options outside curly braces are global. Those placed inside curly braces are relevant to whatever scope is defined using the braces. The only option here that is defined with a non-global scope is the range option, which is defined within a subnet/netmask scope.

All option commands correspond specifically to options that the client is given. With the preceding options, a client gets a default lease length of 1 day with a maximum lease length of 1 week. It also is given a domain name, a subnet mask, a broadcast address, a router (or gateway) address, a dynamic IP address, and two DNS server addresses.

> **NOTE**
>
> DNS options are negotiated with the client, not assigned. The client has the option of ignoring the options sent it when it gets a lease. Most don't, however, unless they are told specifically to override what they get from the DHCP server.

All dynamic IP address ranges must be placed within subnet declarations; all subnets must be declared with a subnet statement. To specify a static IP address for a specific client, wrap it around a host scope, as shown in Listing 13-3.

Listing 13-3 The portion of the /etc/dhcpd.conf file dealing with static IP addresses.

```
host client1 {
    hardware ethernet 00:50:04:83:A5:5B;
    fixed-address 192.168.1.15;
}
```

This tells the DHCP server to give IP address `192.168.1.15` and hostname client1.cheek.com to the machine with Ethernet hardware address `00:50:04:83:A5:5B`. You need to know the client PC network card's hardware address to define a static IP address.

Starting and Stopping DHCP

To stop and start the DHCP daemon by hand, use the *rc* script `/etc/rc.d/init.d/dhcpd`. Type the following commands respectively:

```
/etc/rc.d/init.d/dhcpd stop

/etc/rc.d/init.d/dhcpd start
```

After starting the DHCP server, you see text similar to the following (if it worked correctly):

```
Starting DHCP Server:  dhcpd

Internet Software Consortium DHCPD $Name: V1-0-2 $

Copyright 1995, 1996 The Internet Software Consortium.

All rights reserved.

Listening on Socket/eth0/192.168.1.0

Sending on   Socket/eth0/192.168.1.0

 route(eth0).
```

NOTE

When the DHCP server starts, it adds a static route for 255.255.255.255 on the primary network interface, generally eth0. This is normal. It is deleted if you exit the DHCP server.

To enable or disable the DHCP server from starting at boot time, use *COAS* to enable or disable the DHCP and BOOTP boot server. (Using *COAS* is described in Chapter 2, "Configuring OpenLinux's Basic Network.")

Troubleshooting DHCP

Each lease that the DHCP server gives is logged to the file `/var/state/dhcpd.leases`. Most of the time, if a lease is not working properly, this is the file to check. It gives you the status of the leases for different machines. If you can't find a current lease for a particular machine, the server does not currently recognize a lease for that machine.

This text file is also used to keep track of the current state of leases; it must not be changed while the DHCP server is running, or the server cannot track current leases. The server rotates the logs every so often, renaming the old file to `dhcpd.leases~`. If for some reason the `dhcpd.leases` file gets destroyed or corrupted, this file can be used to restore an old version of the file. This is preferable to simply creating a new file.

dhcpd cannot start if the `dhcpd.leases` file is missing. If this is the case, and there is no `dhcpd.leases` file to restore as a backup, you must create the file by hand. Use the `touch /var/state/dhcpd.leases` command to create an empty `dhcpd.leases` file.

For More Information

To learn more about *telnet*, *ssh*, and DHCP on the Internet, visit these sites.

URL	Resource Name
http://www.ssh.fi	*ssh* Communications Home Page
ftp://ftp.cs.hut.fi/pub/ssh/	Helsinki University of Technology *ssh* FTP Site
http://www.datafellows.com/products/cryptography	Data Fellows Corporation Secure Shell Products
http://www.linuxdoc.org/HOWTO/mini/DHCP-4.html	DHCP Mini Howto
http://linuxkb.cheek.com/page.php?security	Linux Knowledge Base Security Page (includes *ssh*, TCP wrappers)

PART IV

Appendixes

A Recompiling the Caldera OpenLinux 2.3 Kernel

B What's on the CD?

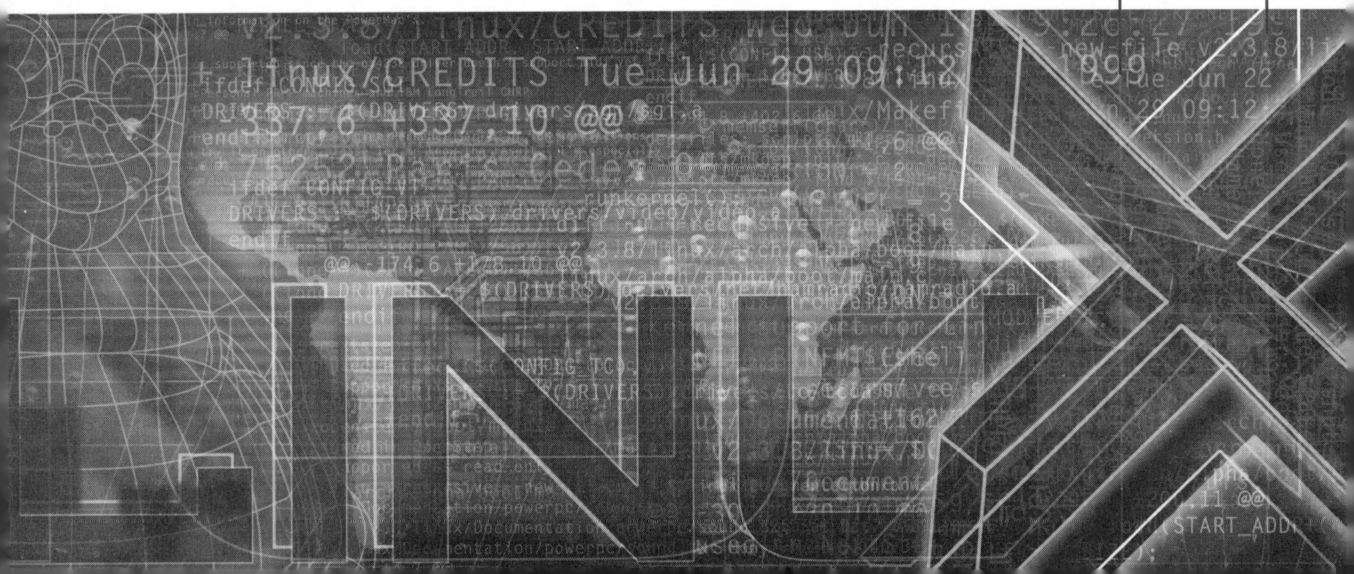

Appendix A: Recompiling the Caldera OpenLinux 2.3 Kernel

Obtaining and Installing the Latest Kernel Source

Configuring the Kernel

Compiling the Kernel and Modules

Installing the New Kernel

OpenLinux 2.3 comes with Linux kernel 2.2.10 preconfigured for many major devices. There are certain times, however, when it is necessary to compile a new kernel. Most of the time, this is for one of two reasons:

- You need a hardware driver that was not preconfigured with the stock kernel.
- You need to load the latest kernel (to patch a bug, or to add a new feature, for example).

Sometimes you can gain a performance increase by recompiling the OpenLinux kernel and including only the bare necessities. Omitting extraneous drivers and functionality can give you a smaller, quicker kernel. The kernel source for 2.2.10 is included with the CD-ROM in this book. I suggest downloading the latest 2.2.x kernel (currently 2.2.13 as of late November 1999), and installing that at the same time.

NOTE

The 2.2 kernel series contains the stable kernels; 2.3 kernels are for testing use only. When 2.4 is released, you might want to migrate to that, but the procedure to do that is not described in this book.

TIP

You can obtain the latest kernel version via FTP from **ftp.us.kernel.org**, in the directory `/pub/linux/kernel/v2.2/`. Kernel 2.2.13, for example, is in the file `linux-2.2.13.tar.gz`.

Regenerating the kernel is a multi-step process. The steps are

- Obtaining and Installing the Latest Kernel Source
- Configuring the Kernel
- Compiling the Kernel and Modules
- Installing the New Kernel

Obtaining and Installing the Latest Kernel Source

When you get a new kernel, it is in a file like `linux-2.2.13.tar.gz`. This file needs to be placed in the `/usr/src` directory. This file is large, around 15 Megabytes in size, so if you plan to get it from the Internet, you need a fast connection.

> CAUTION
>
> Recompiling the OpenLinux kernel requires about 100 Megabytes of free disk space; make sure you have that much space free before attempting a kernel recompilation. To check free space, use the `df -h` command and look for free space on the `/usr` partition—or on the root partition, if no `/usr` partition exists.

In `/usr/src`, you see a subdirectory named `linux-2.2.10` and one named `linux`, which points to the `linux-2.2.10` subdirectory. Create a subdirectory for the new kernel, using the same `linux-2.2.x` convention. If the kernel you are ready to compile is 2.2.13, create a subdirectory called `linux-2.2.13`.

```
mkdir linux-2.2.13
```

Remove the `linux` directory and recreate it, pointing to the new directory.

```
rm linux

ln -s linux-2.2.13 linux
```

You now are ready to extract the new kernel source from the file you downloaded.

```
tar xvzf linux-2.2.13.tar.gz
```

It takes a few minutes for all the files to unpack. After this is complete, change to the `linux` directory.

Configuring the Kernel

Most of the kernel configuration and installation from this point on is done with the `make` command. By configuring the kernel, you tell it which drivers to include. You should include drivers for all hardware you use (as well as hardware you are likely to use in the near future), and for anything else with which you either need or want to play. You can do this with one of three `make` commands: `make config`, `make menuconfig`, or `make xconfig`. If you are in the X Windowing System, you might want to use `make xconfig`; otherwise, use either `make config` or `make menuconfig`. This section assumes you choose `make xconfig`, after which you are shown the menu in Figure A-1.

```
make xconfig
```

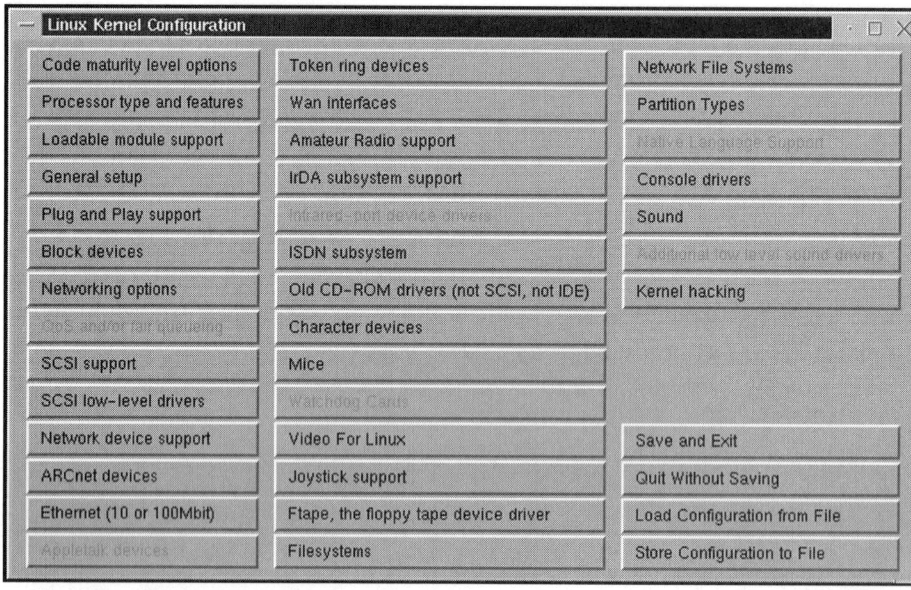

Figure A-1 *The Linux Kernel Configuration main menu*

Each button in the menu corresponds to an area of the kernel that needs to be configured. Click the first one, Code Maturity Level Options, which opens the menu in Figure A-2.

The dialog in this menu asks whether you want to include any drivers that are still in development and not known to be stable yet. Most of the time, you can say no here. Notice that each option has a Y and an N option, for yes and no, but many also have a third option, M, for module. Drivers built as modules are not loaded with the kernel; rather, they are loaded after boot. Building a driver as a module allows you to have a smaller kernel, at the expense of extra overhead later—when you are loading that module into memory. There are buttons at the bottom marked Next and Prev; these take you to the next or previous section. When you reach the end, click the button marked Main Menu, and then choose Save and Exit to save your changes.

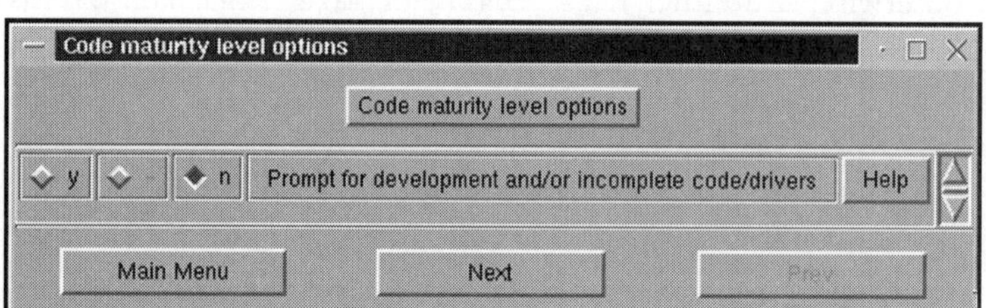

Figure A-2 *The Code Maturity Level Options menu*

Finally, regardless of which flavor of `make` you used, Dependency Information needs to be generated from the selections you just chose. At the shell prompt, type `make dep`.

```
make dep
```

Compiling the Kernel and Modules

You can start the actual compiling now, with the **make bzImage** command. If you have an extremely fast system, it only takes a few minutes; otherwise, it takes up to 40 minutes, so be patient. The kernel recompilation did not compile any drivers you chose to build as modules; issue the command **make modules** to build those.

```
make bzImage

make modules
```

Installing the New Kernel

Use the command **make modules_install** to put the modules you just built into place so you can find them after reboot. You can find the new kernel in the `/usr/src/linux/arch/i386/boot` directory as the file `bzImage`. Copy this file to the spot where you want to keep the new kernel, typically in the `/boot` directory.

```
make modules_install

cp /usr/src/linux/arch/i386/boot/bzImage /boot
```

CAUTION

> If you rebuilt your kernel before, be careful not to overwrite your existing `/boot/bzImage` file! Don't overwrite the existing kernel image file until you fully test the new one. Give the new kernel image a different name, such as `/boot/bzImage.new`.

To test the new kernel, you must reboot. Before you do that, you must tell *LILO* that you built a new kernel.

LILO's options are configured in the `/etc/lilo.conf` file. Your existing `lilo.conf` file should look something like Listing A-1.

Listing A-1 The default /etc/lilo.conf file.

```
#
# /etc/lilo.conf - generated by Lizard
#

# target

boot = /dev/hda3
install = /boot/boot.b

# options

prompt
delay = 50
timeout = 50
message = /boot/message

default = linux

other = /dev/hda1
        label = win

image = /boot/vmlinuz-pc97-2.2.10-modular
        label  = linux
        root   = /dev/hda3
        vga    = 274
        read-only
         append = "debug=2 noapic nosmp"
```

Everything after `image =` tells *LILO* about your kernel and how to load it. Copy those lines so there are two sets of `image =` lines, followed by their options. Change the first one so that it gives the pathname of the new kernel you just generated, and change the second one so that the label becomes `linux.old`. Listing A-2 shows what your result should look like.

Listing A-2 A modified /etc/lilo.conf file.

```
#
# /etc/lilo.conf - generated by Lizard
#

# target

boot = /dev/hda3
install = /boot/boot.b

# options

prompt
delay = 50
timeout = 50
message = /boot/message

default = linux

other = /dev/hda1
        label = win

image = /boot/bzImage
        label  = linux
        root   = /dev/hda3
        vga    = 274
        read-only
        append = "debug=2 noapic nosmp"

image = /boot/vmlinuz-pc97-2.2.10-modular
        label  = linux.old
        root   = /dev/hda3
        vga    = 274
        read-only
         append = "debug=2 noapic nosmp"
```

Now, rerun *LILO* with the command `lilo`. Then reboot your system to try it out. You can reboot into your new Linux kernel by choosing `linux` at the `LILO:` prompt, or into your old system by choosing `linux.old` at the same prompt.

```
lilo

reboot
```

For More Information

URL	Resource Name
http://www.linuxdoc.org/HOWTO/Kernel-HOWTO.html	The Linux Kernel HOWTO
http://linuxkb.cheek.com/page.php?kernel	Linux Knowledge Base Kernel Page

Appendix B: What's On the CD?

Running the CD

The Prima License

The Prima User Interface

The CD that accompanies this book contains an assortment of powerful networking utilities, sample configuration files referenced in the book, and the complete Cheek Consulting Knowledge Base.

Running the CD

To make the CD more user-friendly and take up less of your disk space, no installation is required. This means that the only files transferred to your hard disk are the ones you choose to copy or install.

CAUTION

> This CD has been designed to run under Linux. However, you may open and navigate the CD in any Operating System that has a graphical HTML viewer.

Linux

1. Open the CD tray and insert the CD.
2. As root, type the following at the command line: ***mount /dev/cdrom /tmp*** (replace */tmp* with wherever you want to mount the CD).
3. Start an X session (*startx* in most cases).
4. Open Netscape Navigator.
5. Choose Open from the File menu, and then click the browse button.
6. Browse to start_here.html.

Windows 95/98/NT4

1. Insert the CD in the CD-ROM drive, and close the tray.
2. Go to the Control Panel and double click the CD-ROM Drive.
3. Open start_here.html (works with Netscape and Internet Explorer).

The Prima License

The first window you will see is the Prima License Agreement. Take a moment to read the agreement, and click the "I Agree" button to accept the license and proceed to the user interface. If you do not agree with the license, click the "I Disagree" button and the CD will not load.

The Prima User Interface

The opening screen of the Prima user interface contains a two-panel window. The left panel contains the structure of the programs on the CD. The right panel displays a description page for the selected entry in the left panel.

Resizing and Closing the User Interface

To resize the window, position the mouse over any edge or corner, hold down the left mouse button, and drag the edge or corner to a new position.

To close and exit the user interface, select File, Exit (your specific X setup may have a unique graphical means of closing Netscape).

Using the Left Panel

If you want to view a Tool, click on Tools. A drop-down menu appears, listing the various Tools on the CD. Then simply click the tool you wish to download or view and it will open in the right window. The procedure is the same for Scripts, Modules, and Help.

Using the Right Panel

The right panel displays a page that describes the entry you chose in the left panel. Use the information provided to learn details about your selection -- such as what functionality an installable program provides. To download the particular file, follow the directions that appear in the left panel.

Index

A

B

C

F

G

H

I

K

L

M

Q

R

S

T

U

V

W

Z

Notes

Notes

Notes

How Often Are You Getting It?

PRIMA TECH's Linux series helps you get it.

Providing high-quality material on Linux-related topics, PRIMA TECH is *the* source for Linux. Divided into the following four categories—Programming and Development topics, Networking and Administration, Installation and Configuration, and Applications—PRIMA TECH's Linux series proves to be a trusted resource for anyone working in Linux.

Install, Configure, and Customize Red Hat Linux 6.1
0-7615-2306-5 ♦ $39.99

Guerrilla Guide to Great Graphics with The GIMP
0-7615-2407-X ♦ $39.99

PHP Essentials
0-7615-2729-X ♦ $39.99

Programming with Python
0-7615-2334-0 ♦ $39.99

Sun StarOffice 5.1 for Linux
0-7615-2454-1 ♦ $29.99

PRIMA TECH's LINUX® SERIES

Applications
Install/Configure
Networking/Administration
Programming/Development

PRIMA TECH
A Division of Prima Publishing
www.prima-tech.com

PRIMA TECH's SAP BOOK SERIES

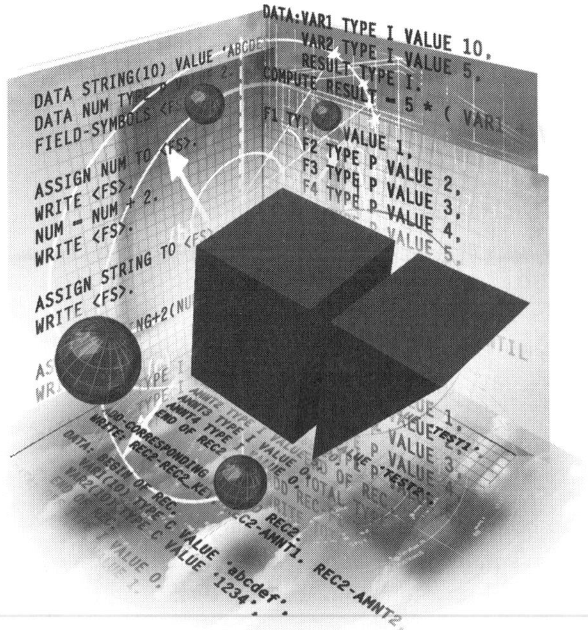

The IT Professional's Resource for SAP

The demand for SAP programming and support expertise is exploding. PRIMA TECH'S SAP book series is designed to prepare IT professionals for a successful career using the world's leading ERP application. From ABAP programming to preparing an effective organizational structure for the support of an SAP installation to providing guidance on becoming an SAP consultant, PRIMA TECH'S SAP book series is the most comprehensive resource available for IT professionals.

Available Now

Introduction to ABAP/4 Programming for SAP
Revised and Expanded Edition
0-7615-1392-2 • $50.00

Supporting SAP R/3
0-7615-1750-2 • $50.00

Getting Started with SAP R/3
0-7615-1904-1 • $29.99

Becoming an SAP Consultant
0-7615-1884-3 • $29.99

Also Available

ALE, EDI, & IDoc Technologies for SAP
0-7615-1903-3 • $69.99

Advanced ABAP Programming for SAP
0-7615-1798-7 • $69.99

Basis Administration for SAP
0-7615-1887-8 • $69.99

Coming Soon

Business Information Warehouse for SAP
0-7615-2335-9 • $69.99

Java & BAPI Technology for SAP
0-7615-2305-7 • $49.99

PRIMA TECH
A Division of Prima Publishing
www.prima-tech.com

Call Now to Order (800) 632-8676 ext. 4444

License Agreement/Notice of Limited Warranty

By opening the sealed disk container in this book, you agree to the following terms and conditions. If, upon reading the following license agreement and notice of limited warranty, you cannot agree to the terms and conditions set forth, return the unused book with unopened disk to the place where you purchased it for a refund.

License:

The enclosed software is copyrighted by the copyright holder(s) indicated on the software disk. You are licensed to copy the software onto a single computer for use by a single concurrent user and to a backup disk. You may not reproduce, make copies, or distribute copies or rent or lease the software in whole or in part, except with written permission of the copyright holder(s). You may transfer the enclosed disk only together with this license, and only if you destroy all other copies of the software and the transferee agrees to the terms of the license. You may not decompile, reverse assemble, or reverse engineer the software.

Notice of Limited Warranty:

The enclosed disk is warranted by Prima Publishing to be free of physical defects in materials and workmanship for a period of sixty (60) days from end user's purchase of the book/disk combination. During the sixty-day term of the limited warranty, Prima will provide a replacement disk upon the return of a defective disk.

Limited Liability:

The sole remedy for breach of this limited warranty shall consist entirely of replacement of the defective disk. IN NO EVENT SHALL PRIMA OR THE AUTHORS BE LIABLE FOR ANY other damages, including loss or corruption of data, changes in the functional characteristics of the hardware or operating system, deleterious interaction with other software, or any other special, incidental, or consequential DAMAGES that may arise, even if Prima and/or the author have previously been notified that the possibility of such damages exists.

Disclaimer of Warranties:

Prima and the authors specifically disclaim any and all other warranties, either express or implied, including warranties of merchantability, suitability to a particular task or purpose, or freedom from errors. Some states do not allow for EXCLUSION of implied warranties or limitation of incidental or consequential damages, so these limitations may not apply to you.

Other:

This Agreement is governed by the laws of the State of California without regard to choice of law principles. The United Convention of Contracts for the International Sale of Goods is specifically disclaimed. This Agreement constitutes the entire agreement between you and Prima Publishing regarding use of the software.